Introduction to Accounting for Finance

Alastair Matchett

Cover design:	Loraine Machlin Marsha Cohen
Illustrations:	Jacque Auger
Proofreaders:	Mary Jane Kaplan Katharine McMaster Truly Donovan
Content review:	Ross Wisdom, CPA
Editor:	Kieran Maguire

Published by Adkins Matchett & Toy LLC

Manufactured in the United States of America

ISBN 1-891112-67-8

Fourth edition, 2007
Originally published in 1997 and revised and republished in 2002 as *Accounting: A Brief Introduction* by South-Western, a division of Thomson Learning, and offered as a college text without answer keys. The fourth edition is not substantially revised from the third edition but like the first and second editions includes answer keys and can be used as a self-study text.

Toll-free order line: **1 888 414 0999**

Visit us at **www.amttraining.com**
www.crunchthenumbers.com

Offices in: London, New York, Mumbai, Italy, Bangkok

About this book

It will help you ***succeed***

Your knowledge of basic accounting skills is one of the most significant predictors of your success as a financial analyst.

It's ***streamlined***

This book is not a detailed general accounting course. It focuses only on the accounting and financial skills you need to understand financial statements and analyze company performance.

It's ***self-paced***

Move at your own pace. Go straight to the checkout tests if you already know the material in a section and simply want to check yourself.

How to use this book

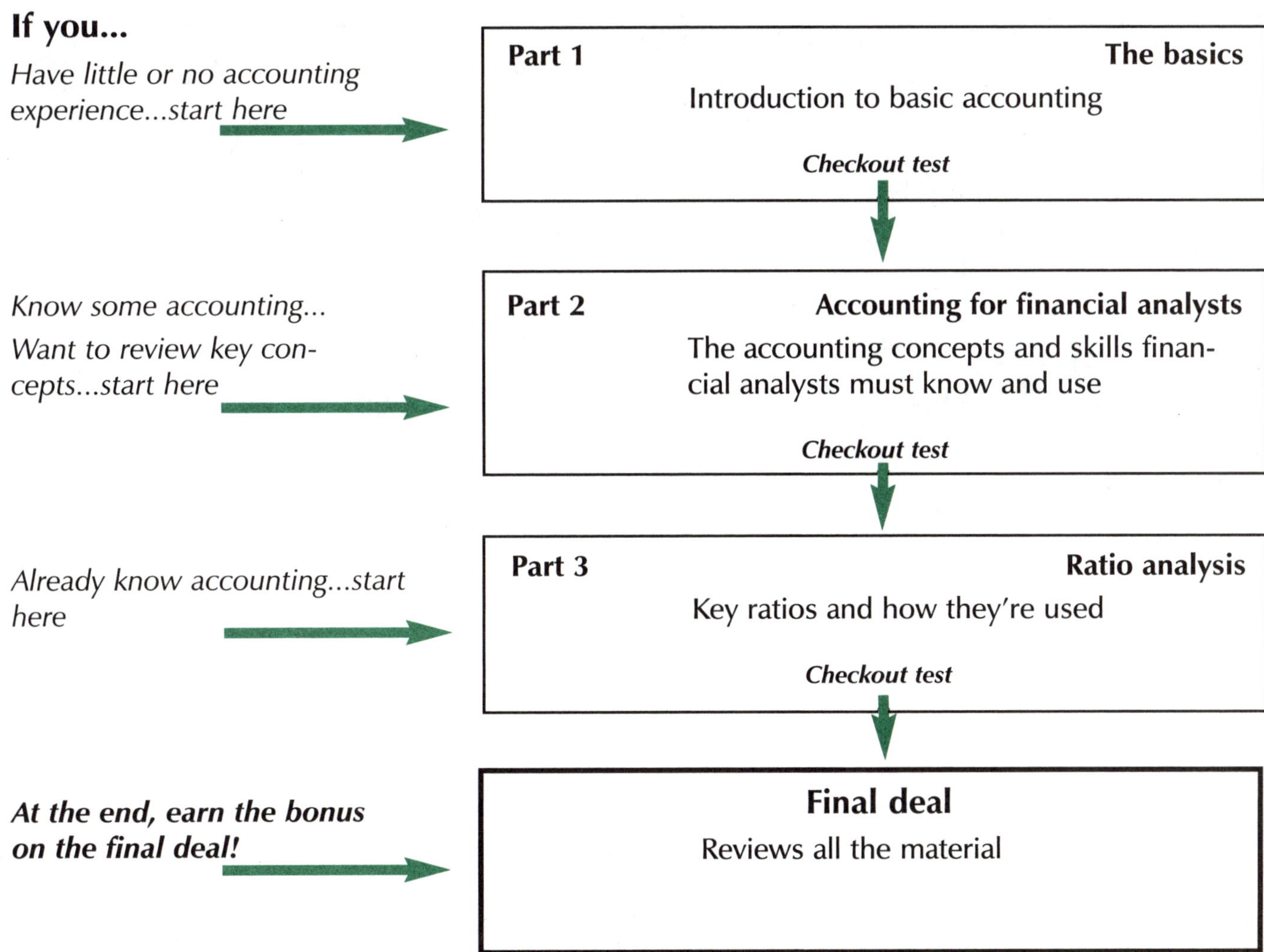

Contents

Contents, *continued*

Contents, *continued*

Part 3 Ratio analysis

Billion dollar deal

Appendices

Index

Coca-Cola's annual report

See the separate booklet that contains answers and the Coca-Cola annual report.

Answers

See the separate booklet that contains answers and the Coca-Cola annual report.

INTRODUCTION

Accounting performs three helpful tasks

1. It **uses numbers** to describe companies and other entities (like governments, individuals, and non-profit organizations) **and their activities**.
2. It organizes the information into **financial statements**.
3. It **provides a standard** so you can compare the performance of different companies, or examine the same company's performance over time.

Think of accounting as the language of business

Accounting helps different businesses **describe their activities consistently and clearly**. A fashion retail business and an auto parts manufacturer can both use accounting to communicate the results of their activities.

Companies in different countries use slightly different "dialects" of the accounting language. The accounting language of the United States describes some procedures slightly differently than the accounting language of the United Kingdom. For example, a British company's accounts record the purchase of another company differently than a US company's accounts do.

Accounting follows a set of agreed-upon concepts, principles, and procedures called Generally Accepted Accounting Principles (**GAAP**). GAAP ensures that a company's financial statements present its business activities fairly.

Each country has its own set of GAAP procedures, such as US GAAP, UK GAAP and French GAAP. There is a common standard called International GAAP which is used in many countries, either as an addition to the local GAAP or as the basis on which the financial statements are prepared. All listed companies in the EU produce accounts using International GAAP for example.

Accounting represents information about an entity

Companies, individuals, organizations and governments can all be **entities**. Financial statements report information about an entity. They do not report information about the owners', customers', or employees' activities.

EXERCISE 1
Accounting entities

Answers are in the separate booklet at the back

Accounting entities

Apply the entity concept to the Chase Bank. Check the items you would include in Chase's financial statements.

- ❑ 1. One Chase shareholder owns three red Ferraris.
- ❑ 2. A Chase employee spent $1,000 on a flight to Argentina to meet with a client.
- ❑ 3. Another Chase employee recently bought a $300,000 apartment in Manhattan.
- ❑ 4. Toyota borrowed $200m from Chase to buy a parts supply company.

THE BALANCE SHEET

1. THE PARTS OF A BALANCE SHEET

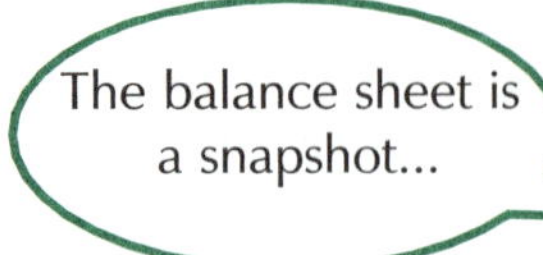

Accounting organizes financial information about an entity into financial statements. One very important financial statement is the ***balance sheet***.

It takes a picture of the assets a company owns at one moment in time. It also shows how those assets were ***funded*** (paid for). The balance sheet for an entity changes each time a new transaction is recorded.

The balance sheet has two lists or sides

One list or side of the balance sheet records resources the company owns/controls (***assets*** is the correct accounting term). The other list shows you how the company funded those assets. Printed copies of the balance sheet may show the two lists side by side or one above the other.

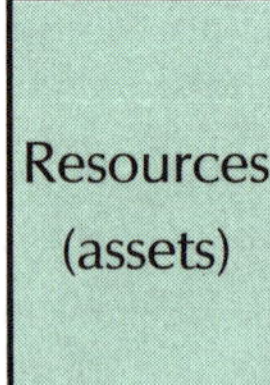

The two sides of the balance sheet

Each side of the balance sheet contains lists of different accounts. Each account represents a particular type of asset or funding.

ASSETS: THE RESOURCES SIDE OF THE BALANCE SHEET

A person may own a house to live in, a business may own a factory to manufacture products, and a bank has cash on hand for its tellers.

Accounting refers to these resources as ***assets***.

The word from GAAP

"Assets are probable future economic benefits obtained or controlled by a particular entity."

An asset must satisfy three requirements before you can record it on the balance sheet:

☑ 1. The entity must ***own/control*** it.

☑ 2. It must be ***valuable*** to the entity *("provide probable future benefit")*.

☑ 3. It must be acquired at a ***measurable cost.***

EXERCISE 2
Find the assets

Recording assets on the balance sheet

Which assets would General Motors record on its balance sheet?

Hint: Use the three requirements

- ❑ 1. Cash
- ❑ 2. Employees
- ❑ 3. Trees next to the factory
- ❑ 4. Machinery for manufacturing cars in its factory
- ❑ 5. Inventories of cars ready to be sold
- ❑ 6. An office building that GM owns

The balance sheet shows the original cost of assets

The balance sheet lists the assets a company owns and tells you the dollar price it paid for them. Assets appear on the **left side** of the balance sheet.

THE FUNDING SIDE OF THE BALANCE SHEET

If an entity owns assets, it must have paid for them in some way. The **right side** of the balance sheet shows how a company funds the assets recorded on the left side. A company can fund assets by either **liabilities** or **equity**.

Liabilities

Liabilities record what you owe to other entities. A liability must satisfy two requirements:

- ☑ 1. It must be a ***measurable obligation***.
- ☑ 2. It must be ***likely to happen*** *("probable")*.
- ☑ 3. It must be ***due to a past event***.

The word from GAAP

"Liabilities are probable future sacrifices of economic benefit arising from present obligations of a particular entity."

Example

Your company orders 500 cases of paper. The bill for $1,000 is due at the end of the month.

The unpaid bill is a liability of $1,000.

Your company borrows $100,000 from the bank.

The loan is a liability of $100,000.

Your company owes $20,000 in taxes but has not yet paid them.

The unpaid taxes are a liability of $20,000.

EXERCISE 3
Find the liabilities

Find the liabilities

Check the liabilities GM would record on its balance sheet:

- ☐ 1. A $100m loan
- ☐ 2. Taxes of $10,000 owed to the government
- ☐ 3. $1,000 in cash in GM's bank account
- ☐ 4. The possibility that an earthquake might hit GM's Los Angeles office

Liability holders can claim your assets

Everything has a price! In return for helping your company get resources, liability holders have a claim against all your company's assets. If you don't pay your liabilities when they are due, the entity that supplied you with resources (the paper supply company, the bank, the government) can claim your assets. The liability holders have a right to make a claim on any of your assets, not just the ones they supplied. Liability is limited to the assets of the company, and does not include the personal assets of the shareholders.

Equity represents the owner's investment

Owners of a corporation are called **shareholders**. Their investment in the company appears in the **equity section** on the **right** *(funding)* **side** of the balance sheet.

Equity has two elements:

1. ***Paid-in capital***

   In return for supplying funds to the company, investors receive **shares** of stock. The funds they supplied are recorded as **paid-in-capital (PIC)** on the balance sheet.

2. ***Retained earnings***

   A company's after-tax profits are available to its shareholders. The company can either pay out profits to shareholders as **dividends** or retain profits in the business.

   Profits retained in the business are recorded as **retained earnings**. A company pays dividends to shareholders out of its store of retained earnings.

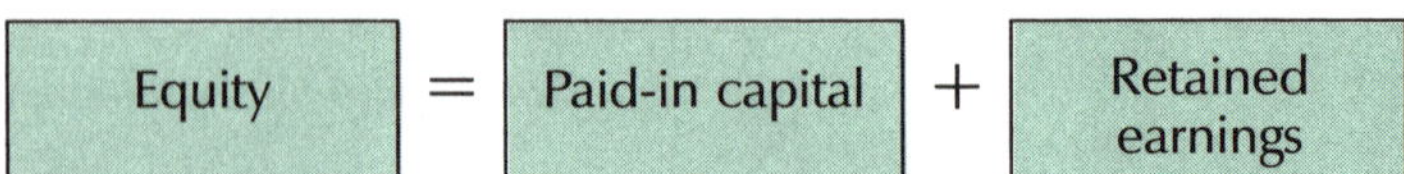

Both paid-in capital and retained earnings help fund the assets on the left side of the balance sheet.

EXERCISE 4
CloseShave's equity accounts

Changes in the equity accounts

1. When a shareholder invests money in a business, in which account does the company record the shareholders' interest?
   ❑ Paid-in capital ❑ Retained earnings

2. If CloseShave's shareholders supplied an additional $200m in cash to the company, which equity account would rise and which asset account would rise? *(Hint: Cash is an asset account.)*

Assets	**Equity**

3. If CloseShave retained $900m profit in one year, which equity account would rise and by how much?

   ____________________ [ ]

Equity holders take more risk

Shareholders also have a claim against the assets of a business. However, their claim on the assets ranks after the claims of owners of liabilities *(creditors)*. If a company goes bankrupt, the owners of liabilities are first in line for the proceeds.

Because they don't have first claim on the assets, owners of equity take more ***risk*** than owners of liabilities.

EXERCISE 5
Equity and risk

Liabilities, equity and risk

You recently started your job as a financial analyst on Wall Street. Your vice president asks you to look at the following balance sheet:

CloseShave's Balance Sheet on December 31, 2006

Assets	$8,940m	Liabilities	$5,040m
		Equity	$3,900m
Total	**$8,940m**	**Total**	**$8,940m**

Then she asks you the following questions:

1. [ ] What if the CloseShave company went bankrupt? How much of the total assets would CloseShave's liability holders claim?

2. Whose claim would be paid first in question 1?
   ❑ Liability owners' claims ❑ Equity owners' claims

3. Which is riskier to own, a company's ❑ equity or ❑ debt?

The two sides must balance

RESOURCES MUST EQUAL FUNDING

Total resources on one side of the balance sheet must always equal the total funding on the opposite side.

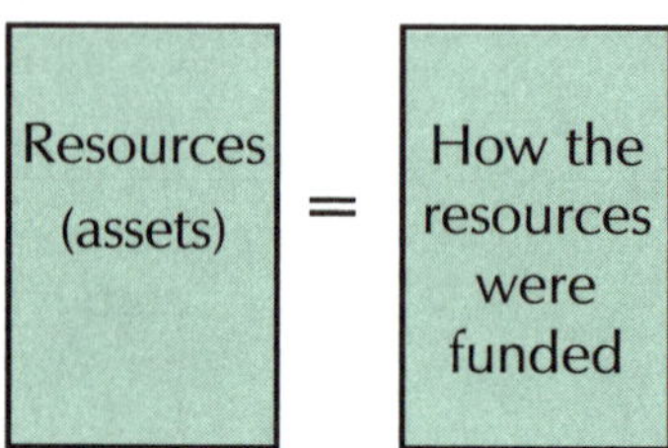

The totals on both sides of the balance sheet must be equal

If you increase or decrease only one side, you must make another change so that the two sides are equal again.

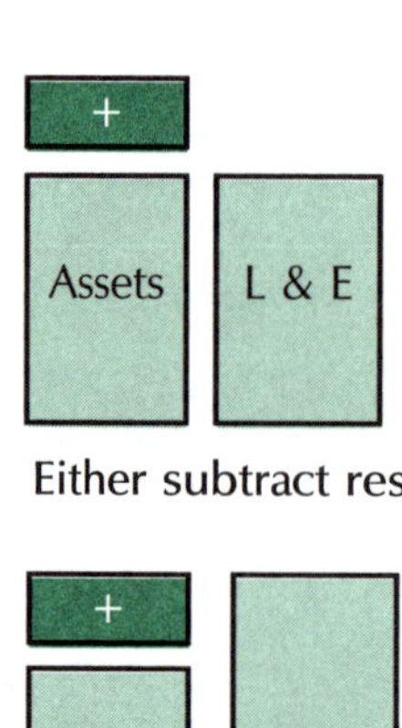

If you add **resources** to a company's balance sheet, you must...

Either subtract resources...

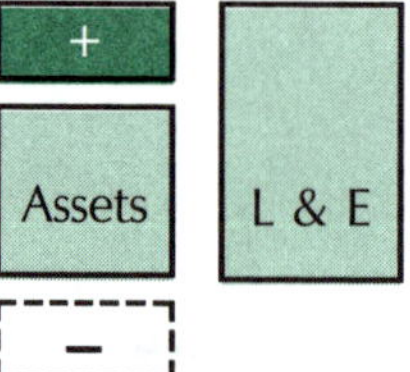

...or add funding

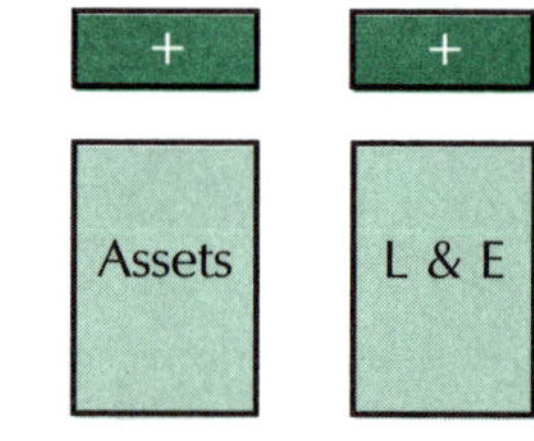

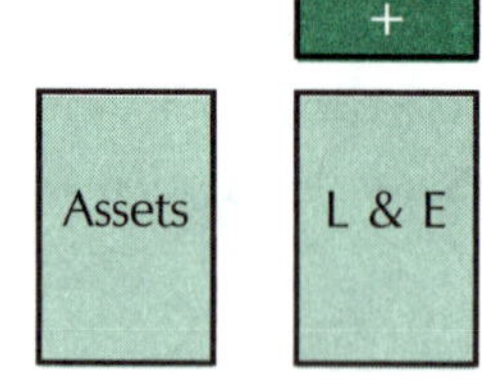

If you add **funding** to a company's balance sheet, you must...

Either subtract funding...

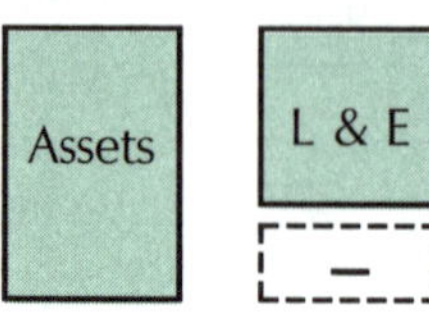

...or add resources

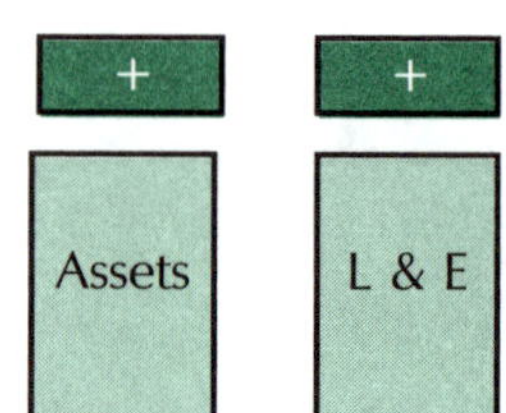

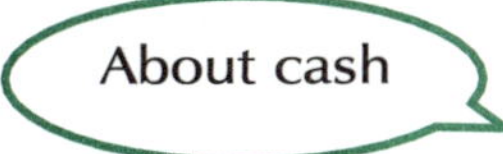

In Exercise 6, you need to know that when accounting refers to "cash," it can mean any of the following:

- Bills and coins
- Money orders
- Very liquid securities (US Treasury bills)
- Checks
- Wire transfers

EXERCISE 6
The clothing company

Create a balance sheet

Imagine you own a retail clothing company. You have $340m worth of resources which you paid for by a $340m bank loan. Your balance sheet would look like this:

Balance sheet

Total resources	=	Total funding
$340m		$340m

1. [ ] If you went to the bank and raised another $10m of loans, what would your total funding be?

2. [ ] The $10m loan was in the form of cash. What is the amount of your total resources now?

3. Now update your balance sheet:

Balance sheet

Total resources	=	Total funding
[ ]		[ ]

Hint: Remember that your balance sheet must always balance.

Suppose you decide to reduce the amount of your bank loan by paying $30m cash back to the bank:

4. [ ] What would be your new total funding? *(Use your new balance sheet totals)*

5. [ ] What would be your new total resources? *(Use your new balance sheet totals)*

6. Now update your balance sheet.

Balance sheet

Total resources	=	Total funding
[ ]		[ ]

Financial analysis tip

Sources and uses of funds

Financial analysts refer to **sources and uses of funds.** Companies spend money on assets, so they represent *uses of funds.* Liabilities and equity show where the funding comes from, so they are *sources of funds*.

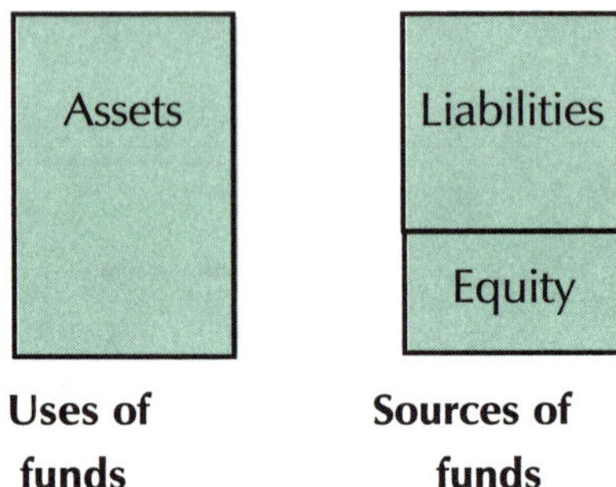

You now know...

- ☑ The balance sheet must balance.
- ☑ The assets a company owns appear on the left side.
- ☑ Assets are funded by liabilities and equity, which appear on the right side.
- ☑ Assets must equal liabilities plus equity: **A = L + E.**
- ☑ Financial analysts refer to **sources and uses of funds**.

2. BUILDING A SIMPLE BALANCE SHEET

Now you're ready to build a simple balance sheet. First, look at some examples.

Balance an increase in assets by...

Example

Suppose Goldman Stanley *(not a real company!)* buys a car for one of its officers. The car costs $50,000. Goldman Stanley has 3 choices:

Option 1 Goldman Stanley takes out a loan to finance the car. It adds $50,000 to assets and $50,000 to liabilities.

...increasing liabilities...

Assets		**Liabilities & Equity**	
Car	$50,000	Loan	$50,000
		Paid-in capital	$0
Total	**$50,000**	**Total**	**$50,000**

Option 2 Goldman Stanley raises money from shareholders to buy the car. It adds $50,000 to assets and $50,000 to equity.

...or increasing equity...

Assets		**Liabilities & Equity**	
Car	$50,000	Loan	$0
		Paid-in capital	$50,000
Total	**$50,000**	**Total**	**$50,000**

Option 3 Goldman Stanley uses its available cash.

...or reducing another asset

Assets		**Liabilities & Equity**	
Cash	$100,000	Loan	$0
		Paid-in capital	$100,000
Total	**$100,000**	**Total**	**$100,000**

The cash originally came from selling stock. First Goldman Stanley issues $100,000 of stock and receives cash.

Now Goldman Stanley uses some of its cash to buy the car. Remember the balance sheet must still balance. Goldman Stanley's cash balance falls by $50,000 but it adds a new asset, the $50,000 car.

Assets		**Liabilities & Equity**	
Cash	$50,000	Loan	$0
Car	$50,000	Paid-in capital	$100,000
Total	**$100,000**	**Total**	**$100,000**

Goldman Stanley reduces one asset and adds a new asset, adjusting only one side of the balance sheet.

EXERCISE 7
Greg's rental agency
Part 1

Greg's rental agency, Part 1

Greg sets up a rental agency for summer houses in the Hamptons (a resort area outside New York City, popular with investment bankers). You have volunteered to keep his accounts for him.

Add the appropriate accounts to your balance sheet for each transaction below. Keep a running total from balance sheet to balance sheet.

1. Greg invests $1,000 cash as paid-in capital to set up the company.

Balance sheet

Assets			**Liabilities**
Cash	____________		____________
			Equity
		PIC	____________
Total assets	____________	**Total L&E**	____________

2. Greg gets a $1,000 loan from the bank and receives cash.

Balance sheet

Assets			**Liabilities**
Cash	____________	Loan	____________
			Equity
		PIC	____________
Total assets	____________	**Total L&E**	____________

3. Greg buys a beach hut for an office for $500. He pays cash.

Balance sheet

Assets			**Liabilities**
Cash	____________	Loan	____________
Beach hut	____________		**Equity**
		PIC	____________
Total assets	____________	**Total L&E**	____________

continued on next page

EXERCISE 7
Greg's rental agency
Part 1, *continued*

Greg's rental agency, part 1, *continued*

4. Greg buys a car for $200 with a new bank loan.

Balance sheet

Assets		**Liabilities**	
Cash	______	Loans	______
Beach hut	______	**Equity**	
Car	______	PIC	______
Total assets	______	**Total L&E**	______

5. Greg buys stationery and other office incidentals for $100 cash.

Balance sheet

Assets		**Liabilities**	
Cash	______	Loans	______
Beach hut	______		
Car	______	**Equity**	
Stationery	______	PIC	______
Total assets	______	**Total L&E**	______

6. Greg decides the car is no use on the beach. He sells the car for $200 and pays back the $200 bank loan. He also purchases a bicycle for $50 cash.

Balance sheet

Assets		**Liabilities**	
Cash	______	Loan	______
Beach hut	______		
Bicycle	______	**Equity**	
Stationery	______	PIC	______
Total assets	______	**Total L&E**	______

Making multiple entries for one transaction

In the rental agency exercise, you made two changes to the balance sheet for each transaction. In accounting, each event generates at least two changes to the financial statements.

In some situations, you might have to make three or more entries to make the balance sheet balance. The next exercise gives you an opportunity to make three entries at once.

EXERCISE 8

Greg's rental agency

Part 2

Continue working with Greg's rental agency

Greg's current balance sheet

Balance sheet			
Assets		Liabilities	
Cash	$1,350	Loans	$1,000
Beach hut	$500		
Bicycle	$50	Equity	
Stationery	$100	Paid-in cap.	$1,000
Total assets	**$2,000**	**Total L&E**	**$2,000**

1. Greg's rental agency business really took off. At the end of the year he decided to build an office. The building work cost $100,000. To pay for this Greg took out a $50,000 bank loan and asked friends to invest $50,000 in exchange for equity in his company.

   Help him change the balance sheet to account for the transactions. Remember, Assets = Liabilities + Equity.

Balance sheet			
Assets		**Liabilities**	
	________		________
	________		
	________		
	________	Equity	
	________		________
Total assets	________	**Total L&E**	________

continued on next page

EXERCISE 8
Greg's rental agency
Part 2, *continued*

Greg's rental agency accounts, part 2, *continued*

2. Greg invests a further $100,000 in the business. He uses the money to buy office furniture for $20,000. He puts the rest into the company's bank account.

Balance sheet			
Assets		**Liabilities**	
	________		________
	________		
	________		
	________		
	________	**Equity**	
	________		________
Total assets	________	**Total L&E**	________

3. Greg decides to sell half the building for $50,000 in cash. With the extra cash he pays back $40,000 of the bank loan.

Make sure the balance sheet balances!

Balance sheet			
Assets		**Liabilities**	
	________		________
	________		
	________		
	________		
	________	**Equity**	
	________		________
Total assets	________	**Total L&E**	________

Facts must be measurable in money

What financial statements can't tell you

Financial statements measure facts about an entity in units of money. But some facts about an entity and its resources cannot be accurately measured using money.

For example, ***employees*** are one of an entity's most important assets. How do you measure how much a company's employees are worth? You can't, because they are priceless in terms of having no agreed market value (the one exception here is sports players who can be traded between clubs). Financial statements do not report facts that cannot be reliably measured in money. This fact is called the **money as unit of measurement concept.**

Financial statements are not complete because they don't measure some things, and focus on cost rather than value. But they do give you valuable information.

EXERCISE 9
What can be measured?

What can be measured?

Which facts are included in a company's financial statements?

- ❑ 1. The size of a company's bank debt
- ❑ 2. Employee job satisfaction
- ❑ 3. The amount of cash a company has in the bank
- ❑ 4. The company's customer list
- ❑ 5. The number of cars a company leases

EXERCISE 10
Cleo's relocation service

Build a balance sheet

Record each transaction in the blocks below.

1. Cleo thinks there is a significant opportunity to provide a relocation service to financial analysts. She starts a new company called IBRelocate Inc. and invests $50,000 of her own money in its equity. The new company now has $50,000 in cash.

Assets	Liabilities
	Equity
Total Assets ______	Total L & E ______

2. She spends $10,000 of this cash on a car to drive around New York.

Assets	Liabilities
	Equity
Total Assets ______	Total L & E ______

continued on next page

EXERCISE 10

Cleo's relocation service, *continued*

Build a balance sheet, *continued*

3. She then goes to the Bank of New York and takes out a $200,000 loan to really get the business moving. She receives cash from the bank.

Assets		Liabilities	
		Equity	
Total Assets	________	Total L & E	________

4. She purchases a building for $50,000 in the Meat Packing District as her new offices. She pays in cash.

Assets		Liabilities	
		Equity	
Total Assets	________	Total L & E	________

5. Two days after she moves in, the new nightclub Stylo opens next door. The new club stays open until 11am. The music is so loud she cannot use her offices before that time.

Assets		Liabilities	
		Equity	
Total Assets	________	Total L & E	________

Review and reinforcement

- ☑ ***The balance sheet must balance.***

  Assets must equal liabilities and equity.

- ☑ ***Every transaction has at least two equal entries.***

- ☑ ***Only assets and liabilities that can be reliably measured by money appear on the balance sheet.***

Deal #1

SCORE PAD

Each right answer is worth $10,000.

1. ____________
2. ____________
3. ____________
4. ____________
5. ____________
6. ____________
7. ____________
8. ____________
9. ____________
10. ____________

Close the deal #1

It's time for you to earn your first "tombstone"! On Wall Street, a tombstone is a clear plastic block announcing a successful deal or project.

You must make $90,000 to earn your tombstone. If you make less than $90,000, review the material before you go on.

1. What is the "unit of measurement" concept?
2. Is a liability a ❑ source of funding or a ❑ resource?
3. Name two components of equity.
4. If a company's assets are $300,000 and its liabilities are $145,000, what is its equity?
5. How would General Motors account for the threat of a strike at its major manufacturing facility?
6. A company buys a new building for $40,000, two new cars for $30,000 each and new office furniture for $10,000. It also issues $50,000 of equity. Will the company have to borrow additional resources from the bank? Assume the company has no spare cash available. ❑ Yes ❑ No

   If yes, how much? ____________
7. How often does a balance sheet change?
8. Who has a prior claim on a company's assets?

   ❑ Equity holders ❑ Liability holders
9. When you account for a transaction on the balance sheet, at least how many entries do you have to make?
10. What three characteristics must assets have to be included on a company's balance sheet?

3. DIVISIONS WITHIN A BALANCE SHEET

The balance sheet sorts assets and liabilities into current and non-current accounts.

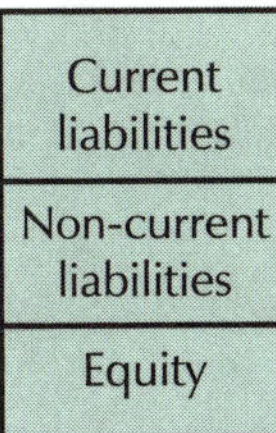

Current and non-current accounts

Current assets

Current: Lifespan of a year or less

Current assets are short-term assets. They are expected either to turn into cash ***within a year*** or to be used up ***within a year***.

Example

Cash	
Accounts receivable	Money that customers owe but haven't yet paid
Inventory	Goods waiting to be sold
Investments	Short term ownership or maturing in less than one year

Current liabilities

Current liabilities are bills or loans that are due within a year. They are generated when a company uses or purchases resources but does not pay for them immediately or borrows money for less than one year.

Example

Accounts payable	Bills for items bought on credit
Loans	Loans due within a year

Non-current assets (also called long-term assets)

Non-current: Lifespan of more than a year

Assets which are expected to be useful for longer than a year.

Example

Property, plant & equipment (PP&E)	Buildings, land, machinery, furniture
Investments	Long-term ownership stakes or loans to other companies.

Non-current liabilities (also called long-term liabilities)

Bills, loans or other obligations that you expect to last longer than one year.

Example

Long-term debt	A loan due more than a year from now. Sometimes a loan may have to be divided into long and short term elements, depending upon when repayments are due.

EXERCISE 11
Long-term vs. Short-term

Understanding long and short-term assets and liabilities

1. Show what each item is by writing in the box:

CA	*Current (short-term) asset*	**CL**	*Current (short-term) liability*
NCA	*Non-current (long-term) asset*	**NCL**	*Non-current (long-term) liability*
		E	*Equity*

☐ a. Cash in the cash register

☐ b. A shareholder's investment in a business

☐ c. An unpaid electricity bill

☐ d. A three-year bank loan

☐ e. Investment bonds maturing in nine months

☐ f. A factory building

☐ g. Income accumulated from previous years

☐ h. Bills owed to suppliers

☐ i. Money that customers owe you

☐ j. Stocks of goods waiting to be sold

☐ k. Office furniture

2. Describe assets and equity.

3. Which is riskier to own? ❑ Liabilities ❑ Equity
   Why?

Record assets at purchase cost

The cost concept

If you record an asset on the balance sheet, you are attaching a dollar value to something that will benefit the company in the future. For example, a company buys an empty plot of land because it expects benefit from the land ***in the future***.

However, the market value of an asset may change. The company's plot of land may be worth three times as much next year.

What amount should appear on the balance sheet for the land?

Accounting rules require the land to be recorded at its **original purchase cost** on the company's balance sheet.

EXERCISE 12
Sarah's balance sheet

Cost concept

Sarah, a friend of yours, is an experienced analyst. Over the years she has amassed some valuable assets. To help you practice your accounting skills, she asks you to prepare her balance sheet at the end of the year.

- She has $7,000 in her bank account.
- She owns a Van Gogh sketch which cost her $10,000 and was recently valued at $15,500.
- Her apartment on the Upper West Side was purchased for $150,000. She took out a $110,000 mortgage to help meet the purchase price. The apartment was recently valued at $180,000.
- She owns jewelry worth $14,590. It originally cost $11,000.

1. Write out her balance sheet using the cost concept.

Assets	Liabilities & Equity

2. [ ] What is her equity according to the rules of accounting?

3. Does your answer reflect her true net worth?
❑ Yes ❑ No

4. Why is there a difference between the accounting value of her assets and their market value?

[ ]

Financial analysis tip

The balance sheet may not be a good indicator of the market value of assets and liabilities. It tells you only what their original purchase price was. The potential sale value of an asset could be higher.

A financial analyst who is trying to determine the sale value of a company's assets and liabilities can't just look at a company's balance sheet. Asset values shown on balance sheets can be misleading.

EXERCISE 13
Aunt Kate's accounts

Understanding long and short-term assets and liabilities

Your aunt Kate, a successful fashion designer, is having difficulty sorting out her financial situation. She doesn't know accounting, so you offer to help. She says she wants to determine the amount of her total equity, also known as her net worth.

You ask her to list the following:
all her cash receipts and purchases during the year
all her assets
all her liabilities

Here's her list:

- During the year she paid into her bank account her salary of $300,000 (after tax) and her year end bonus of $1,500,000 (after tax). She also purchased a country house for $400,000 in cash and a $10,000 drum kit.
- She owns a $600,000 apartment in midtown New York.
- She has a $400,000 mortgage on the New York apartment.
- She has a $40,000 bank loan payable in six months.
- She owes $3,000 in unpaid household bills.
- She owns $5,000 of Government bonds maturing in six months.
- She owns $50,000 of stocks held as long-term investments.

Remember:
If she purchased assets with cash, her cash balance will fall.

As you prepare her balance sheet, round her financial figures to the nearest thousand. Write your answer (to the nearest thousand) in the following table. The template in the margin will help you calculate the ending cash balance. *(Add receipts, add payments, subtract payments from receipts.)*

Cash balance

Receipts	Payments

Balance sheet

Assets		Liabilities	
Cash			
Total CA		**Total CL**	
		Tot. Liab.	
		Equity	
		Tot. Equity	
Tot. NCA			
Tot. Assets		**Tot. L&E**	

Deal #2

SCORE PAD

1. ______
2. ______
3. ______
4. ______
5. ______
6. ______
7. ______
8. ______
9. ______
10. ______

Total

Close the deal #2

Get another "tombstone" by earning $100,000 or more. If you earn less than $100,000, review the material before you go on.

1. What is the difference between current and non-current liabilities?
2. What are accounts payable? Are they a current or non-current liability?
3. What are inventories and are they a current or non-current asset?
4. At the beginning of the year a company buys a building for $200,000. At the end of the year the accountants are told the building is worth $500,000. What amount do the accountants record on the balance sheet?
5. If financial analysts are asked to value a company's assets, why can't they just look at the balance sheet?
6. Name two current liabilities.
7. Name two long-term assets.
8. What does the asset side of the balance sheet tell you?
9. What does the liabilities and equity side of the balance sheet tell you?
10. If a company has $40,000 of equity, $50,000 of liabilities and $77,000 of non-cash assets, how much cash is recorded on the balance sheet?

4. Introducing T&J's

You are now going to look at a more detailed balance sheet. T&J's Inc. is a large ice cream manufacturer based in Vermont. On December 31, 2005 its balance sheet looked like this:

Your first real balance sheet

T&J's Balance Sheet on 31 December 2005

	$000s		*$000s*
Cash & cash equivalents	46,591	Accounts payable	38.915
Accounts receivable	18,833	Other current liabilities	5,627
Inventories of ice cream	13,937	**Total current liabilities**	**44,542**
Other current assets	7,986		
Total current assets	**87,347**	Long-term debt & leases	16,669
		TOTAL LIABILITIES	**61,211**
Property & equipment net	56,557		
Investments	200		
Other non-current assets	6,498		
Total non-current assets	**63,255**	Paid-in capital	40,678
		Retained Earnings	48,713
		TOTAL EQUITY	**89,391**
TOTAL ASSETS	**150,602**	**TOTAL L&E**	**150,602**

Notice how T&J's summarizes some sets of accounts. For example, Property, Plant & Equipment includes all buildings, equipment, and land the company owns.

Preparation for Exercise 14

Examine the T&J's balance sheet. Then update the balance sheet to include the following changes that happened during 2006. Always remember that Assets must equal Liabilities + Equity. There are lots of flows in and out of the cash account so use the table on the side to keep account of them.

EXERCISE 14
T&J's balance sheet

A real-life balance sheet

Note: all figures in thousands ($000)

- T&J's received $2,000 in cash from people who owed it money (accounts receivable). *Hint: cash increases, accounts receivable decreases.*
- The Company bought 50,000 gallons of milk to turn into ice cream inventory. The farmer who sold them the milk gave them credit for the entire price of $5,000. The Company then logged this $5,000 in accounts payable. *Hint: inventory increases and accounts payable also increases.*
- The Company purchased a new property for $10,000 paying for it in cash. *Hint: cash falls and property and equipment rises.*
- The Company issued $10,000 of new shares and received cash. *Hint: paid-in capital rises and cash rises.*
- The Company used $5,000 of the cash it raised from its share issue to pay down its long-term debt. *Hint: cash falls and long-term debt falls.*
- The company sold $200 of its investments for cash, equal to the original cost of the investments. *Hint: cash rises and investments fall.*
- Assume all other accounts remain the same.

Fill out T&J's balance sheet.

T&J's balance sheet on 31 December 2006

ASSETS	*$000s*	*LIABILITIES*	*$000s*
Cash & cash equivalents		Accounts payable	
Accounts receivable		Other	
Inventories of ice cream		**Total current liabilities**	
Other current assets			
Total current assets		Long-term debt	
		Other L-T liabilities	
Property & equipment net		**Total non-current liabs.**	
Investments		**TOTAL LIABILITIES**	
Other non-current assets			
Total non-current assets		Paid-in capital	
		Retained Earnings	
		TOTAL EQUITY	
TOTAL ASSETS		**TOTAL L&E**	

Cash balance

Receipts	**Payments**

New meanings for old words

Journal entries: an easy way of ensuring A = L + E

The next part of this course is crucial for your understanding of accounting. Start by setting aside your current definitions of "Debit" and "Credit."

Consumers think of credit as a good thing. For a business owner, a credit on the books represents an increase in a liability or equity or a reduction in an asset.

You'll have to work with these terms until you are comfortable making journal entries and you understand why debits must equal credits.

This is tricky...

New meanings for two old words: Debit and Credit

Assets		**Liabilities & Equity**	
Increases	= Debits	Increases	= Credits
Decreases	= Credits	Decreases	= Debits

Journal entries help you organize changes you make to the balance sheet.

...but it helps organize your work

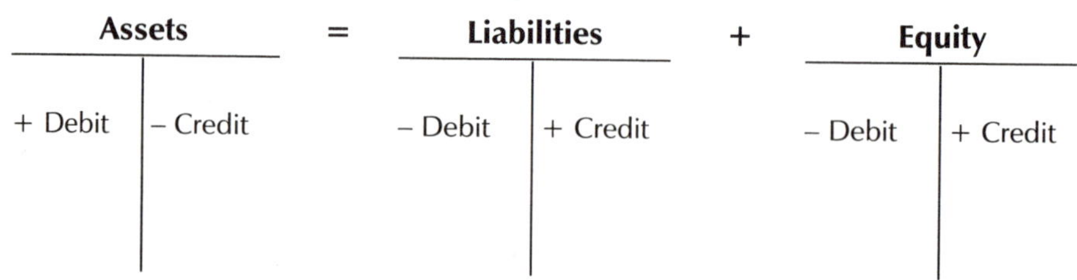

Total debits always must equal total credits.

Example

Examples of journal entries using debits (*Dr*) and credits (*Cr*):

T&J's receives $2,000 in cash from people who owed it money.

Debit	Cash	$2,000	
Credit	Accounts receivable		$2,000

T&J's issues $10,000 worth of new shares and receives cash.

Debit	Cash	$10,000	
Credit	Paid-in capital		$10,000

T&J's uses $5,000 of its cash to pay down its long-term debt.

Debit	Long-term debt	$5,000	
Credit	Cash		$5,000

*Note: **Debit** is often written as **Dr**, **Credit** as **Cr***

EXERCISE 15
Journal entries

Journal entries

You are going to record several debit and credit transactions for T&J's. Write out the proper debits and credits. Include the name of the account. The templates at the bottom of the page will help you.

Debits are traditionally written on the left and credits on the right.

Example

The company purchases $2,000 of inventory using cash.

Debit	Inventory	$2,000	
Credit	Cash		$2,000

1. The company issues $1,000 worth of shares for cash.

   Debit ______________________

   Credit ______________________

2. The company buys $4,000 of chocolate *(inventory)* for cash.

   Debit ______________________

   Credit ______________________

3. The company purchases new equipment worth $10,000. It takes out an $8,000 loan (lasting five years) to do this. It pays for the remaining $2,000 with cash.

   Debit ______________________

   Credit ______________________

   Credit ______________________

4. The company buys a van for $5,000. It uses $3,000 of cash and takes out a short-term loan to pay the remaining $2,000.

   Debit ______________________

   Credit ______________________

   Credit ______________________

For more debit and credit practice, turn to Appendix A in the back of the book.

Use these T-accounts to help find the answers

Assets		=	**Liabilities**		+	**Equity**	
+ Debit	– Credit		– Debit	+ Credit		– Debit	+ Credit

Use this form to help track journal entries

	Account	Debits	Credits
Dr	________	________	
Cr	________		________
Dr	________	________	
Cr	________		________
Dr	________	________	
Cr	________		________
Dr	________	________	
Cr	________		________
Dr	________	________	
Cr	________		________
Dr	________	________	
Cr	________		________
Dr	________	________	
Cr	________		________
Dr	________	________	
Cr	________		________

Check your work.

Do debits = credits?

Total debits ________

Total credits ________

Close the deal #3

Get another "tombstone" by earning $50,000 or more. If you score less than $50,000, review the material before you go on.

1. Put yourself in T&J's shoes when they first set up their company. Assume they made the following transactions in the first month the company was set up:

   a. T&J each put in $40,000 cash to get the company started. In return for their investments they each received shares.

   b. They also went to their local bank to take out a loan for $50,000. They received cash.

   c. They purchased two ice cream-making machines for $10,000 each in cash.

   d. They also purchased $4,000 of ingredients including 500 gallons of milk from the local dairy (record as inventory). They asked the farmer to give them credit for this order (record as an account payable).

   e. During the first week they bought a truck. They paid $2,000 in cash.

   f. They purchased an old garage to house their ice-cream making operations. The garage cost $10,000 in cash.

   g. During the second week they ordered more milk from the dairy for $500. The dairy said they must wait for the delivery of the milk. They did not have to pay for the milk until it was delivered.

   h. In the third week they bought a computer for their accounting. The computer cost $1,000 in cash.

   i. In the fourth week one of the ice cream-making machines broke down.

   j. In the fifth week they repaid $20,000 of the $50,000 loan to the bank.

   Record these transactions on the left. Then build their balance sheet at the end of the month.

T&J's, Inc. balance sheet

Assets	**Liabilities & Equity**

continued on next page

Deal #3

SCORE PAD

1. ______________
2. ______________
3. ______________
4. ______________
5. ______________

Total

Debits and credits got you down?

Do the extra exercises in Appendix A!

Close the deal #3, *continued*

2. Name four sources of funds.

a. ______ b. ______

c. ______ d. ______

3. If a company increases its total resources what must it also do?

4. What is the difference between a current and a non-current asset?

5. Name two of T&J's current assets.

a. ______ b. ______

Debit – credit workout

If you need more practice with debits and credits, do the exercises in Appendix A.

THE INCOME STATEMENT

1. OVERVIEW

The income statement shows you how a company has performed over a period of time. All companies prepare income statements annually, at the same time that they prepare their balance sheets. Companies traded on the US stock market also provide quarterly statements.

The income statement is a summary...

Unlike the balance sheet which records conditions at one instant in time (usually the end of the fiscal year), the income statement is a **summary**. It summarizes information about revenues and expenses that have accumulated over an entire time period, usually a whole fiscal year.

The income statement records the sales a company generated during the accounting period and the costs it incurred to generate those sales. It has several sections.

The income statement

...of revenue

...and expenses

...ending with net income

Sales made in the **whole accounting period**	Sales
Production expenses generated by the sales	Cost of goods sold
Overhead expenses during the **whole period**	Sales, general and administrative costs
Infrequent or unusual income for the **whole period**	Other income
Infrequent or unusual expenses for the **whole period**	Other expenses
Income from cash and investments or the cost of debt for the **whole period**	Interest expense or income
Tax a company estimates it will have to pay on the period's profit	Tax
Net income (income after all expenses) generated over the **whole period**	Net income

EXERCISE 16
Chugger's

Build an income statement

Chris, the owner of a new cafe bar called Chugger's, sits down to do his accounts. In front of him are scraps of paper in no particular order. He needs to sort them into a proper income statement which will show how much business he has done over the last month:

- He estimated his tax bill for the month would be $4,000.
- He received a $2,000 bill from his bank for a month's interest.
- His first month's sales, general and admin costs were $3,000.
- His cost of goods sold was $10,000 for the month.
- He made $50,000 in sales during the month, all in cash.
- He had no other income or expenses.

Help him by building his income statement using the above information. Some subtotals are already included.

Income statement for Chugger's

Sales	
Direct costs of sales	
Gross profit	40,000
	Hint: gross profit = sales minus direct costs
Sales, general and administrative costs	
Operating profit	37,000
	Hint: operating profit = gross profit minus SG&A costs
Other income or expense	
	Hint: if any. Remember the entity concept.
Interest income and expense	
Profit before tax	35,000
Tax	
Net Income	
	Hint: all revenue and income less all expenses

The income statement

2. REVENUE

The first section of the income statement deals with ***revenues***. Revenues includes sales, fees for services, and royalties.

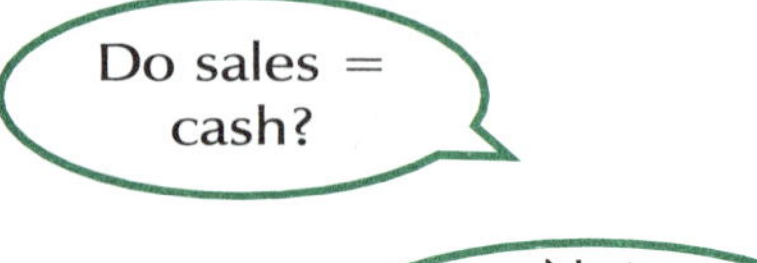

Not necessarily!

Sales made do not always equal cash received

The problem in using the receipt of cash to record sales *(cash accounting)* is that it does not capture sales made on credit. Imagine a store like Macy's measuring its sales by the amount of cash it collects. Because many customers use credit cards, cash accounting would not give Macy's management an accurate picture of how many sales they made on one day.

Manufacture, deliver, *then* record the sale

Sales are recorded when they are delivered

An important aspect of GAAP accounting is the question: ***when should a company recognize revenue from a sale?*** Under GAAP, sales are recognized **when the goods are delivered** to the customer. Not when they are manufactured, not when the contract is signed, not when the cash is received.

If you sell a service, record the revenue **when the service is performed.**

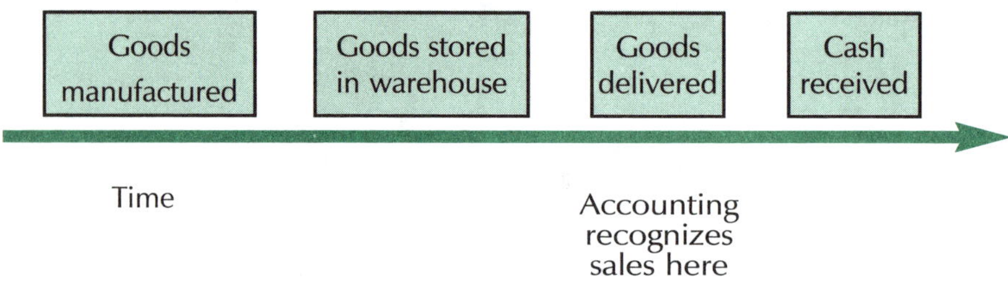

Example

A grocer delivers $30 worth of bananas to a local store on credit. His cash does not increase but he successfully generates $30 of revenues. He is certain the store will pay and wants to record the benefit of these sales in his accounts.

	Monday	**Tuesday**	**Wednesday**
	Grocer agrees to sell $30 of bananas.	Grocer delivers $30 of bananas	Grocer gets paid $30 in cash for bananas.
Sales	$0	+ $30	$0
Cash	$0	$0	+ $30

By recording the sales on delivery rather then waiting until he receives the cash, his financial statements better reflect the true performance of his business.

EXERCISE 17
New York supermarket

Recognizing sales

1. A New York supermarket telephoned T&J's and ordered 2,000 tubs of pralines and cream @ $1.50 per tub, to be delivered in a month. How would T&J's account for the transaction on their income statement that day? Assume each tub cost $1 to make.

2. When T&J's delivered the ice cream to the supermarket, they were paid $3,000 in cash. How would T&J's account for this transaction on their income statement?

3. If the supermarket paid for the ice cream before T&J's had delivered it, would T&J's record the sales on their income statement?
❑ Yes ❑ No

3. EXPENSES

Revenues
Expenses

The income statement

The income statement separates normal business expenses into two categories:

☑ Direct production costs (also called the cost of goods sold or **COGS**)

☑ Sales, general and administrative costs, or **SG&A**

MATCHING EXPENSES TO REVENUES

Record expenses...

When you record revenues, you also record (or ***match***) the expenses that directly helped to generate that revenue.

Some costs don't relate directly to revenue.

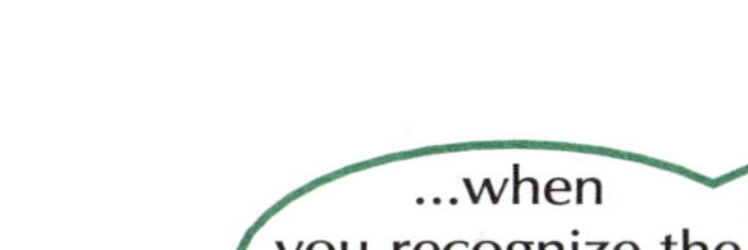

Cash spent on manufacture	Sale recorded Costs of manufacture expensed (recorded) in COGS
Goods Manufactured	Goods Delivered

Time →

What about stuff like insurance?

Some costs don't relate directly to revenue

Some costs cannot be directly matched to revenue. For example, insurance expense on a factory building occurs regardless of how many orders the sales team generates. In these circumstances, companies expense (record on their books) the insurance during the period it was used.

Expenses don't always equal cash costs

A business can incur costs by purchasing goods and services on credit. So expenses can be recorded without using up cash.

A company can also buy goods and services and store them for future use (think of an insurance policy, for example, or inventory). They have spent cash, but they don't record an expense on their income statement.

EXERCISE 18
Disneyland

Matching expenses with revenue

T&J's buys $100,000 of milk in March. In April it uses the milk to manufacture 100 tons of ice cream. It sells all 100 tons to Disneyland for $200,000. Disney takes delivery of half the ice cream in May, a quarter in June and a quarter in July. T&J's receives cash from Disneyland in August.

1. Track the cash receipts, payments and revenue on the following table:

	Mar	Apr	May	Jun	Jul	Aug
Revenue						
Milk expenses						
Change in cash						

2. T&J's buys a 5-month insurance policy in March for $600. The policy starts in May. Track the insurance expense recognition and the change in cash each month.

	Mar	Apr	May	Jun	Jul	Aug	Sep
Insurance expense							
Change in cash							

Don't overlook this concept!

The conservatism concept

Accounting is conservative when recording revenue and losses.

Accounting recognizes revenue when it is **reasonably certain**.

Accounting recognizes losses when they are **reasonably possible**

(GAAP calls it "reasonably determinable.")

EXERCISE 19
Kalvin Kleen

Conservatism and recognition

Kalvin Kleen recently opened a sock warehouse in New York. Business was brisk in the first few months after opening. One day he received a call from a large uptown department store who wanted to order $2,000 worth of men's socks. Kalvin had heard that the store's buyer is notoriously fickle and changes his mind like the weather.

1. In order to fulfill the concepts of realization and conservatism, when does Kalvin recognize the $2,000 of revenue?

   ❑ When the socks are ordered ❑ When the socks are delivered

   ❑ When Kalvin receives the cash

In the end the department store did want the socks. Kalvin dispatched them by courier. At five o'clock that day the department store still had not received the order. Eventually the courier company called and said that their messenger had disappeared without a trace that afternoon. The messenger was known to have a penchant for Kalvin Kleen socks.

2. Kalvin would like to wait until next month before he accounts for the loss. After all, the missing socks may turn up. Under the rules of accounting, when should Kalvin account for the loss of the socks?

   ❑ The same day ❑ Next week ❑ Next month

   Hint: remember the conservatism concept and be conservative

3. Above Kalvin's shop is an apartment. Kalvin decided to rent the apartment as a source of additional revenue. A new tenant moved in on June 1 and paid Kalvin $6,000 for six months rent upfront in cash. When should Kalvin account for this revenue?

   How much in:

   June? ____________ July? ____________

   August? ____________ September? ____________

   October? ____________ November? ____________

COGS is linked to sales...

COGS tends to fall and rise with the level of sales

Costs of goods sold (COGS) represent costs that are directly related to the manufacture of a product or service. These costs/expenses tend to rise or fall according to how much is sold during the accounting period.

Examples The cost of milk that T&J's uses to make ice cream.

The cost of the labor that mixes the ice cream.

SG&A costs tend to remain stable

Sales, general and administrative costs are costs or expenses that a company incurs to keep the organization running. SG&A costs are not directly related to production.

Examples Maintenance costs for the president's company-owned BMW.

The salaries of employees in the accounting department.

EXERCISE 20
The clueless bookkeeper

COGS or SG&A?

At the end of the year, T&J ask you to prepare an income statement to reflect the business the company did during the year. Your bookkeeper asks you the following questions.

1. "I have a bill here for milk. In which cost category should I put it?"
   ❑ COGS ❑ SG&A
2. "The bill for my salary has come in. Where should it go?"
   ❑ COGS ❑ SG&A
3. "Should I put interest expense into COGS or SG&A?"
   ❑ COGS ❑ SG&A ❑ Neither
4. "Here's the printer's bill for the sales brochure. Where does it go?"
   ❑ COGS ❑ SG&A
5 "We bought a $100,000 ice cream-making machine using cash last year. What journal entries should I make?"

Debit ______________ ________

Credit ______________ ________

Unusual or infrequent income and expenses

Other income and expenses

This category includes the other income and expenses not included in the COGS or SG&A category. Other income and expenses are unusual or infrequent items that are not part of a company's normal operations.

Example Gain on the sale of equipment

Interest income and expense

Interest income	Cash in the bank can generate interest income. The more cash a company has, the higher its interest income. Interest income can also be generated from investments.
Interest expense	Outstanding loans generate interest expense. The larger the loan, the greater the interest expense.

Net income increases equity, not cash

At the end of an accounting period, the accountant adds net income to retained earnings on the balance sheet. The increase in retained earnings increases a company's equity balance. As revenues increase net income, they help to increase retained earnings (equity) in the business. As expenses decrease net income, they decrease equity.

Net income is not cash income. A company can recognize revenue before it receives any cash, and it can record expenses before it pays any cash.

4. JOURNAL ENTRIES ON THE I/S

More debits and credits...

An easy way to organize your additions and subtractions to the income statement is to use journal entries.

- Expenses or costs are **debits** on the income statement.
- Revenue or sales and income are **credits** on the income statement.

Income statement		**Equity**	
Increases	= credits	Increases	= credits
Decreases	= debits	Decreases	= debits

Notice that the income statement and the equity accounts use debits and credits the same way, ***because net income and retained earnings are linked***.

...this time on the Income Statement

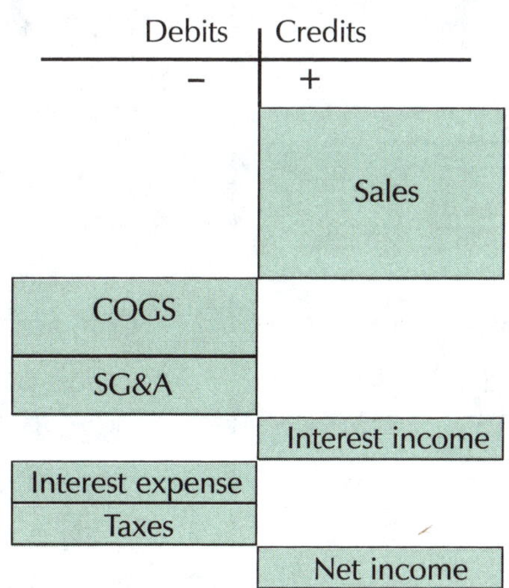

EXERCISE 21
Credits and debits

Need more credit and debit help? Go to Appendix A.

Increase (+) or decrease (-) in equity? Debit or credit?

Try this exercise to get more insights into credits and debits on the income statement.

	+ or – in equity?	**Debit or credit?**
1. An increase in sales is		
2. An increase in costs is		
3. Tax expense is		
4. Interest income is		

Deal #4

SCORE PAD

1. ______
2. ______
3. ______
4. ______
5. ______
6. ______
7. ______
8. ______
9. ______
10. ______

Total

Close the deal #4

Win another "tombstone" by earning $100,000 or more. If you earn less than $100,000, review the material before you go on.

1. When does a company account for revenue?

2. Does the income statement measure changes in cash or equity?
   ❑ Cash ❑ Equity
3. As a company's cash balance grows, what will probably happen to its interest income? ❑ Rise ❑ Fall ❑ Remain unchanged
4. You set up a curtain-making business. In one year you made 100 curtains for $10 each. You sold them all for $50 each. Your accountant's charges were $1,000 and you paid yourself as chief executive $2,000. Your interest income on the cash in your bank account was $500. You also purchased a 2-year insurance policy for $200. You pay tax on your profits at 50%. Prepare your income statement for that year:

Curtain business income statement

Revenue	______
COGS	______
Gross profit	______
SG&A	______
Operating profit	______
Interest income	______
Earnings before tax	______
Tax	______
Net income	______

5. What is the conservatism concept in accounting?

6. What does COGS stand for? ______
7. What does SG&A stand for? ______
8. If you reduce your bank loans, what will probably happen to your interest income? ❑ Rise ❑ Fall ❑ Remain unchanged
9. If you buy inventory on credit what happens to your cash balance?
   ❑ Rises ❑ Falls ❑ Remains unchanged
10. Which accounts would change in Question 9?

LINKS

Financial analysts must understand the ***links*** between the balance sheet and income statement. Many activities change both the income statement and the balance sheet at the same time. You'll now look at some of the important links between these financial statements.

NET INCOME  AND RETAINED EARNINGS

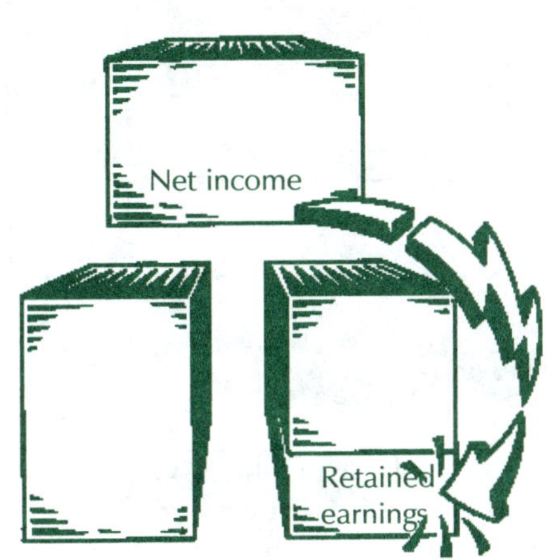

The most important relationship between the income statement and balance sheet is the link between net income and retained earnings.

During the year a company creates net income by generating more revenue and income than expenses. The company then adds its net income for the year to retained earnings. If net income is negative, the loss is subtracted from retained earnings.

Net Income, Dividends and Retained Earnings

Dividends are paid out of ***retained earnings***, not net income. A good way of understanding the flows in and out of retained earnings is to use **B-A-S-E** analysis.

B-A-S-E analysis is a simple technique to help you understand the flows into and out of an account over a period of time.

B A S E analysis: a useful tool

B	balance at **B**eginning of period	150
A	**A**dditions during the period	+ 60
S	**S**ubtractions during the period	- 10
E	The balance at the **E**nd of the period	200

Example

As of December 31, 2004, T&J's had retained $45,328,000 of earnings in its business from previous years. In the year ending December 31, 2005, it generated $3,385,000 of net income. It paid no dividends during the year.

T&J's retained earnings (B A S E analysis)

B	Beginning balance	$45,328,000
A	Additions	$3,385,000
S	Subtractions	$0
E	Ending balance	$48,713,000

You can use this information to establish the flows in and out of T&J's retained earnings account in 2006.

EXERCISE 22

T&J's retained earnings

B A S E analysis

Assume that in the year January 1 to December 31 2006 T&J's Inc., generated $10,567,000 of net income. It also decided to pay $6,000,500 in dividends to its shareholders. Now fill in the following B-A-S-E analysis table:

B	Beginning balance, retained earnings	48,713,000
	Beginning balance from the previous year's info, above	
A	Additions	
S	Subtractions	
E	Ending balance	

REVENUE  CURRENT ASSETS

Another important link connects revenue and the balance sheet. When a company records a sale, its net income goes up. Link 1 showed you that if net income goes up, so does equity. If equity goes up, something else has to change to make the balance sheet balance.

The account that changes will be either cash or accounts receivable (A/R).

- ☑ ***When customers pay on the spot, cash goes up.***
- ☑ ***When the company gives credit, A/R goes up.***

Revenue

Current assets

Either way, the increase in equity is balanced.

Think of the link another way. If a company makes a sale, what happens?

Cash or A/R rises...

therefore total assets rise...

therefore you need a balancing entry.

But wait! The sale added revenue to the income statement, which...

Increases net income, which...

+

increases retained earnings, which...

increases equity.

+

Now the balance sheet balances again.

More about accounts receivable

When you deliver goods to a customer, you recognize the revenue by recording it on the income statement. But what if the customer buys on credit and pays later?

If you record the sales on your income statement...

your equity will rise...

therefore you need a balancing entry....

so record the credit sales as accounts receivable on the asset side of the balance sheet.

EXERCISE 23

Ice cream sales

Revenue and the balance sheet

1. T&J's sold $50,000 of ice cream during the year. $30,000 of the sale was on credit. The rest was paid for in cash.

   Debit: ____________________ __________

   Debit: ____________________ __________

   Credit: ____________________ __________

   Hint: increase cash and accounts receivable

2. During the year customers with outstanding accounts paid $25,000 to T&J's. *Hint: increase cash and reduce accounts receivable.*

   Debit: ____________________ __________

   Credit: ____________________ __________

3. [ ] Assuming no other sales, what would be the balance (the remaining amount) of accounts receivable after question 2?

4. What happened to equity when the $25,000 was paid in question 2?
   - ❑ Nothing; equity already went up when the sale was recorded
   - ❑ Equity went up by $25,000
   - ❑ Equity went down to balance the drop in accounts receivable

COGS AND INVENTORIES

When a company records cost of goods sold on its income statement, net income falls. If net income falls, retained earnings fall and equity also goes down. If equity falls, something else has to change so that the balance sheet will balance. The account that changes is inventory.

☑ ***When COGS goes up, inventory goes down.***

Think of the link another way. If goods are delivered from inventory to a customer, what happens?

Inventory falls...

...Therefore total assets fall...

...Therefore you need a balancing entry.

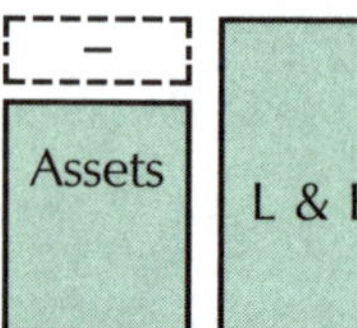

But wait! The cost of inventory hits COGS in the income statement only when the goods are delivered and sales are recognized.

Therefore, when inventory falls...

...COGS goes up, which...

...Decreases retained earnings, which ...

...Decreases equity.

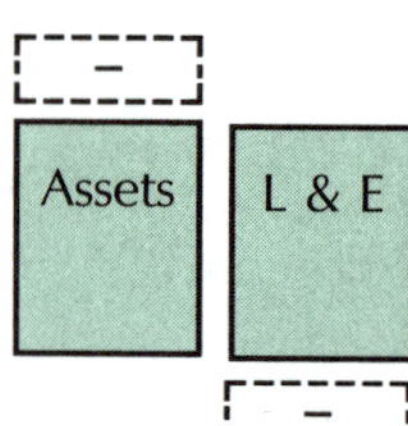

Now the balance sheet balances again. The journal entries look like this:

Debit: Increase cost of goods sold

Credit: Inventories in balance sheet

EXERCISE 24
Avocado Explosion

COGS and inventories

T&J's decided to launch a new ice cream called Avocado Explosion. They bought the following ingredients:

- $2,000 worth of avocados, paid for with an IOU. *Hint: increase accounts payable and inventories.*
- $5,000 worth of milk, paid for with an IOU to the farmer *Hint: increase accounts payable*

Then they delivered $3,000 worth of Avocado Explosion to a trendy restaurant in New York. *Hint: increase COGS, decrease inventory.*

T&J's charged $5,000 for the ice cream. The restaurant paid $2,500 in cash and said they would pay the balance in one month.

1. After the transaction, what would the balance sheet and income statement look like? (Assume no taxes are paid.)

Assets	
Cash	
Inv.	
Acct. Recv.	
Total	

L & E	
Acct Pay	
Ret earnings	
Total	

Inc. Statement	
Sales	
COGS	
Net income	

2. [ ] What is T&J's gross profit on the sale?

INTEREST AND THE BALANCE SHEET

Interest expense

Long term liabilities are mostly debt accounts. A company is charged interest on its outstanding loans, which are recorded on the balance sheet. The larger a company's outstanding loans, the larger its interest expense, assuming interest rates stay constant.

Interest income

The amount of a company's interest income depends on the amount of its interest-bearing assets. These include:

- Cash in deposit accounts
- Loans to other entities
- Bonds

The larger a company's interest-bearing accounts, the larger its interest income, assuming interest rates stay constant. Interest income is shown on the income statement after the company's operating profit line, usually above the interest expense account.

EXERCISE 25
Interest income and expense

Interest income and expense

1. If a company increases the loans on its balance sheet, what will happen to the interest expense on its income statement?
   ❑ Increase ❑ Decrease ❑ Stay the same

2. Suppose a company's interest income rises and interest rates stay the same. What does this suggest about its interest-bearing assets like bonds and cash in deposit accounts?
   ❑ They increased ❑ Decreased ❑ Stayed the same

3. A company took out a \$40,000 loan at the beginning of the year. The bank charges interest at 7% per annum. What would be the journal entries for interest expense at the end of the year assuming the company paid the bank in cash?
   Debit ____________________ __________
   Credit ____________________ __________

4. Another company had an exceptionally good year. At year end it put \$67,000 on deposit at its bank at 6.2% interest. How would journal entries record the interest at the end of the following year?
   Debit ____________________ __________
   Credit ____________________ __________

EXERCISE 26
The links

Use this form to help track journal entries

	Account	*Debits*	*Credits*
Dr	________	________	
Cr	________		________
Dr	________	________	
Cr	________		________
Dr	________	________	
Cr	________		________
Dr	________	________	
Cr	________		________
Dr	________	________	
Dr	________	________	
Cr	________		________
Dr	________	________	
Cr	________		________
Dr	________	________	
Cr	________		________
Dr	________	________	
Cr	________		________
Dr	________	________	
Cr	________		________

Check your work.
Do debits = credits?

Total debits ________
Total credits ________

Links between balance sheet and income statement

1. Using the T&J's balance sheet below, create an income statement and new balance sheet for 2006.
   - T&J bought milk for $150,000. The farmer gave them credit.
     Hint: Increase inventories and increase accounts payable.
   - T&J bought a new machine for $80,000 cash.
   - During the year they paid their management $49,000 in cash.
     Hint: Increase SG&A
   - The bank charged 12% on their existing loans. They paid in cash.
   - During the year, T&J generated $200,890 in revenue. $10,000 was on credit, the rest was in cash.
   - T&J's sales cost them $130,000.
     Hint: Reduce inventory and increase COGS
   - T&J's other administration costs were $10,890, paid in cash.
     Hint: Increase SG&A.
   - T&J's paid dividends of $1,000 in cash. *Hint: debit Ret. earnings.*
   - Assume they recorded and paid $3,851 of tax in cash during 2006.
   - ***Assume all other accounts remain the same.***

   Use journal entries, the cash balance template and B A S E analysis to calculate inventories and retained earnings.

Continue on Page 44 after you finish Question 1

T&J's balance sheet on 31 December 2005

ASSETS	*$000s*	*LIABILITIES*	*$000s*
Cash & cash equivalents	46,591		
Accounts receivable	18,833		
Inventories of ice cream	13,937	Accounts payable	38,915
Other current assets	7,986	Other current liabilities	5,627
Total current assets	**87,347**	**Total current liabilities**	**44,542**
Property & equipment net	56,557		
Investments	200	Long-term debt	16,669
Other non-current assets	6,498	**TOTAL LIABILITIES**	**61,211**
Total non-current assets	**63,255**		
		Paid-in capital	40,678
		Retained Earnings	48,713
		TOTAL EQUITY	**89,391**
TOTAL ASSETS	**150,602**	**TOTAL L&E**	**150,602**

Retained earnings

Beg

Add

Sub

End

Inventories

Beg

Add

Sub

End

T&J's income statement on 31 December 2006

Revenue/sales
Cost of goods sold
Gross profit

SG&A
Operating profit
Interest expense
Profit before tax

Tax
Net income

Cash balance

Receipts	Payments

T&J's balance sheet on 31 December 2006

ASSETS	*$000s*	*LIABILITIES*	*$000s*
Total curr. assets		**Total curr. liabs**	
Total NCA		**Total NCL**	
		TOT. LIABILITIES	
Total NCA		**TOTAL EQUITY**	
TOTAL ASSETS		**TOTAL L&E**	

EXERCISE 26
The links, *continued*

Links between B/S and I/S, *continued*

2.a. Where are dividends paid from?

❑ Retained earnings ❑ Net income ❑ Sales

A company pays cash dividends of $28,000. What journal entries does it make?

Dr ____________ ____________

Cr ____________ ____________

b. A company has accumulated $3,200,894 of earnings from previous years. It generates $134,892 of income during the year, and pays $90,891 in dividends during the year. What are its year-end retained earnings?

Year-end retained earnings ______________________

3a. Name two links between the balance sheet and the income statement.

Link 1.

Link 2.

b. What's the difference between accounts receivable and accounts payable ?

4a. A company buys $100,000 of inventory on credit. What journal entries does it make?

Dr ____________ ____________

Cr ____________ ____________

b. A company delivers goods that cost $3,589 to produce. What journal entries must it make?

Dr ____________ ____________

Cr ____________ ____________

END OF PART 1

You have reached the end of Part 1. Now take the ***Checkout Test*** and score at least 90%. If you do not score at least 90%, you should review Part 1 again and then retake the test.

Don't go on to Part 2 until you have taken the test and scored at least 90%. If you don't know this material, you probably won't be able to complete the assignment at the end of the book.

Turn the page to start the test.

This test will probe your understanding of basic accounting. You should meet standards (90% or $900,000) in this test before moving to Part 2.

CHECKOUT TEST FOR PART 1

Section 1

You are the Chief Financial Officer for FizzCo. Your bookkeeper gives you the information below to build year-end financial statements for 2005.

Figures are in millions.

- ❑ Create FizzCo's income statement for the year ending Dec. 31, 2005.
- ❑ Create a balance sheet for FizzCo as of Dec. 31, 2005.

Fill in the blank forms on the opposite page.

Round your answers to the nearest million

Income statement

1. Sales for the year were $20,438.
2. Other operating costs were equal to 0.675% of sales for the year.
3. COGS was $7,943.
4. Interest income was $76, interest expense $221.
5. FizzCo recorded $1,027 worth of income taxes during the year.
6. SG&A costs were equal to 44.7% of sales for the year.

Balance sheet *(as of December 31, 2005, except when otherwise noted)*

1. Just before FizzCo paid its dividend, the company's cash and cash equivalents on its balance sheet amounted to $2,126.
   Hint: Remember to remove dividends from the cash balance.
2. Other current liabilities amounted to $120.
3. FizzCo owed $2,346 in long-term debt. Other long-term liabilities were $4,908.
4. Customers owed FizzCo $1,764.
5. FizzCo paid a dividend of $796.
   Hint: Use this to help calculate ending retained earnings and cash.
6. Retained earnings were $4,878 at the beginning of the year.
7. FizzCo had short-term bills *(accounts payable)* outstanding of $3,815.
8. On December 31, FizzCo had $905 worth of inventories.
9. Other current assets were $570.
10. Property plant and equipment was $5,438.
12. FizzCo owned $2,978 of long-term investments.
13. Other long-term assets amounted to $5,319.
14. Paid-in capital was $984.

Checkout test continued on next page

FizzCo's Income Statement (in millions)
Year ending December 31, 2005

Net Sales	________
Cost of Sales	________
Gross Profit	________
Selling General and Administrative Expenses	________
Other Operating Costs	________
Operating Profit	________
Equity Income	________
Interest Income	________
Interest Expense	________
Earnings Before Tax	________
Provision for Income Taxes	________
Net Income	________

FizzCo's Balance Sheet (in millions)
Year ending December 31, 2005

ASSETS		**LIABILITIES AND SHAREHOLDERS' EQUITY**	
Cash and cash equivalents	________	Accounts payable	________
Accounts receivable	________	Other current liabilities	________
Inventories	________	**Total current liabilities**	________
Other current assets	________	Long-term debt	________
Total current assets	________	Other long-term liabilities	________
Investments	________	**Total liabilities**	________
PP&E	________	Paid-in capital	________
Other long-term assets	________	Retained earnings	________
		Total shareholders' equity	________
Total assets	________	**Total liabilities and shareholders' equity**	________

Section 2

1. Explain the meaning of the matching concept:

2. In 2005 T&J's, Inc. made $400,000 in sales, 35% on credit and 65% for cash. Fill in the journal entries:

   Dr ____________ ____________

   Dr ____________ ____________

   Cr ____________ ____________

3. What does **GAAP** stand for?

4. Which, if any, personal assets of Deutsche Lazard's employees are included in the financial statements of Deutsche Lazard?

5. Explain "Accounting represents information about an entity."

6. Name four current assets or current liabilities:

   a. ____________

   b. ____________

   c. ____________

   d. ____________

7. Describe what equity represents on the balance sheet.

8. Name two things financial statements cannot tell you:

   a. ____________

   b. ____________

Checkout test continued on next page

Score pad

Section 1

Income statement correct

Worth $300,000

Balance sheet correct

Worth $300,000

Your score:

Section 2

Each correct question is worth $25,000. All parts of the question must be correct.

Your score:

Section 3

Each correct question is worth $25,000. All parts of the question must be correct.

Your score:

TOTAL SCORE

Section 3

1. What is the difference between cost of goods sold and sales, general and administrative costs?

2. The balance sheet reflects operating activities over the year.
   - ❑ True ❑ False

3. Which balance sheet account is net income added to?

4. What does the income statement measure?
   - ❑ Changes in equity ❑ Changes in cash

5. When are revenues recognized?

6. Describe non-cash current assets.

7. How is inventory linked to the income statement?

8. If a company's cash balance grows, what will happen to:
   - Interest income ______________________
   - Interest expense ______________________

END OF CHECKOUT TEST FOR PART 1

If you don't earn $900,000 on this test, go back and review the concepts you missed.

ABOUT PART 2

Now you'll start to apply your basic accounting skills by analyzing the Coca-Cola Company's financial statements. Like a detective, you'll find crucial information, which you'll use to understand more about the company's performance.

What you'll learn

When you finish Part 2, you will understand what a company's financial statements can tell you. You will know:

- ☑ What you can find in a company's **financial statements**;
- ☑ What the **individual accounts** on the balance sheet and income statement tell you;
- ☑ How to calculate a **cash flow statement**;
- ☑ What the numbers tell you about the **company's business**.

Introduction to Coca-Cola's annual report

...develops your financial accounting skills

You'll find Coca-Cola's financial statements in the attached booklet. You'll be referencing the information frequently for the rest of this book. Here is a summary of its key elements:

P 2 – 3	Selected financial data
P. 4 – 5	The balance sheet
P. 6	The income statement
P. 7	The cash flow statement
P. 8	Statement of shareholders equity
P. 9 – 58	Notes to the accounts

Look for this icon

Every time you see this icon, you'll be looking for information in Coca-Cola's annual report.

Here we go!

Turn the page and let's get started.

Financial analysis tip

Your information source

One of your major sources of information about a company is the financial statements and other information in its ***annual report***. In Part 2, you will extract and interpret key data from Coca-Cola's annual report, skills every analyst must know how to use.

Different annual reports will have different layouts. However, most companies with publicly traded shares will include the information listed below.

Guide to the typical annual report

Section	Description
Financial highlights, Table of contents	Opening remarks.
Chairman's letter to shareholders	Overview of the company's activities during the year. General statements about the company's future plans and strategy.
Review of operations	A rich source of information for you. May include a breakdown of revenues and profitability by region and sector, a clear idea of investment plans and a lot of information about individual divisions.
Financials	The most important part for you. Financials are divided into into three sections:
1 Financial commentary	Includes useful information about ratios, margins and subsidiaries.
2. Financial statements	A summary of the company's financial statements for the full year. They include: *Income statement* *Balance sheet* *Cash flow statement* *Statement of shareholders equity*
3. Notes to the financial statements	Important: they include additional data about accounts and describe the company's significant accounting policies.
Report of independent auditors	The auditors check to see if the accounts are a fair and true reflection of the company's activities during that year.
Board of directors	Key management and the board of directors

THE BALANCE SHEET

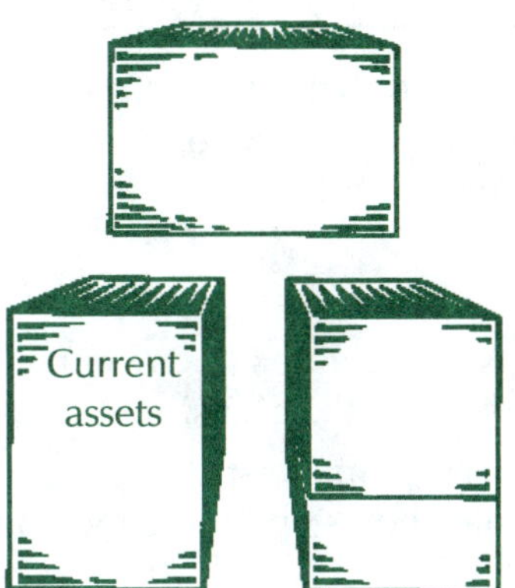

1. CURRENT ASSETS

CASH AND CASH EQUIVALENTS

Nearly all companies need cash to run their business.

- They need cash to pay salaries and bills.
- A retail store needs to give change when making sales.

Most companies' cash balances are small compared to their annual sales. They keep just enough ready cash to run their operations smoothly.

However, the cash situation changes when a company wants to make a big investment. Say Coca-Cola wanted to acquire a large bottling plant for $500 million. Coca-Cola may amass a large amount of cash in preparation for the acquisition. Then the amount of cash on the balance sheet would be far greater than needed just for everyday operations.

When a company is not using its cash balance it may invest its cash in very low risk ***liquid*** *(easily sold)* securities so it can generate interest income. Therefore very liquid securities are sometimes called ***cash equivalents***.

Typical cash equivalent: US Government treasury bills

EXERCISE 1
Coke's cash

For most of the exercises in Part 2, you will need to use the Coca-Cola financial statements in the separate booklet.

Coca-Cola's cash and cash equivalents

1. [ ] How much cash and cash equivalents did Coca-Cola have in 2004?
2. Is this a large or small amount compared with total sales? Use a ratio to help make your decision. Divide the cash and cash equivalents figure by the 2004 sales figure.

   Ratio: Cash & equivalents to sales [ ]

   ❑ Large ❑ Small
3. Do you think Coke is planning to use this cash for an acquisition?
   ❑ Yes ❑ No
4. Look at Coca-Cola's significant accounting policies in the notes to its accounts *(note 1)*. How does it describe cash equivalents?

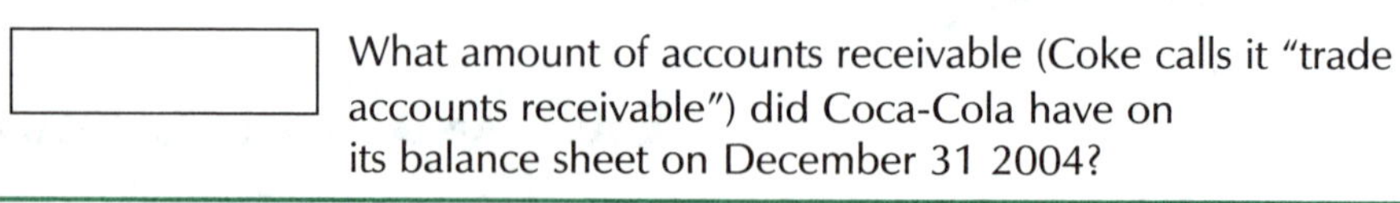

Accounts receivable

You already know that accounts receivable are sales that a company has made on credit. It has delivered the product to the customer but it has not collected the cash yet.

What amount of accounts receivable (Coke calls it "trade accounts receivable") did Coca-Cola have on its balance sheet on December 31 2004?

Allowances for bad debts

When a company sells goods on credit, it trusts customers to pay in the future. But some of those customers may default on their bills.

To prepare for some nonpayments, the company **estimates** that a proportion of its credit sales will **go bad**. This estimate shows up on the income statement as a bad debt expense. This expense is usually charged to SC&A in the income statement.

SG&A increases and profits fall due to bad debts

Example

Gross Profit	1,000
SG&A including bad debts	250
Net profit	750

If net income changes, equity changes too. If income falls, equity will fall. The assets side of the balance sheet will need a balancing entry.

That balancing entry is a separate account called ***bad debt allowance***, a contra account.

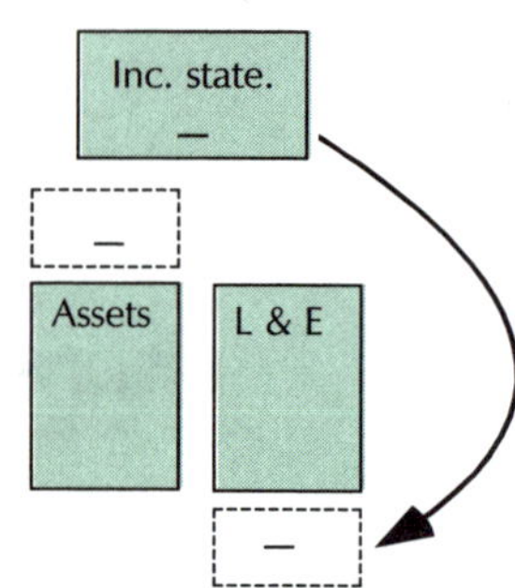

Contra accounts

A contra account is like a parasite. It lives off another account – its host. If the contra account grows, the "host" gets smaller. The bad debt allowance is attached to accounts receivable, which is its host.

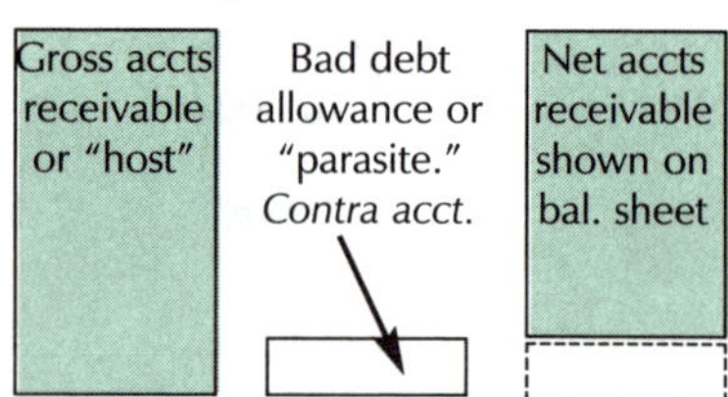

Journal entries for contra accounts are confusing because credits normally *decrease* asset accounts. But this credit *increases* the bad debt allowance. Because the bad debt allowance is a contra account, it reduces accounts receivable as it grows. So indirectly the credit decreases an asset account.

Example

Debit	Accounts receivable (B/S)	$1,000	
Credit	Revenues (I/S)		$1,000
Debit	Bad debt expense (I/S)	$50	
Credit	Bad debt allowance (B/S)		$50

When a company knows exactly which customer is not going to pay, it ***writes off*** (removes) that particular receivable and reduces its bad debt allowance.

Debit: Bad debt allowance (I/S)

Credit: Accounts receivable (B/S)

When the company writes off an accounts receivable, its net accounts receivable balance does not change.

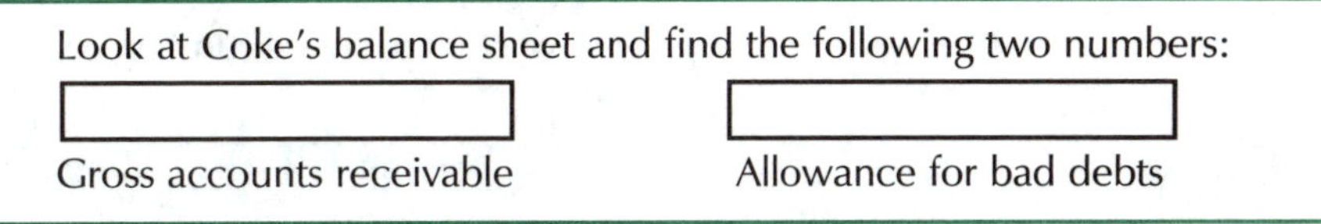
Look at Coke's balance sheet and find the following two numbers:

Gross accounts receivable	Allowance for bad debts

EXERCISE 2
Bad debts

All about bad debts

1. Assume you set up a clothes store in downtown New York. You estimate that 10% of your credit sales will never be paid. In the next year you make $240,000 of credit sales.

   ________ What is your bad debt allowance for the year?

   Fill in the journal entries:

   Debit: ________ ________

   Credit: ________ ________

2. Assume you are the financial director of Coca-Cola and you see a recession coming. You decide to increase your bad debt allowance to 5% of gross accounts receivable. Fill in the following table:

	Existing amount	+	Additional allowance	=	Ending amount
Gross accts. recv.	____	+	____	=	____
Bad debt allowance	____	+	____	=	____
Net accts. recv.	____	+	____	=	____

3. One of your customers in Texas goes bust. They owe you $2 million. You decide write it off as a bad debt. Fill in the following table:

   Debit ________ ________

   Credit ________ ________

4. ________ What is your new net accounts receivable balance for Coca Cola?

Financial analysis tip

More assets aren't always better

If you give customers credit you want them to pay you as soon as possible. It costs money to "fund" those assets on your balance sheet. Good management will try to reduce the amount of money tied up in accounts receivable.

Up until now you might have thought, *The more assets a company has, the better*. But that's not usually true! Follow this reasoning:

Shareholders want the company to generate as much income as possible for their investment. If income remains constant and assets rise, the company must increase its funding to make the balance sheet balance. It has two choices:

- It can raise debt. But then it must pay more interest expense, which reduces net income.
- It can raise equity. But then its net income is watered down because it's spread among more shareholders.

In either case, the percentage return of the shareholders' investment will fall.

*Account driver**

**The factors that make an account change from accounting period to accounting period.*

Pay attention to account drivers as you go through this book. They're important in financial analysis.

Financial analysis

The level of accounts receivable is driven by:

- The company's credit management;
- The proportion of credit sales to total sales;
- Selling conditions in the industry.

Analysts use the *receivable days ratio* to compare different companies' ability to manage their accounts receivable.

$$\text{Receivable days} = \frac{\text{Average accounts receivable}}{\text{Credit sales}} \times 365$$

Note: to calculate average accounts receivable, take last year's amount, add it to this year's and divide by two. Usually you won't be able to find credit sales, so most analysts use total sales.

Receivable days tells you the average number of days between the sale and the receipt of cash. A comparatively high receivables days figure tells you a company is not chasing people who owe it money fast enough.

Not a good situation! Such a "lazy" company has to fund more accounts receivable on its balance sheet, which costs money and lowers profitability.

Less accounts receivable = fewer assets to fund = greater profitability

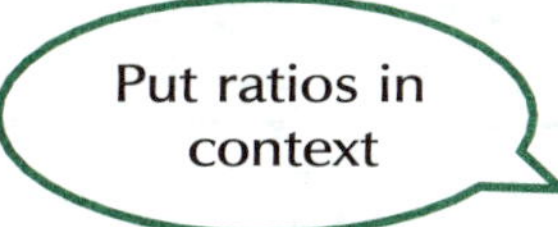

Analysts use ratios frequently. Remember that ratios are only meaningful ***in context***. You must:

- Compare them to other companies **in a similar business**.
- Look at them **over time**. Are they going up or down or remaining stable?

EXERCISE 3
Coke's receivable days

What About Coca-Cola's receivable days ratio?

1. [ ] Calculate Coca-Cola's receivable days using trade receivables after the allowance for bad debts. You won't find the credit sales figure so assume all the sales Coca-Cola made were on credit.
2. Suppose 3 competitors had the following receivable days ratios:

Competitor A	38
Competitor B	41
Competitor C	42

What does this suggest about Coke's management of its receivables?

Your conclusions

INVENTORIES

Inventory on a company's balance sheet consists of three things:

- Raw materials to be used in the production process·
- Products in the production process that are incomplete
- Finished products ready for sale

Inventory also includes the direct costs of producing goods, such as labor, storage and freight costs.

Name two items in Coca-Cola's inventory figure:

1. 2.

Hint: Look in the notes to the financial statements

EXERCISE 4
Inventory detection

Coca-Cola's inventory

Look for Coca-Cola's inventory on its balance sheet.

1. [ ] What was Coca-Cola's inventory at the end of 2004?

2. Coca-Cola started 2004 with $__________ worth of inventory.
   Hint: look at last year's ending balance

3. Coca-Cola took $__________ out of the inventory account in 2004.
   Hint: look on the income statement for cost of goods sold

4. Now use **B A S E** analysis to help you work out what Coca-Cola added to its inventory account during the year:

Beginning balance in 2004	
Additions in 2004	
Subtractions in 2004	
Ending balance in 2004	

Inventory records can be...

Simple inventory accounting

If you make only a few sales a year, it's easy to figure out the worth of your inventory. You can keep a ***perpetual inventory record***, which tracks the cost and sale price of each piece of inventory.

- If you are a top art dealer, you may sell only ten very expensive paintings a year. When you make a sale, you can easily identify the inventory you used to generate it.

Complex inventory accounting

Tracking each item of inventory is not practical for most businesses.

- Coca-Cola sells millions of cases of soft drinks each year. Can you imagine tracking the manufacturing cost and sale price of each can of Coke sold?

Companies like Coca-Cola use detective work to solve the problem of accounting for inventories. They can easily identify how much they spend increasing their inventory. It's harder for them to identify ***which*** items they sold ***when.***

Most companies record how much stock they have in their warehouse only periodically. This is called a ***periodic inventory record***.

Defining cost of goods sold

Over the course of a year the prices of Coca-Cola's raw materials will probably rise due to inflation. Therefore the Coke it manufactured at the beginning of the year costs less than the Coke made at the end of the year.

If Coca-Cola doesn't track the manufacturing cost of each gallon of Coke, how will it determine the cost of the Coke it sells? It can't. Instead, Coca-Cola will ***deduce*** the cost of goods sold.

Three ways to value inventory

There are three ways to "value" inventory:

LIFO	Last in, first out
FIFO	First in, first out
Average cost	

The following example demonstrates the three different methods. Note, while all three methods are allowed under US GAAP, under International GAAP LIFO is not allowed, so you would not see it when analyzing the financial statements of a European company.

Example

Assume you set up a gas station in Los Angeles. Getty delivers gas to you each month. Each delivery is poured into a storage tank at the back of the station.

Over the last four months you sold 36,000 gallons of gas and took the following deliveries:

	May	June	July	August
Gallons	15,000	15,000	15,000	15,000
Price per gallon	$0.30	$0.70	$1.00	$1.10
Total invoice	$4,500	$10,500	$15,000	$16,500

Because oil prices were very volatile during the four months, the price you paid for gas rose from $0.30 to $1.10. You can't easily establish your cost of gas sold because all the deliveries were poured into the same tank at the back of your station. GAAP accounting gives you three ways to work out your cost of goods sold at the end of four months:

* **Last in First Out (LIFO)**
  This method assumes you sold the gas which was delivered last (the newest gas) first:

Delivery			**COGS**
15,000	$1.10 * 15,000	=	$16,500
15,000	$1.00 * 15,000	=	$15,000
6,000	$0.70 * 6,000	=	$4,200
36,000			**$35,700**

continued on next page

Example

* **First in First Out (FIFO)**

This method assumes you sold the oldest gas (the first gas delivered) first:

Delivery		COGS
15,000	$0.30 * 15,000 =	$4,500
15,000	$0.70 * 15,000 =	$10,500
6000	$1.00 * 6000 =	$6,000
36,000		**$21,000**

* **Average cost**

This method uses the average cost of all the gas you bought to work out your cost of goods sold:

Delivery		Delivery cost
15,000		$4,500
15,000		$10,500
15,000		$15,000
15,000		$16,500
60,000		**$46,500**
Average cost =	**$46,500/60,000 =**	**$0.78**
COGS =	**$0.78 * 36,000 =**	**$28,080**

Summary

LIFO gives you the highest COGS figure but the lowest inventory figure.

FIFO gives you the lowest COGS figure but the highest inventory figure.

Average cost COGS and inventory figures will always fall between LIFO and FIFO.

Try the next exercise using the three different ways companies deduce their COGS and value their inventory.

EXERCISE 5
Inventory party

Companies can choose how they report inventory

Inventory accounting

Assume you operate a snack stand on the beach. During July you make several purchases of Coca-Cola at the following prices.

Date	Unit price per gallon	Gallons ordered	Total cost
July 1	$2.10	300	$630
July 5	$3.00	200	$600
July 10	$4.00	350	$1,400
July 17	$4.10	100	$410

During the month you sell 500 gallons of Coke. You only have one refrigerator, so you can't tell how much each gallon originally cost.

At the end of the month you take a periodic inventory to help deduce your cost of goods sold. You have 450 gallons of Coke left. You had no Coke at the start of the month.

What unit cost do you apply to the Coke you sold? Under U.S. GAAP, you have three choices:

Average cost method — You could take the average unit cost of all the Coke you bought.

FIFO — You could assume you sold the oldest Coke in the refrigerator first. *(First in first out or **FIFO** method of inventory valuation.)*

LIFO — You could assume you sold the newest Coke in the refrigerator. *(Last in first out or **LIFO** method of inventory valuation.)*

Average cost, FIFO, or LIFO

1. Find the cost of goods sold for each method of inventory valuation.

a. [ ] Average cost method

b. [ ] FIFO method

c. [ ] LIFO method

2. Which method uses the lowest cost of goods sold?
❑ Average cost method ❑ FIFO ❑ LIFO

3. Which method will give the company the highest net income?
❑ Average cost method ❑ FIFO ❑ LIFO

4. Will the amount of tax the company expenses be higher or lower using FIFO instead of the other methods? ❑ Higher ❑ Lower

continued on next page

Inventory accounting, *continued*

5. If you compare the ratio of net income to sales for a company that uses LIFO to the ratio for a company that uses FIFO, what fact should you consider?

6. Read note 1 ("significant accounting policies") in Coca-Cola's annual report. What does it say about Coke's inventory accounting policy?

Levels of inventory

Account driver

Usually the higher a company's sales the more inventory it needs (particularly true if a company is opening up new sales units).

Management can also have an impact on the level of inventories. If a company manages its warehouses more efficiently, it can support its sales with less inventory.

Normally inventories will remain the same proportion of a company's cost of goods sold each year.

Financial analysis

Managing inventory effectively is a big challenge for companies. Financial analysts are interested in how well – or how badly – a company is meeting the challenge. They use a ratio called ***inventory days*** to find out.

$$\text{Inventory days} = \frac{\text{Average inventory}}{\text{Cost of goods sold}} \times 365$$

The inventory days ratio tells you approximately how many days it takes inventory to move through a business. Generally, a comparatively low inventory days figure is better, because a faster-moving inventory means you can support the same amount of sales with less inventory assets. Faster moving inventory also reduces the likelihood of slow moving (obsolescent) items arising, that the business may be forced to sell at a loss , and warehousing costs are lower too.

Financial analysis tip

Less inventory = fewer assets to fund = greater profitability

EXERCISE 6
Inventory days

Coca-Cola's inventory days

1. [ ] Calculate Coca-Cola's inventory days in 2004.

2. Suppose Coca-Cola's three closest competitors had inventory days ranging from 42 to 47 in 2004. What conclusions can you draw about Coke's inventory management?

[ ]

Your conclusions

PREPAID EXPENSES

When you purchase insurance you pay your premium at the beginning of the policy. In effect you prepay for the benefit of having the insurance in the future. When a company prepays for a service we call it a ***prepaid expense***.

Prepaid expenses are intangible. You cannot physically touch them. Accounting treats "pre-paid" expenses as unexpired (unused) costs. Prepaid expenses go on the _________ side of the balance sheet.

PREPAID EXPENSES  I/S

Example

You agree to rent an apartment in New York and pay $6,000 (2 months' rent) in advance. Your payment is a prepaid expense.

After the two months is up, you can record the "use" of your apartment on your income statement as SG&A.

How it looks on your financial statements

	May 1	July 1
Income statement		
Rent expense (SG&A)	-no entry-	-6,000
Balance sheet		
Cash	-6,000	-no entry-
Prepaid expenses	+6,000	-6,000

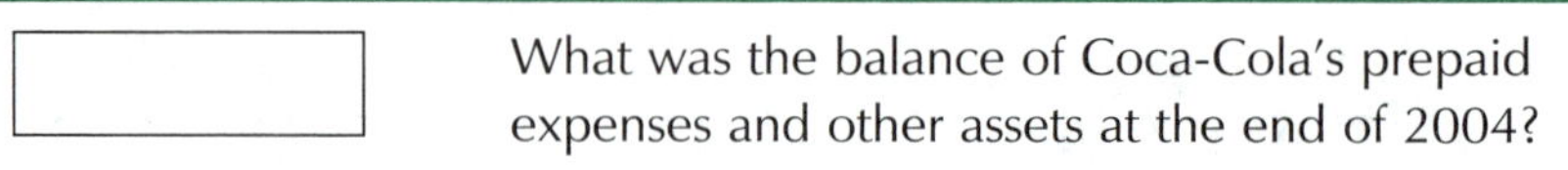

What was the balance of Coca-Cola's prepaid expenses and other assets at the end of 2004?

Prepaid expenses are linked to SG&A costs (and sometimes COGS) on the income statement.

Account driver

Prepaid expenses follow SG&A

Prepaid expenses usually remain the same proportion of SG&A from year to year. For example, a portion of Coca-Cola's prepaid expenses is advertising costs which are part of SG&A. If Coke spends proportionally more on advertising, SG&A and prepaid expenses will rise.

EXERCISE 7
Your new apartment

Prepaid rent

Write out the appropriate journal entries for the following transactions:

1. You move into a new apartment. The landlord asks for $10,000 for six months' rent in advance. You reluctantly hand over a check:

   Dr __________ __________

   Cr __________ __________

2. Three months later you recalculate your balance sheet. How do you account for the prepaid rent that expired?

   Dr __________ __________

   Cr __________ __________

3. Which of the following assets are prepaid expenses?

   a. ❑ Yes ❑ No Goods waiting to be sold.
   b. ❑ Yes ❑ No One rent payment for the following 12 months
   c. ❑ Yes ❑ No A payment for a bottling machine at Coca-Cola
   d. ❑ Yes ❑ No Wages paid in cash by Coca-Cola
   e. ❑ Yes ❑ No Insurance premium paid by Coke for next year.

4. [ ] How much advertising had Coke prepaid at the end of 2004? *Hint: look at note 1 in the annual report.*

OTHER CURRENT ASSETS

Those "other" accounts

Companies often combine small accounts into an "**other**"category. Sometimes the company will include information about this category in the notes to the financial statements. Always check the notes in the annual report when you are unclear what an account represents.

Financial analysis tip

Financial analysis tip

Many times you will be unable to find out what these "other" accounts really are. One technique financial analysts use is to track their proportion of sales or total assets over time.

If the account remains a stable percentage of sales, it's likely to be driven by everyday ***operational activities,*** like making sales. Current assets or liabilities are also more likely to be driven by operational activities.

If the account remains the same $ amount over time it is likely to be driven by a one-off event like taking out a loan.

EXERCISE 8
Recap

Recap current assets

1. ❑ Yes ❑ No Most current assets are resources that are essential to a company's operations.
2. ❑ Yes ❑ No Current assets typically become expenses or turn into cash within a year.
3. ❑ Yes ❑ No Cash is a current asset.
4. ❑ Yes ❑ No If a company takes out a loan it is accounted for as a current asset.
5. ❑ Yes ❑ No The buildings a company owns are current assets.

2. CURRENT LIABILITIES

Now you're going to jump across to the other side of the balance sheet to check out the current liabilities. These are obligations that are generated in the ordinary course of a company's business and are due within one year.

ACCOUNTS PAYABLE

You already know accounts payable are bills owed to other people, usually for inventory purchased on credit. Typically these bills are interest free: the person you owe money to probably won't charge you interest on your overdue account. Therefore **accounts payable are cheap funding for you!**

Generally a higher accounts payables figure is better as you are getting more free credit. However, you must be careful not to pay your bills too late or your suppliers might stop selling to you.

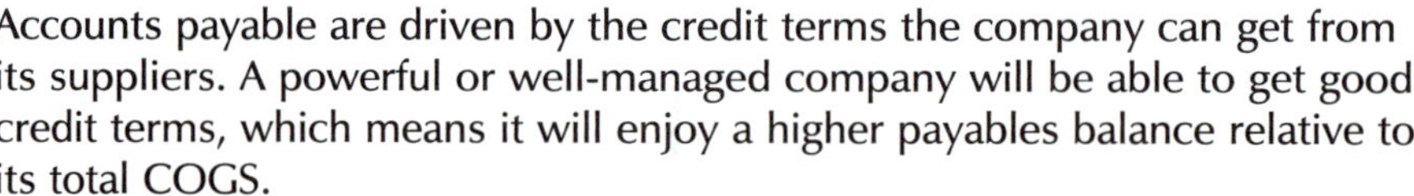

Accounts payable are driven by the credit terms the company can get from its suppliers. A powerful or well-managed company will be able to get good credit terms, which means it will enjoy a higher payables balance relative to its total COGS.

Account driver

A company's accounts payable are likely to remain the same proportion of cost of goods sold over time if industry practices or management doesn't change.

ACCRUED EXPENSES

Accrued expenses are the opposite of prepaid expenses. You have used services or received goods but have not yet been billed for them.

Salaries are a good example. Most people get paid in arrears. The company you work for ***accrues*** your wages. Do you charge interest on your unpaid salary? No! Again, this is another account that provides free funding for a company.

ACCRUED EXPENSES AND THE I/S

Accrued expenses are usually linked to SG&A costs on the income statement. Companies usually accrue expenses for services like utilities and labor. Some accrued expenses may be linked to COGS, for example, the accrued wages of factory workers.

Example

Assume you are paid $8,000 at the end of each month. Just before you get your check, the company has finished accruing your $8,000 salary expense.

How it looks on your financial statement

	March 30	March 31
Income statement		
Salaries (SG&A)	-8,000	-no entry-
Balance sheet		
Cash	-no entry-	-8,000
Accrued expenses	+8,000	-8,000

EXERCISE 9
Free credit

Accounts payable and accrued expenses

Notice how Coke lumps accounts payable and accrued expenses together on the balance sheet.

1. [ ] What was the balance of accounts payable and accrued expenses in 2004?

2. How does Coca-Cola break down its accounts payable and accrued expenses in the notes? *Hint: see note 5*

Name of division	Amount in $s
______	______
______	______
______	______
______	______
______	______
______	______

3. [ ] Coca-Cola also has an account called accrued income taxes (taxes expensed on the income statement and due within one year). How much were they in 2004?

Hold on for short-term debt

Short-term debt (loans due within a year or less and current maturities of long-term debt) is also a current liability. You'll learn about it later.

3. WORKING CAPITAL

Working capital is an important analytical concept. It's the difference between current assets and current liabilities.

Working capital	=	Current assets	–	Current liabilities

If a company's working capital is positive, its current assets are larger than its current liabilities. Some of its current assets will need financing through equity or long-term debt.

Example

A company has the following current assets and liabilities:

Cash	110	Short-term debt	105
Receivables	150	Payables	200
Inventory	200	Accrued expenses	100
Total	460	Total	405

Working capital = 55 (460 - 405)

This company has $55 more current assets than liabilities. It has to fund these assets in some way. Therefore, it needs financing, which it can get either through debt or equity.

EXERCISE 10
Working capital

Calculate working capital

1. Which accounts are included in working capital?
   - ❑ Yes ❑ No Cash
   - ❑ Yes ❑ No Buildings, land & equipment
   - ❑ Yes ❑ No Long-term debt

2. Calculate working capital using the following balance sheet info:

Cash	53
Receivables	68
Inventory	150
Short-term debt	80
Accounts payable	54
Accrued taxes	20

Working capital = ______

3. A company increases its inventory. What happens to working capital?
   ❑ Increases ❑ Decreases ❑ Remains the same

4. A company takes out a short-term loan. What happens to working capital?
   ❑ Increases ❑ Decreases ❑ Remains the same

5. A company pays a bill with cash. What happens to working capital?
   ❑ Increases ❑ Decreases ❑ Remains the same

Working capital measures risk

How do analysts use working capital?

Analysts use working capital to measure a company's ability to pay its current bills. In other words, working capital is a test of liquidity.

If a company has more current assets than current liabilities *(positive working capital)*, it can probably pay its current bills easily. Why? Because it can turn its short-term assets into cash within a year.

Another way to describe working capital is as a ***measure of risk***. Does a company have enough liquid resources to withstand a sudden downturn? Positive working capital means the company can liquidate current assets to raise cash in an emergency.

EXERCISE 11
Changes in working capital

Changes in working capital

What will happen to a company's working capital balance if:

1. A company adds more inventory to support an increase in sales.
   ❑ Increases ❑ Decreases ❑ Remains the same
2. A company takes out a new short-term note for cash.
   ❑ Increases ❑ Decreases ❑ Remains the same
3. A company takes out a new long-term loan, which increases cash:
   ❑ Increases ❑ Decreases ❑ Remains the same
4. A company issues $150m of equity for cash:
   ❑ Increases ❑ Decreases ❑ Remains the same
5. A company sells off $200m of PP&E and uses the money to pay off its long-term debt:
   ❑ Increases ❑ Decreases ❑ Remains the same
6. A company faces strong competition. It decides to increase its receivable days by 14 days. It funds this increase in its accounts receivable with short-term debt:
   ❑ Increases ❑ Decreases ❑ Remains the same

OPERATING WORKING CAPITAL

Some financial analysts use ***operating working capital*** instead of working capital. Operating working capital excludes current assets and liabilities ***not*** driven by day-to-day operating activities.

Operating activities Anything that helps a company carry out its day-to-day activities, such as making sales, purchasing supplies, paying bills to suppliers, and paying salaries.

Operating working capital does not include any accounts driven by investing or financing decisions.

Investing activities	Anything related to PP&E, investments in stocks and bonds, and other long-term assets.
Financing activities	Anything related to raising money through debt or equity.

Comparing working capital & operating working capital

Analysts use operating working capital because it's a better measure of the funding needed for the company's daily activities (operating activities).

In addition, a company can't manipulate its operating activities as easily as its investing or financing activities. A company can always wait to buy that new factory; it can't wait to replace the inventory it sold.

Operating working capital	Includes only current assets and liabilities that move with operating decisions.
Working capital	Includes all current assets and liabilities.

Example

A company has the following current assets and liabilities:

Cash	110	Short-term debt	105
Receivables	150	Payables	200
Inventory	200	Accrued expenses	100
Total	460	Total	405

Operating working capital = $50 (350 – 300)

Notice that cash and short-term debt are not included.

As a general rule:

Operating working capital = Current assets – cash – Current liabilities – debt

Negative operating working capital

Operating working capital is not always positive. Some companies can have negative operating working capital. They are companies whose current operating liabilities are greater than their current operating assets. For these lucky companies, operating working capital serves as a source of funds.

For example, magazine publishers collect subscription revenues in advance covering magazine deliveries for the next year. These advance revenues are recorded as a current liability. Receivables and inventory requirements are relatively low, resulting in a negative operating working capital figure which serves as a source of funds for the business.

EXERCISE 12
Coke's operating working capital

Calculate operating working capital for Coca-Cola

$ in millions

1. Calculate Coca-Cola's operating working capital for 2003 and 2004.
   *Hint: do **not** include finance subsidiary receivables in your calculation!*

	2003	2004
Sales		
Accounts receivable		
Inventories		
Prepaid expenses		
Accounts payable		
Accrued taxes		
Operating working capital		
Op. w. cap. as % of sales		

Estimating the level of operating working capital

Three key drivers of a company's operating working capital:

1. Its type of business and product

- ☑ Does the company manufacture products? Manufacturing companies usually have a high operating working capital/sales ratio due to large amounts of inventory.
- ☑ How long does it take for the company to manufacture the product? The longer it takes to manufacture a product the higher the level of inventories.
- ☑ Does the company provide a service? Service companies usually have a relatively low operating working capital/sales figure due to low inventory balances.

Account driver

2. Industry practices and management decisions

- ☑ Do customers pay cash or take credit? Higher credit sales mean higher accounts receivable.
- ☑ Can the company buy on credit or does it have to pay cash? More credit purchases mean higher accounts payable and accrued expenses.
- ☑ Does the management like to hold large stocks of inventory?·
- ☑ How much power does the company have over its customers and suppliers? More power means you are paid earlier by your customers, but you pay your suppliers later.

3. Accounting practices

- ☑ Does the company use LIFO or FIFO to account for its inventory? When prices are rising FIFO produces a higher inventory figure as you use your old inventory first.

EXERCISE 13
One last time

Coke's operating working capital, again

Use your solution to Exercise 12 to answer the following questions.

1. Why has Coca-Cola's operating working capital changed as a % of sales?

2. Will Coca-Cola's working capital increase or decrease?
   - ❑ Increase
   - ❑ Decrease

3. What does Coca-Cola's operating working capital balance suggest about its power over its suppliers?

Deal #5

SCORE PAD

1. ______
2. ______
3. ______
4. ______
5. ______
6. ______
7. ______
8. ______
9. ______
10. ______

Total

Close the deal #5

Get another tombstone by earning $100,000 If you make less than $100,000, review the material before you go on.

1. Calculate operating working capital and working capital for the following company:

CloseShave, 2006

Income taxes payable	319.4
Cash and equivalents	81.6
Accounts payable	1,609.8
Short-term investments	1.6
Loans payable (short-term)	634.7
Curr. portion of LTD	26.5
Accounts receivable	2,290.8
Inventories	1,267.6
Prepaid expenses	199.3
Other current assets	246.8

Operating working capital *Working capital*

2. What is the key difference between operating working capital and working capital? Why would you use operating working capital?

3. A company uses LIFO to calculate its ending inventory at the end of the year. If it used FIFO would its inventory be higher or lower? Assume prices are rising. ❑ higher ❑ lower

4. If a company pays $10m cash for insurance a month before the policy starts what would the journal entries be?

Dr ______ ______

Cr ______ ______

5. ______ If a company starts paying its bills later, which account on the balance sheet will rise?

6. ______ If a company never made any sales on credit, what account would be missing from their balance sheet?

continued on next page

Close the deal #5, *continued*

7. Which method of inventory accounting will yield a larger positive operating working capital? Assume prices are rising.

   ❑ LIFO ❑ FIFO

8. Which of the following accounts should ***not*** be included in an operating working capital calculation? Explain each answer.

   ❑ Accounts receivable ______________________________

   ____

   ❑ Marketable securities which are cash equivalents __________

   ____

   ❑ Accrued expenses ______________________________

   ____

   ❑ Inventories ______________________________

   ____

   ❑ Other current liabilities related to new debt financing

   ____

   ❑ Accounts payable ______________________________

   ____

9. A company makes $100,000 of credit sales and estimates 5% of its customers won't pay. How does it account for the sales?

   Dr __________ __________

   Cr __________ __________

   How does it account for its estimate for bad debts?

   Dr __________ __________

   Cr __________ __________

10. Suppose you run a large pharmaceutical company. If the US government deregulated the healthcare industry resulting in greater competition in your business sector, what is likely to happen to your accounts receivable?

    ❑ Rise ❑ Fall ❑ Remain the same

4. DEBT

SHORT-TERM DEBT

Debt that is borrowed for periods of less than one year is a current liability.

EXERCISE 14
Debt due within 12 months

Current debt liabilities

1. Name the two current debt accounts on Coca-Cola's balance sheet:

   a. ______________________________

   b. ______________________________

2. When will Coca-Cola have to pay this debt back?

   ____

   ____

3. Look at the notes under short term borrowings and credit arrangements. What do Coca-Cola's loans and notes payable (corporate bonds) consist of? *Hint: Look in Note 6.*

Current portion of long-term debt

"Current portion of LTD" is exactly what it says it is – the long-term debt you have to pay back in the next twelve months. So Coca-Cola has to pay back $1,490m worth of debt between December 31 2004 and December 31 2005.

This $1,490m was taken from last year's long-term debt account in the long-term liabilities section of the balance sheet.

Example

You are Coca-Cola's chief financial officer and you take out a $100m loan. You must pay the loan off over five years starting in the middle of year one:

End of...	Year 1	Year 2	Year 3	Year 4	Year 5	Year 6
Current maturity of LT debt	20	20	20	20	20	0
Long-term debt	80	60	40	20	0	0
Total debt outstanding	100	80	60	40	20	0

LONG-TERM DEBT

Long-term debt is debt originally raised for periods longer than one year.

EXERCISE 15
Long-term debt

Coca-Cola's long-term debt

- In 2004 Coca-Cola's total long-term debt amounted to $2,647m.
- $1,490m of this debt was due in the next twelve months.
- Assume that the company issues no more long-term debt in 2005 and answer the following questions:
  Hint: Read note 7 in the financial statements

1. [ ] What will be Coca-Cola's current maturity of long-term debt in 2005?
2. [ ] What will be Coca-Cola's long-term debt on its 2005 balance sheet?

A key part of a financial analyst's job in an investment bank is to help clients get funding at the lowest cost possible. One of the ways a company can fund itself is by using ***debt***.

Unlike equity, debt funding must be paid back. The easiest way to think about debt is as a series of cash flows.

Financial analysis tip

Cash flows

Borrowers ***receive*** cash	when they raise money;
Borrows ***pay out*** cash	either as interest or principal during the life of the loan.

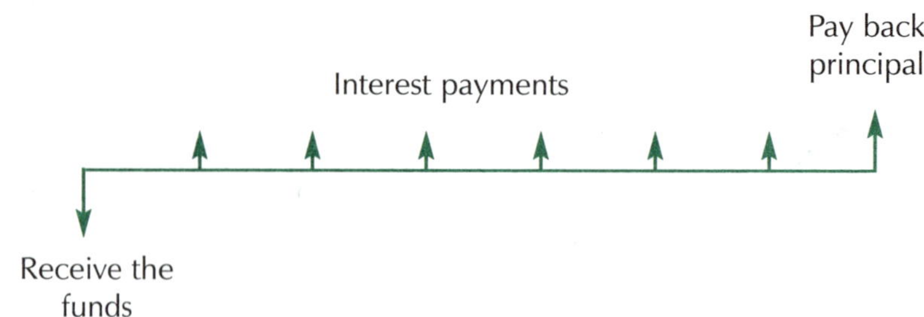

Principal — The amount of the loan. It's the money you agree to pay back when the loan is due. It is also known as the face amount of the loan.

Debt capital is riskier than equity...

...from the company's point of view

Companies are legally obliged to pay the interest and principal due to debt holders. A company is ***not*** legally obliged to pay dividends to equity holders. Therefore funding with debt capital is riskier to the company than funding with equity capital.

You usually see the total long-term debt outstanding on a company's balance sheet. You have to look in the notes to the financial statements to find when and how much the company raised at one particular time. Remember, the current portion of long-term debt is recorded in current liabilities.

EXERCISE 16
Debt close-up

Coca-Cola's long-term debt in detail

Look at Coca-Cola's balance sheet.

1. [ ] How much of Coca-Cola's long-term debt comes due in 2005?
2. Which debt "issues" come due in 2005?

Hint: look in the notes to the financial statements

3. How much long-term debt does Coca-Cola have to pay back in the following years? *Hint: look in the notes*

	2005	2006	2007	2008	2009
LT Debt to be repaid					

4. If Coca-Cola raised $400m of debt in the financial markets, what would be the new balances of assets, liabilities and equity?

Assets **Liabilities**

Equity

5. If Coca-Cola repaid $300m of its existing debt early, what would be the new balances of assets, liabilities and equity?

Assets **Liabilities**

Equity

5. TANGIBLE LONG-TERM ASSETS

Long-term assets are expected to be valuable to the entity for ***longer than one year***. There are two types of long-term assets:

- Those you can physically touch, called ***tangible assets.***
- Those you cannot see or feel, or ***intangible assets.***

PP&E

Tangible long-term assets are physical resources that the entity owns. They include buildings, machinery, land, cars, office equipment, etc. They are also known as **property, plant and equipment** (sometimes ***fixed assets***).

Look at Coca-Cola's annual report. List the tangible assets (Property, Plant & Equipment) on its balance sheet:

1. ______________________________
2. ______________________________
3. ______________________________
4. ______________________________

Notice the category called *buildings and improvements*. This records the original cost of buildings bought by Coca-Cola and the cost of improvements to them.

Recording PP&E on the balance sheet

You record PP&E (fixed assets) on the balance sheet at their ***original cost***. You add to this all the costs involved in getting the asset ready for its intended use, such as legal fees, transportation to the current location, necessary testing and non-recoverable taxes. You ***do not*** record PP&E at its market value.

EXERCISE 17
Watch those legal fees

Recording the full cost of equipment

Assume Coca-Cola buys a new bottling machine for $300,000. It spends $3,000 in legal fees to write a contract with the manufacturer. It is charged a $10,000 installation fee and a $1,000 transportation charge. At what cost would the bottling machine be recorded on Coca-Cola's balance sheet?

PP&E and fixed assets: two names for the same thing

Terms you should know

Property, Plant & Equipment	All the buildings, factories, warehouses, land, and equipment a company owns combined into one account. Abbreviated PP&E or PPE.
Capital expenditure	Additions to the property, plant and equipment account. Abbreviated CAPEX.
Sales of fixed assets	Reductions in PP&E.
Gross PP&E	Original cost of the assets owned at the year end.
Net PP&E	Gross PP&E - accumulated depreciation

DEPRECIATION

How to recognize wear and tear on assets

Most assets fall in value over time. They get "used up." This is true of most office buildings if they are not renovated on a regular basis, and it's especially true of machinery. For example, an aircraft might have a life of 20,000 flight hours, a piece of machinery could be measured as being useful to the business for 5 years, and so on.

Apart from land, most long-term tangible assets lose their value over time unless more money is spent on them. An exception is assets that become valuable to collectors. For example, a building's design or location might suddenly become "classic" or very fashionable. But accounting recognizes only the historical cost of an asset, not its market value.

Depreciation records wear and tear

Accounting records the gradual loss of an asset's usefulness in an account called ***accumulated depreciation***.

	Original cost of PP&E	Original purchase cost of asset
–	Accumulated Depreciation	Total value consumed so far
=	Net PP&E	Total value remaining

Another contra account, like bad debt allowance

Accumulated depreciation is a ***contra asset account***, which is a negative account. You can think of it as a parasite to its host account, PP&E. When accumulated depreciation goes up, Net PP&E must fall.

Net PP&E is simply gross PP&E less accumulated depreciation. All three accounts appear on the balance sheet, but Net PP&E is the only account which is added to total assets.

Example

Assume you buy a new car for $25,000. You assume it will last five years and will have no salvage value. Here's your balance sheet when you buy the car:

PP&E (car)	$25,000
Accum. depr.	$0
Net PP&E	$25,000

After 2 years, your balance sheet looks like this:

PP&E (car)	$25,000
Accum. depr.	($10,000)
Net PP&E	$15,000

After 5 years, your balance sheet looks like this:

PP&E (car)	$25,000
Accum. depr.	($25,000)
Net PP&E	$0

Financial analysis tip

You can tell how old a company's fixed assets are by dividing its accumulated depreciation by its PP&E (gross fixed assets).

The larger this number is, the older the company's fixed assets.

EXERCISE 18
The logging mills

Analyzing PP&E

1. You are advising a paper manufacturing company which wants to acquire a logging mill. After a few days of research you find two suitable targets. One of your client's key requirements is to purchase the company with the most up-to-date plant and equipment. Which company would you recommend to your client?

❑ **Watermill Logging Inc**

Gross plant and equipment	5,000,000
Accumulated depreciation	(1,000,000)
Net plant and equipment	4,000,000

❑ **Oregon Loggers Inc**

Gross plant and equipment	5,000,000
Accumulated depreciation	(4,000,000)
Net plant and equipment	1,000,000

2. Does Coca-Cola have relatively old or new property plant and equipment compared to its competitor below? ❑ Old ❑ New

	PepsiCo
Gross plant and equipment	15,930
Accumulated depreciation	(7,781)
Net plant and equipment	8,149

	PepsiCo	**Coke**
Accumulated depreciation / Gross PP&E		

How to account for depreciation

When you add depreciation to the balance sheet...

Your accumulated depreciation rises...
Your total assets fall...
And your balance sheet no longer balances.

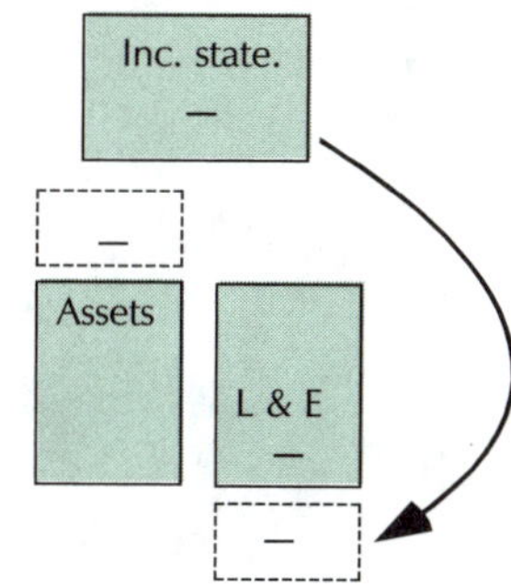

To bring the balance sheet back into balance, you record depreciation on the income statement as an expense so that...

Your net income falls...
Your retained earnings fall...
And your balance sheet balances.

Here's how it looks as a journal entry:

Debit	Depreciation expense *(I/S)*	
Credit	Accum. depreciation	*(B/S)*

	What was Coca-Cola's depreciation expense in 2004? *Hint: look in the Selected Financial Data section of Coca-Cola's annual report under Balance Sheet Data*
	What was Coca-Cola's gross PP&E in 2004? *Hint: look on the Balance Sheet*
	What was Coca-Cola's accumulated depreciation in 2004?
	What was Coca-Cola's Net PP&E in 2004?

Calculating depreciation

When a company buys a new fixed asset, it estimates how many years of useful life the asset will have and its expected salvage value at the end of its life.

	Original cost of asset
–	Estimated salvage value
=	Total depreciation

Two methods for calculating depreciation

Each year the company will expense part of the asset's total depreciation. It has a choice of two ways to calculate its yearly depreciation expense:

- Straight-line depreciation
- Accelerated depreciation

Straight-line depreciation in three easy steps

1. **Subtract** your estimate of the salvage value from the asset's original cost to get your total depreciation.
2. **Estimate** how many years you expect the asset to last.
3. **Divide** your total depreciation by the number of years you expect the asset to last.

Result: the yearly depreciation expense over the life of the asset.

When you have fully depreciated the asset, only the salvage value will be left on the balance sheet.

Example

Black Diamond Ski Stores, Inc., purchased a delivery truck which cost $50,000. Management expected the truck to last three years and have a residual value of $5,000.

	Year 1	Year 2	Year 3	Year 4
Income statement				
Depreciation expense	15,000	15,000	15,000	0
Balance sheet				
Gross PP&E	50,000	50,000	50,000	50,000
Accumulated depreciation	15,000	30,000	45,000	45,000
NET PP&E	35,000	20,000	5,000	5,000

EXERCISE 19
The bottling machine

Calculate straight-line depreciation

Assume that Coca-Cola bought a new bottling machine for $314,000 (including installation and setup costs). Now assume that Coca-Cola expects the machine to last for five years and have a salvage value of $10,000 at the end of that time.

[ ] Calculate how much Coca-Cola would depreciate this asset each year, using straight-line depreciation.

Accelerated depreciation

Accelerated depreciation means:

1. ***Higher*** depreciation in the early years;
2. ***Lower*** depreciation in the later years.
3. The total depreciation expense is the same as with the straight line method but the ***timing*** is different.

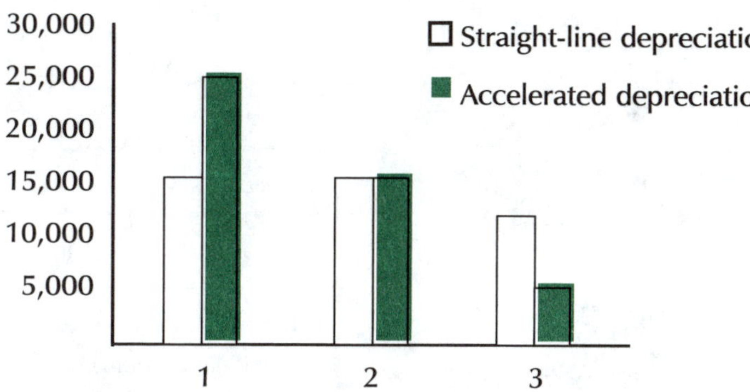

Straight-line vs. accelerated depreciation

Example

Assume Black Diamond decided to use accelerated depreciation. See the graph above.

	Year 1	Year 2	Year 3	Year 4
Income statement				
Depreciation expense	25,000	15,000	5,000	0
Balance sheet				
Gross PP&E	50,000	50,000	50,000	50,000
Accumulated depreciation	25,000	40,000	45,000	45,000
NET PP&E	25,000	10,000	5,000	5,000

Look at Coca-Cola's annual report.

What method of depreciating assets does Coca-Cola typically use?

❑ Straight line ❑ Accelerated

Hint: look in the note to the accounts headed "Accounting Policies."

Depreciation and the income statement

Where is depreciation expense recorded on the income statement?

Answer: It depends on the type of fixed assets you are depreciating.

Production assets:	Add depreciation to **COGS**
Non-production assets:	Add depreciation to **SG&A**

EXERCISE 20
Depreciation Workout

Depreciation

A company had the following assets in its accounts:

Production fixed assets		**Non-production fixed assets**	
Original cost of production equipment	500,000	Headquarters building	50,000
Accum. depreciation	150,000	Accum. depreciation	20,000
Net production assets	350,000	Net non prodn. assets	30,000

Assume the company uses straight-line depreciation.

1. The company is depreciating the headquarters building by $5,000 each year. The expected residual value of the building is $10,000. How long did the company estimate the building will last?
2. How much depreciation will the company expense for its headquarters building next year? Where would you find it on the income statement?
3. If the production equipment had no salvage value and an estimated life of ten years, how many years has the company owned the equipment?
4. How much depreciation expense will the company include in its COGS next year?
5. What was the company's total depreciation expense this year?
6. Does the net asset value necessarily reflect the market value of a company's fixed assets? ❑ Yes ❑ No

Selling non-current assets

Although companies buy fixed assets to hold for long periods, they may want to sell them before their original cost is fully depreciated.

When you sell an asset, you must remove from the balance sheet **both** the accumulated depreciation and the gross PP&E assigned to the asset.

Carrying value = Net PP&E value

When you sell an asset you typically receive cash. If the cash you receive does not equal the ***carrying value*** *(net PP&E value)* on your balance sheet, the balance sheet won't balance after you record the transaction. Therefore:

- If the cash you receive is lower than the asset's carrying value, record ("expense") a ***loss*** on the income statement.
- If the cash you receive is higher than the asset's carrying value, record a ***gain*** on the income statement.

Example

Assume you own a van that originally cost $10,000. So far, you have $3,500 of accumulated depreciation recorded against it, making its carrying value, also known as *book value*, $6,500.

Suppose you decide to sell it.

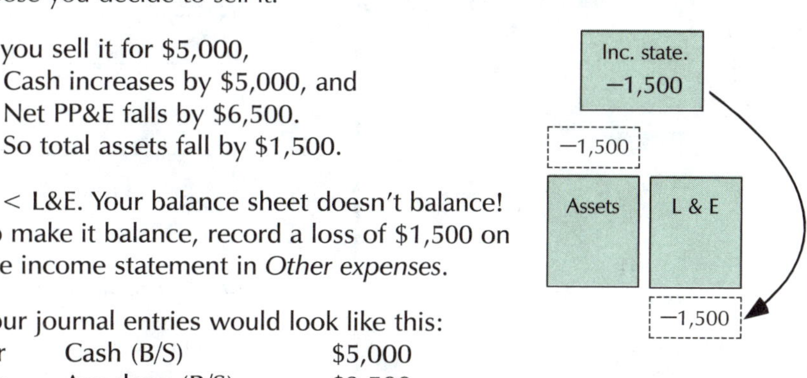

1. If you sell it for $5,000,
   - Cash increases by $5,000, and
   - Net PP&E falls by $6,500.
   - So total assets fall by $1,500.

   A < L&E. Your balance sheet doesn't balance! To make it balance, record a loss of $1,500 on the income statement in *Other expenses*.

   Your journal entries would look like this:

Dr	Cash (B/S)	$5,000	
Dr	Acc depn (B/S)	$3,500	
Dr	Other expenses (I/S)	$1,500	
Cr	Gross PP&E (B/S)		$10,000

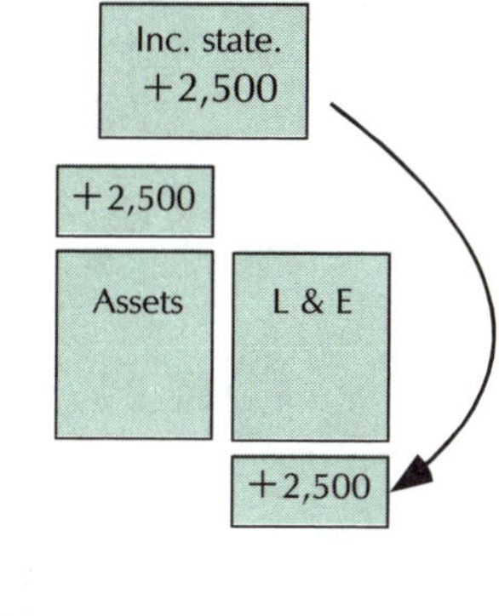

2. If you sell the asset for $9,000:
   - Cash increases by $9,000
   - Net PP&E decreases by $6,500
   - So total assets rise by $2,500.

   A > L&E. Your balance sheet doesn't balance!

   To make it balance, record a gain of $2,500 on the income statement in *Other income*.
   Your journal entries would look like this:

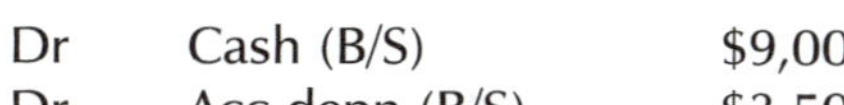

Dr	Cash (B/S)	$9,000	
Dr	Acc depn (B/S)	$3,500	
Cr	Gross PP&E (B/S)		$10,000
Cr	Gain on sale (I/S)		$2,500

EXERCISE 21
That bottling machine again

Coca-Cola's fixed assets, *continued*

1. In 2005 Coca-Cola sold a bottling machine that originally cost $500. Its accumulated depreciation was $200. If it was sold for no gain or loss, show the journal entries.

   Dr ______________ __________

   Dr ______________ __________

   Cr ______________ __________

2. If the same asset is sold for a $250 gain, how would you record the sale?

   Dr ______________ __________

   Dr ______________ __________

   Cr ______________ __________

   Cr ______________ __________

3. If the asset is sold for a $100 loss, how would you record it?

   Dr ______________ __________

   Dr ______________ __________

   Dr ______________ __________

   Cr ______________ __________

4. If an asset is sold at a loss, is it a loss of cash or a paper loss?

   ❑ Cash ❑ Paper

5. Coca-Cola's balance sheet on Dec. 31 2004:

Total property, plant and equipment	$10,149
Accumulated depreciation	$4,058
Net property, plant and equipment	$6,091

Assume that in 2005 Coca-Cola sold property, plant and equipment (PP&E) that originally cost $300m and had $100m of accumulated depreciation allocated to it.

Assume that Coca-Cola also bought $1,000m worth of new PP&E and depreciated its existing PP&E by $500m. Use the following table to calculate Coca-Cola's ending Net PP&E balance in 2005.

	Gross PP&E	Acc depr	Net PP&E
Beginning balance			
Additions			
Subtractions			
Ending balance			

6. INTANGIBLE LONG-TERM ASSETS

Intangible assets are resources you cannot touch. Intangible assets are split into two main categories:

- Goodwill
- Other intangible assets

GOODWILL

When one company buys another company, it is buying more than just assets on a balance sheet. It's also buying some intangibles, like the quality of the employees and client base, its reputation, or its brand name.

Financial analysis tip

You don't normally record these intangibles on a balance sheet because they are difficult to measure. But when you buy another company, you record these valuable intangibles on your balance sheet as ***goodwill***. The purchase price includes these intangibles. If PepsiCo bought Coca-Cola, part of the purchase price would include Coke's brand name and reputation.

Example

Suppose you buy a company's equity for $100 cash. On their balance sheet the equity has a book value of $30.

What you paid	What you got	Difference
$100 cash	$30 equity	$70

The difference between what you paid and what you got is goodwill.

Note: Complex issues cluster around this topic. For more details, look into consolidation accounting.

EXERCISE 22
Goodwill

Goodwill

1. You buy a company for $400m. It has $500m of assets and $350m of liabilities. How much is your goodwill?
2. What does goodwill represent?

AMORTIZATION AND IMPAIRMENT

Tangible assets are depreciated. The depreciation of *intangible* assets is called ***amortization.***

- Intangible assets with an indefinite life are not amortized, for example, goodwill. However such intangibles are subject to ***impairment reviews***. An impairment review involves comparing the balance sheet value of goodwill to its current market value. If the market value is less than the balance sheet figure the difference is charged to the income statement within SG&A costs.
- Intangible assets with a finite life are amortized straight line over their life, for example, patents.
- Intangibles have no salvage value.

Like depreciation, amortization is expensed (recorded) on the income statement and accumulated on the balance sheet. Amortization is incorporated into SG&A on the income statement.

However, unlike depreciation, you are unlikely to see an account called ***Accumulated amortization.*** On the balance sheet, intangible assets are usually shown after accumulated amortization has been subtracted.

EXERCISE 23
Goodwill extravaganza

More goodwill

1. What is the amount of Coca-Cola's goodwill and other intangibles in 2004?

   Goodwill and other intangibles ____________

2. What is Coca-Cola's principal method of treating intangible assets?
   Hint: check note 1

3. Assume Coca-Cola bought a patent and recorded $500m intangible assets. Coca-Cola decided to amortize the patent over ten years. Fill in the following table:

End of	Year 1	Year 2	Year 3	Year 4	Year 5
Amortization expense on the income statement					
Accumulated amortization					
Balance of intangibles on the balance sheet					

4. Is amortization and impairment a cash expense? ❑ Yes ❑ No

5. [ ] What was Coca-Cola's depreciation in 2004? *Hint: look in the selected financial data section*

6. [ ] What was the amount of Coca-Cola's depreciation and amortization in 2004? *Hint: look in the consolidated statement of cash flows.*

7. [ ] Using your answers to the last two questions, find Coca-Cola's amortization expense in 2004.

OTHER INTANGIBLE ASSETS

Other intangibles include:

Other Intangibles
Patents
Franchises
Licenses

Record intangibles only if you purchase them

Intangible assets like franchises and patents are included on the balance sheet only when they are bought from an external entity, not if they are developed internally.

According to some valuation sources its "Coca Cola" brand's real value is over $67 billion in 2005. However, Coca-Cola's total assets on its balance sheet are only $31 billion. Why the discrepancy? Because the Coca-Cola brand has never been properly measured.

When you buy another company's trademark you are also measuring its value so you will record the purchase on your balance sheet as an intangible asset.

Most intangibles are recorded on the balance sheet only when they are purchased from another entity.

EXERCISE 24
What's in a name?

Coca-Cola's brand name

1. Coca-Cola's brand name is estimated to be the most valuable asset the company has. Why is it not shown on the balance sheet?

2. If PepsiCo bought the Coca-Cola brand name for $70 billion in cash how would it account for the purchase?

Dr ____________________ __________

Cr ____________________ __________

Investments on the balance sheet

7. INVESTMENTS

When you buy securities in the financial markets, you are purchasing an interest in another entity which is valuable to you. You hope your purchase will appreciate in value and pay a return.

Financial analysis tip

When a company purchases debt securities like loans or bonds from another entity, it records the purchase as an ***investment*** on its balance sheet. If you are accounting for shares in another company and you have a controlling interest *(this usually means owning more than 50%)* you **consolidate** *(combine)* your accounts with the other company. If you don't own a controlling interest, you must account for the shares as ***investments*** on your balance sheet.

Investments in which you own a controlling interest

You may have noticed the heading at the top of Coca-Cola's balance sheet, "The Coca-Cola Company and its subsidiaries." This tells you you're looking at a ***consolidated balance sheet***. Coca-Cola's accountants have combined all the entities in which Coca-Cola has a ***controlling interest*** *(more than 50%)*.

What does Note 1 say about Coca-Cola's consolidation policy?

Account driver

The amount of investments on a company's balance sheet will depend on the company's strategy. If a company's strategy is to own stakes in other entities, it will have a large amount of investments on its balance sheet.

A good way to understand whether owning investments is part of a company's long-term strategy is to track their proportion of total assets over time.

EXERCISE 25
Equity, cost, or other?

Investments

	1.	What amount of Coca-Cola's investments are recorded using the cost method in 2004?
	2.	What is the amount of Coca-Cola's total marketable securities and other assets in 2004?

Other assets

In many financial statements you will find "mystery" accounts. You can't easily understand what they represent. Don't panic! You must learn to deal with this ambiguity.

Deal #6

SCORE PAD

1. ______

2. ______

3. ______

4. ______

5. ______

6. ______

Total

Close the deal #6

You must make $50,000 to earn this tombstone. If you make less than $50,000, review the material before you go on.

1. What distinguishes tangible and intangible fixed assets?

2. If Coca-Cola bought a building for $1,000,000, spent $50,000 on redecorating before it moved in, and paid its surveyor $5,000 to report on the building, all for cash, how would it account for the purchase of this building?

3. Assume Coca-Cola builds a new bottling plant. The plant cost $550,000 to build. Coca-Cola expects the building to last fifteen years. It also expects to be able to sell the building for $50,000 at the end of its useful life. It paid a lawyer $10,000 to draw up the contract to build the building.

   Fill in the following table setting out the building's net PP&E on Coca-Cola's accounts and its depreciation expense each year. Assume Coca-Cola uses straight-line depreciation. Show your figures in '000's.

End of	2005	2006	2007	2008	2009
Original cost of building	______	______	______	______	______
Accumulated depreciation	______	______	______	______	______
Net PP&E of building	______	______	______	______	______
Depreciation expense	______	______	______	______	______

4. Where would the bottling plant's depreciation expense be recorded on Coke's income statement?

Close the deal #6, *continued*

5. You have a client who is looking at purchasing a transportation company. You look at the company's balance sheet and see that their trucks originally cost $5,000,000. The company had accumulated depreciation related to its trucks of $4,500,000. What advice would you give to your client?

6. You are the CEO of Coca-Cola. You decide to sell two buildings:

   21 Park Street, Atlanta

   You originally bought this building for $1,500,000. Since you bought the building you have accumulated $1,000,000 of depreciation against it. You agreed to sell the building for $600,000 cash.

   Olympic Towers, 100 Center Boulevard, Atlanta

   You originally bought this building for $12,000,000. Since you bought the building you have expensed $10,000,000 of depreciation against it. You agreed to sell the building for $1,200,000 cash.

   Write the journal entries for these transactions:

8. OTHER LONG-TERM LIABILITIES

Mystery accounts

Other long-term *(non-current)* liabilities could include:

Deferred taxes Pension obligations for the company's employees·

The accounting for leases and pension obligations is complex. It's not covered here.

Reminder: When you are not sure what an account is:

1. Look in the notes to the accounts to get more information
2. See if the account is related to other accounts. For example you might want to see if it stays the same percentage of total assets or sales each year.

9. EQUITY

Equity is the difference between assets and liabilities. It represents the company owners' claim against the assets. Remember these points about equity:

Equity reminders

- ☑ Claims against a company's assets by its equity holders are considered ***after*** its debt holders' claims·
- ☑ Paid-in capital is never "repaid" while the company is operating.
- ☑ Holders of equity are entitled to receive dividends. A company does not have to pay dividends.

COMMON STOCK AND APIC

A company raises new equity by selling shares. Most share certificates are issued with a specific amount printed on them (the ***par value***). The total amount of par value on the shares a company has issued is recorded as ***common stock*** on the balance sheet.

If the company sells the shares for more than their par value, the difference is recorded as ***additional paid-in capital (APIC)***, or ***capital surplus***.

Example

Suppose a company issued 2m new shares. Each new share had a par value of $1 but was sold for $50. Here are the journal entries:

Dr	Cash	$100m *(= $50 x 2m)*	
Cr	Common stock		$2m *(= $2m x $1)*
Cr	APIC		$98m *(= $100m – $2m)*

Look at Coca-Cola's balance sheet to find information about its shares:

[   ] What is the par value of each Coca-Cola share?

Understand these definitions before you try Exercise 27.

Number of **issued** shares	=	number of shares sold since incorporation
Number of **outstanding** shares	=	shares owned by other entities

EXERCISE 26
Coke's shares

Shares

1. If Coca-Cola issued 100 new shares and sold them on Wall Street for $60 cash each with a par value of $0.25, what would you record in Coca-Cola's accounts? *Hint: you must make three entries.*

   ____

   ____

   ____

2. [   ] How many shares did Coca-Cola issue in 2004? *Hint: 2004 issued shares – 2003 issued shares*

3. [   ] What is the total number of shares that Coca-Cola has ever issued?

When a company buys back its own stock

TREASURY STOCK

Once a company has sold shares, it can buy them back at a later date. When a company buys back its shares, it records the "repurchase" in an account called ***treasury stock***:

- Enter into the treasury stock account the total price you paid to buy back the shares.
- Common stock or additional paid-in capital does not change.

The treasury stock account is a **contra account** to all the company's equity accounts. Remember how accumulated depreciation is a parasite on gross property, plant and equipment? Treasury stock is a parasite on a company's equity accounts.

Shares outstanding = shares issued – the number of repurchased shares

Example

CyberTech, a software company, wanted to reduce the amount of total equity on its balance sheet. It decided to use excess cash to buy back 2m of its own shares for $5 each.

Dr	Treasury stock	$10m *(2m x $5)*	
Cr	Cash		$10m

At the end of the transaction, CyberTech's total assets and shareholders' equity had both fallen by $10m.

Look at Coca-Cola's annual report.

1. [ ] What was the balance of Coca-Cola's treasury stock in 2004?
2. [ ] Calculate the number of Coca-Cola's outstanding shares as of Dec. 31, 2004.

RETAINED EARNINGS

Retained earnings are previous years' income that is kept in the business. Coca-Cola calls its retained earnings account "reinvested earnings."

The management of a company chooses the amount of dividends to pay out of retained earnings. Normally the amount of dividends is related to the business's profitability.

The payout ratio

Financial analysis tip

$$\text{Payout ratio} = \frac{\text{Dividends}}{\text{Net income}}$$

A fast-growing company will probably have a low payout ratio because it will use its earnings to help fund its future operations. A mature business is more likely to have a high payout ratio as it has less funding needs.

EXERCISE 27
B A S E for Dividends

Dividends

1. Solve the base analysis for Coca-Cola's dividends. (Fill in the other boxes and derive dividends from those figures.) .

Flows in and out of the retained earnings account

B		*Retained earnings, beginning of 2004*
A		*Net income for 2004*
S		*Dividends*
E		*Retained earnings, end of 2004*

2. Calculate Coca-Cola's payout ratio for 2004.

3. If Coca-Cola's 2005 net income was $5,000m and it declared dividends of $2,000m what would be its 2005 reinvested earnings balance?

4. Look at the payout ratios of the three companies below. What do they tell you about the businesses?

Electricity Generating Co *80% payout ratio*	
Joe's Clothing Stores Inc. *35% payout ratio*	
Gates Software Co. *0% payout ratio*	

OTHER EQUITY ACCOUNTS

Look at Coca-Cola's equity accounts.

Which equity accounts have you not yet examined?

- ☑ Retained earnings
- ☑ Common stock
- ☑ Treasury stock
- ☑ Capital surplus
- ❑ ____________________
- ❑ ____________________
- ❑ ____________________
- ❑ ____________________

Multinationals and currency differences

Accumulated other comprehensive income

You will see this account many times in ***multinational*** companies. Companies have to make adjustments for changes in currency exchange rates when they own assets abroad. Coca-Cola probably owns buildings and factories abroad. These are recorded at their original cost in foreign currency on Coca-Cola's foreign subsidiary's balance sheet.

But Coca-Cola's annual accounts are in dollar amounts. Each year when they consolidate their subsidiaries they must convert the original cost of these assets from the foreign currency into dollars. When the exchange rate changes, the original cost in dollars of the asset may rise or fall. These changes are matched by an entry into the other comprehensive income account.

To make sure **A = L + E**, you must make an adjustment. You show this adjustment in the equity accounts an addition to other comprehensive income.

What is Coca-Cola's other comprehensive income on December 31, 2004?

Accumulated other comprehensive income also includes unrealized gains and losses on securities and pensions.

Deal #7

Close the deal #7

Another tombstone opportunity! You must make $90,000 to earn this tombstone. If you make less than $90,000, review the material before you go on.

1. Using the following information, decide which companies' equity investors stand the least chance of getting their money back if the business went bust. *Highest risk = 1*

Company	Total Debt	Total Equity	Risk
New York Building Services	$300m	$200m	
Bishko SunTan Salons	$1,000m	$5,000m	
Midwest Farming Inc	$75,000	$90,000	

SCORE PAD

1. ____________

2. ____________

3. ____________

4. ____________

5. ____________

6. ____________

7. ____________

8. ____________

9. ____________

10. ____________

Total

Close the deal #7, *continued*

2. If Coca-Cola issued $1,000m of new debt on January 1, 2005 what would its new total assets, liabilities and equity balances be?

Assets	Liabilities	Equity

3. ❑ Yes ❑ No — Can Coca-Cola's shareholders ever demand repayment of their original investment?

   ❑ Yes ❑ No — Does Coca-Cola have to pay dividends?

4. If Coca-Cola issued 100m new shares with a $0.25 par value for $50 cash each, what would the journal entries be?

   ____

   ____

   ____

5. What would be the new balances of common stock and capital surplus?

Common stock	Capital surplus

6. [ ] What was Coke's total shareholders' equity at Dec 31 2004?

   [ ] What would equity be if on January 1st, 2005 Coca-Cola bought back 4m shares at $60 each?

7. [ ] If in 2005 Coca-Cola generated $5,000m of Net Income and declared $3,000m of dividends ,what would retained earnings be on Dec. 31, 2005?

8. [ ] If Coca-Cola's net income is $4,600m and it declares dividends of $2,000m, what is its payout ratio?

9. What is a foreign currency adjustments?

   What type of corporation will show foreign currency translation adjustment on its balance sheet?

10. Which is riskier for an investor to own, a company's equity or its debt securities? ❑ Equity ❑ Debt securities

INCOME STATEMENT REVIEW

1. REVENUES, COGS AND SG&A

More about revenues

You learned about revenues in Part 1. Now you'll look at revenues from a financial analyst's point of view.

As a financial analyst, you will want to know what drives a company's revenues. You can start with its income statement, but because it's only a summary you'll get more detail by looking in the notes.

EXERCISE 28
Coke's revenues by operating segment

Coca-Cola's revenues by operating segments

Turn to note 19, "Operating Segments." Notice that each business line is broken down into several different accounts. The corporate segment refers to Coca-Cola's head office activities.

1. Calculate the profitability of each of Coca-Cola's business lines.

	North America	Latin America
Revenues		
Identifiable Operating assets		
Operating profit *(income)*		
Operating profit/revenues		
Operating profit/assets		

	Europe	Asia
Revenues		
Identifiable Operating assets		
Operating profit *(income)*		
Operating profit/revenues		
Operating profit/assets		

Which geographic segment had the best profitability in 2004?

COST OF GOODS SOLD (COGS) RECAP

EXERCISE 29
COGS recap

Cost of goods sold

You learned about cost of goods sold in Part 1. Here's a quick recap:

1. Which balance sheet account is linked to COGS?

2. When is depreciation included in cost of goods sold?

3. Which other income statement account does cost of goods sold track?

4. Explain the matching of costs to revenues.

SG&A RECAP

EXERCISE 30
SG&A recap

SG&A recap

You learned about SG&A in Part 1. Here's a quick recap:

1. Name two accounts linked to SG&A.

2. When is depreciation expense included in the SG&A line?

3. Where do you think Coca-Cola records most of its depreciation expense? ❑ COGS ❑ SG&A

4. Where is amortization expense included in the income statement?

Gross profit and operating profit

Gross profit represents the sales revenue that remains after cost of goods sold including any depreciation related to production activities is taken away.

Gross profit
Revenues
– COGS
Gross profit

Operating profit *(or* ***income****)* tells you the profit that remains after accounting for COGS and SG&A including depreciation and amortization.

Operating profit
Revenues
– COGS
– SG&A
Operating profit

Gross margin = Gross profit / Sales

$$\text{Gross margin} = \frac{\text{Gross profit}}{\text{Sales}}$$

Most costs in the COGS figure are ***variable***. As sales go up, so will COGS. The gross margin ratio shows you this relationship.

Gross margin is usually driven by pricing and production efficiency.

Account driver

▪ If the industry becomes more competitive...	Customers will demand lower prices and companies will see their gross margins fall.
▪ If a company's production line becomes more efficient...	Its gross margin should rise.

EXERCISE 31
Gross margin

Gross margin

1. Use the 'Selected Financial Data' section of Coca-Cola's annual report to track Coke's gross margin ratio over the last ten years:

Gross margin

1995		2000	
1996		2001	
1997		2002	
1998		2003	
1999		2004	

2. What do these ratios suggest about Coca-Cola's production efficiency over the last ten years assuming the price of Coke has not changed?

3. If a company's gross margin ratio includes most of its depreciation *(for instance, if it is largely a manufacturing company)* and it begins a large capital expenditure program, what will happen to its cost of goods sold if other production costs stay constant?

COGS will ❑ rise ❑ fall

Operating margin = Operating profit / Sales

Account driver

$$\text{Operating margin} = \frac{\text{Operating profit}}{\text{Sales}}$$

Most costs in the SG&A figure are ***fixed costs***. If sales go up, SG&A may not be affected. The operating margin ratio shows you this relationship.

EXERCISE 32
Operating margin

Operating margin

1. Track Coca-Cola's operating margin over the last ten years:

$$\frac{\textbf{Operating profit}}{\textbf{Sales}}$$

Year		Year	
1995		2000	
1996		2001	
1997		2002	
1998		2003	
1999		2004	

2. What does this analysis tell you about Coca-Cola's operating performance over the last ten years?

3. Name two expenses that Coca-Cola includes in its SG&A number.

4. Find how much money Coca-Cola spent on advertising over the last two years. *Hint: look in note 1.*

Is this a significant expense for the company? ❑ Yes ❑ No

INTEREST INCOME AND INTEREST EXPENSE

Interest income represents the amount of interest generated from a company's cash balances, investment in debt securities and loans made to outside entities.

Financial analysis tip

Interest expense represents the amount of interest paid on a company's loans from outside entities. You can look at interest expense to estimate a company's average ***cost of debt***.

$$\text{Average cost of debt} = \frac{\text{Total interest expense}}{\text{Average total debt}}$$

Average total debt: add last year's debt and this year's debt and divide by 2.

Beware of companies with seasonal debt funding requirements. Estimating the cost of debt by the averaging method can be misleading if a company takes on a lot of short-term debt between reporting periods.

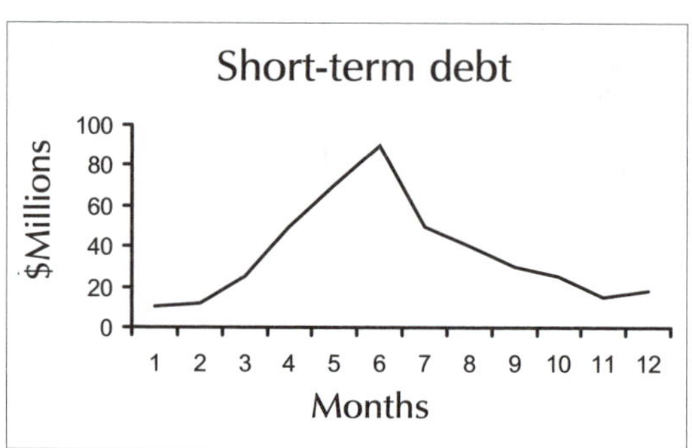

EXERCISE 33
Average cost of debt

Average cost of debt

1. Calculate Coca-Cola's average cost of debt in 2004. *Remember to include the current maturing portion and loans and notes payable.*

2. Why could the above calculation be misleading?

3. Assuming interest rates remain constant, what will happen to a company's interest expense if it takes on more debt?

How invest-ment bankers add value

Interest expense is the cost of using debt to fund assets. Financial analysts help companies reduce their cost of debt by matching debt investors with debt issuers in the most efficient way.

Other income statement accounts

Other expenses and Other income

Many annual reports have accounts called *Other expenses* or *Other income*. These accounts record ***unusual or infrequent income and expenses***.

Coke has three other expense and income accounts. What are they?

1.
2.
3.

Extraordinary items

Extraordinary items are transactions and other events that are:

Significantly different from the company's typical business activities

AND

Not expected to recur frequently

Extraordinary items are shown *net of tax* (with tax taken out)

Extraordinary items appear separately in the income statement, ***net of taxes.*** Extraordinary items are not allowed under International GAAP, but are permitted under US GAAP.

Operating profit
Interest
Taxes
Extraordinary items
Net income

Where extraordinary items appear on the Income Statement

EXERCISE 34
Extraordinary!

Extraordinary items

1. Are the following extraordinary items? *Hint: see test for extraordinary items on previous page*

- ❑ Yes ❑ No Loss on sale of a significant part of a company's assets
- ❑ Yes ❑ No Wages paid to a company's factory workers
- ❑ Yes ❑ No Losses as the direct result of a major natural disaster
- ❑ Yes ❑ No Losses resulting from prohibition under a newly enacted law or regulation

EARNINGS BEFORE INTEREST AND TAXES (EBIT)

Financial analysis tip

EBIT is earnings that can be used to make interest payments. It includes all earnings and expenses **before interest expense** and **taxes**. A company with very large debts might have to use all of its EBIT for interest payments. It might not have any income left over for taxes or shareholders:

EBIT	The pool of available income...
Interest	...paid to debt holders
Tax	...paid to the government
Net income	...available to shareholders

EXERCISE 35
EBIT workout

EBIT workout

Calculate income available to shareholders. Assume a tax rate of 50% and an interest rate of 10% of the outstanding debt balance.

	Scenario 1	*Scenario 2*	*Scenario 3*
Outstanding debt	900	450	100
EBIT	100	100	100
Interest expense			
Profit before tax			
Tax			
Net Income			

2. TAXES

Two sets of accounting records...

Every company has at least two sets of accounts: a set of accounts for ***tax records*** and a set of accounts for ***investors***. Tax accounts use accounting rules laid down by the IRS. Accounts presented to investors use GAAP rules.

Investor accounts	Companies report their income as ***fairly*** as possible.
Tax accounts	Companies try to report taxable income that is as ***low*** as legally possible.

...one for shareholders...

Many tax accounting principles are similar to GAAP rules. But when they are different, the company's taxable income will be different from its GAAP income.

One of the big differences between GAAP and tax accounting is how depreciation expense is calculated.

...one for the government

GAAP	Allows a variety of methods to calculate depreciation expense. A company can depreciate fixed assets using straight line or accelerated methods.
Tax accounting	Usually uses an accelerated method of accounting for depreciation.

Even though a business might use straight line depreciation for GAAP purposes, it can use accelerated depreciation in its tax accounts. Most companies will choose accelerated depreciation for their tax accounts. This choice reduces their taxable income, postponing the payment of taxes. It's better to pay taxes later, not earlier.

GAAP vs. tax accounting

Financial analysis tip

Tax accounts determine how much tax you ***pay*** to the government each year; GAAP accounts determine how much tax you ***expense*** in the financial statements you show to your shareholders.

Why is it important for companies to delay their tax payments? Because they can conserve that cash and invest it in their business for the period before they hand it to the IRS.

Important! Total tax depreciation of an asset is equal to the total GAAP depreciation of the asset. The only difference is in the ***timing***, or when that depreciation is recognized.

Timing differences

Example

Here's an example showing the differences between tax expensed (recorded) and tax paid. Assume the following:

- A company purchases new machinery which cost $100,000.
- The machinery is expected to last 5 years. Tax depreciation is 50,25, 15, 10 and 0 over the five year period.
- The machine has no salvage value.
- The tax rate is 50%.
- Income before depreciation and taxes is $100,000 for the next 5 years.

If the company uses straight-line depreciation in its GAAP accounts and accelerated depreciation to calculate its tax payments, the yearly amount of tax it ***pays*** will be different from the amount it ***expenses***.

(all figures in $000's)	**Year 1**	**Year 2**	**Year 3**	**Year 4**	**Year 5**	**Total**
GAAP Accounts						
Income	100	100	100	100	100	
Depreciation	(20)	(20)	(20)	(20)	(20)	(100)
Profit before tax	80	80	80	80	80	
Tax expensed	(40)	(40)	(40)	(40)	(40)	(200)
Tax Accounts						
Income	100	100	100	100	100	
Depreciation	(50)	(25)	(15)	(10)	0	(100)
Profit before tax	50	75	85	90	100	
Tax paid	(25)	(38)	(42)	(45)	(50)	(200)
Timing difference between tax expensed and paid	**15**	**2**	**(2)**	**(5)**	**(10)**	**0**

EXERCISE 36
Try your hand at taxes

Tax accounting

1. You buy a new car for your business for $50,000. You estimate it will last five years. You expect it not to have any salvage value. Assume your profits excluding the car's depreciation expense are $50,000 each year for the next five years. Assume the tax rate is 50%. Complete a summarized income statement that you will show to your ***investors***:

Year	**1**	**2**	**3**	**4**	**5**
Profit before tax and car depr.	$50,000	$50,000	$50,000	$50,000	$50,000
Car depn expense	($10,000)	($10,000)	($10,000)	($10,000)	($10,000)
Profit before tax					
Tax at 50%					

continued on next page

EXERCISE 36, *continued*
Try your hand at taxes

Tax accounting, *continued*

2. However, in your tax accounts you want to use the largest depreciation deduction possible, which reduces your tax payments in the earlier years. Tax depreciation is $20,000, $15,000, $10,000, $5000 and $Nil respectively. Using a tax rate of 50%, complete the income statement you will present to the ***tax authorities:***

Year	**1**	**2**	**3**	**4**	**5**
Income before tax and car depreciation	$50,000	$50,000	$50,000	$50,000	$50,000
Car depreciation in tax books	($20,000)	($15,000)	($10,000)	($5,000)	($0)
Income before tax					
Tax at 50%					

3. Now calculate the difference between the tax you paid to the tax authorities and the tax you expensed in your GAAP accounts.

Year	**1**	**2**	**3**	**4**	**5**
Difference between tax and GAAP amounts					

DEFERRED TAX LIABILITY

A difference between the tax a company pays and the tax it expenses in its GAAP accounts creates a problem. If you expense $20,000 of tax on the income statement and only pay out $15,000 in taxes to the government, your balance sheet will not balance. You must create an account called a ***deferred tax liability***:

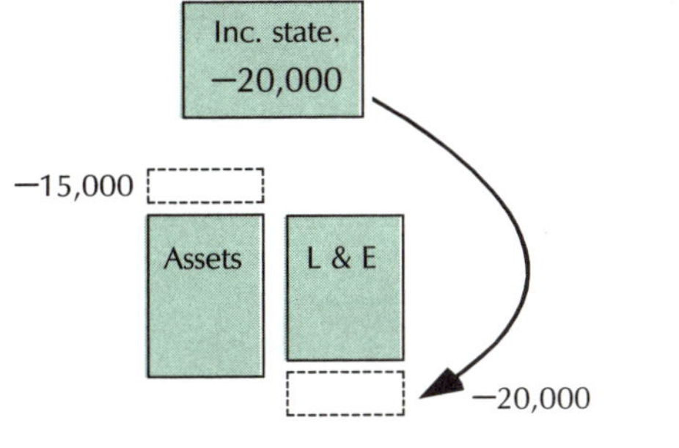

1. Balance sheet doesn't balance. It's off by $5,000.

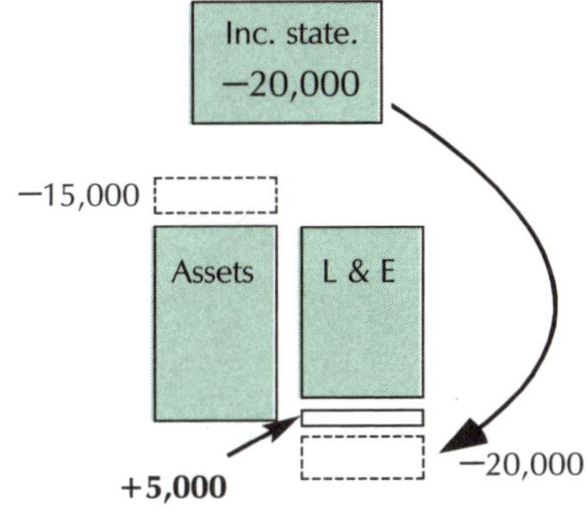

2. A deferred tax liability of $5,000 balances the B/S

Here are the journal entries:

Debit:	Income tax expense	$20,000	
Credit:	Cash		$15,000
Credit:	Deferred tax liability		$5,000

In the last exercise you found the "timing difference" between GAAP and government tax reporting. Here's how GAAP deals with the timing difference in a company's financial statements:

Example

Timing difference (amounts in thousands)	5	2.5	0	(2.5)	(5)
GAAP inc. statement					
Income tax expense	(20)	(20)	(20)	(20)	(20)
Reduction in cash	(15)	(17.5)	(20)	(22.5)	(25)
Change in def. tax liab.	5	2.5	(0)	(2.5)	(5)
GAAP balance sheet					
Deferred tax liability	5	7.5	7.5	5	0

The only accounts that change on the financial statements are income tax expense, deferred tax liability, and cash.

The deferred tax liability account shows you that sometime in the future your income tax ***expense*** will be lower than your income tax ***payment*** to the IRS.

When that time comes, and your expense is lower than your payment,...

your balance sheet won't balance...

so you make up the difference by reducing the deferred tax liability:

Debit:	Income tax expense	$20,000	
Debit:	Deferred tax liability	5,000 *(reduction in account)*	
Credit:	Cash		$25,000

DEFERRED TAX ASSET

When GAAP tax expenses are lower than taxes paid to the government in cash, you put the difference into an account called a ***deferred tax asset***, the opposite of the deferred tax liability.

The deferred tax asset account shows you that sometime in the future your income tax ***expense*** will be higher than your income tax ***payment*** to the IRS.

Deferred tax asset and liability are not linked to each other. They show ***temporary differences*** related to individual events, e.g., depreciation of a particular asset. When enough time passes they are reduced to zero.

EXERCISE 37
Death by taxes

Deferred taxes

1. ☐ What was Coca-Cola's tax expense in 2004?
   Hint: look in note 15 to the accounts
2. ☐ What proportion of Coca-Cola's tax expense was current?
3. ☐ What proportion of Coca-Cola's tax expense was deferred?
4. If Coca-Cola increases its deferred tax liabilities, is it paying more tax than it expenses? ❑ Yes ❑ No
5. If Coca-Cola creates a deferred tax asset, does it pay tax earlier or later than it expenses the tax on its GAAP accounts?
   ❑ Earlier ❑ Later

Deferred tax assets and liabilities are created for many different reasons. If a company continues to add to its deferred taxes, they will probably remain the same proportion of sales over time. If a company's deferred taxes were created by a one-time transaction then they will probably fall over time.

Note that not all items expensed in the income statement are allowable in the tax account. Such items are called permament differences and have no deferred tax impact on the financial statements.

Account driver

Effective tax rate

The effective tax rate is calculated by dividing your income tax expense by your pre-tax income.

$$\text{Effective tax rate} = \frac{\text{Income tax expense}}{\text{Pre-tax income}}$$

EXERCISE 38
The last tax exercise

Coca-Cola's effective tax rate

	What was Coca-Cola's effective tax rate in 2004?

Deal #8

SCORE PAD

1. ______
2. ______
3. ______
4. ______
5. ______
6. ______
7. ______
8. ______
9. ______
10. ______

Total

Close the deal #8

Get your next tombstone by earning $90,000. If you make less than $90,000, review the material before you go on.

1. When is depreciation included in cost of goods sold?

2. Does SG&A include more fixed or more variable costs than COGS?
   ❑ More fixed costs ❑ More variable costs

3. A company recorded the following information in its income statement:

Revenues	$100,000
COGS	$30,000
SG&A	$10,000
Other income	$1,000
Extraordinary items	$500
Interest expense	$2,000

   Calculate the company's operating margin and gross margin.

   Operating margin **Gross margin**

4. The same company had $30,000 of debt outstanding at the beginning of the year and $20,000 at the end of the year.

   Calculate the company's average cost of debt.

5. Is depreciation a cash expense? ❑ Yes ❑ No

6. What are two tests for extraordinary items?
   1)
   2)

7. Assume a construction company sold its stake in a publishing business and made a gain of $10m. Their accountants advised them that the $10m should be categorized as an extraordinary item. The company's tax rate is 40%. What amount would appear on their income statement?

8. Who does a company prepare its tax accounts for?

continued on next page

9. You record a $60m tax expense in your GAAP accounts and pay $40m in taxes to the government. Show your journal entries.

10. Name one event that creates a deferred tax liability.

THE CASH FLOW STATEMENT

In addition to preparing an income statement and balance sheet, a company must prepare a ***cash flow statement***. A cash flow statement simply describes the ***flows of cash*** into and out of different accounts over the course of one year. The cash flow statement is like your bank statement. It shows how cash came in and went out.

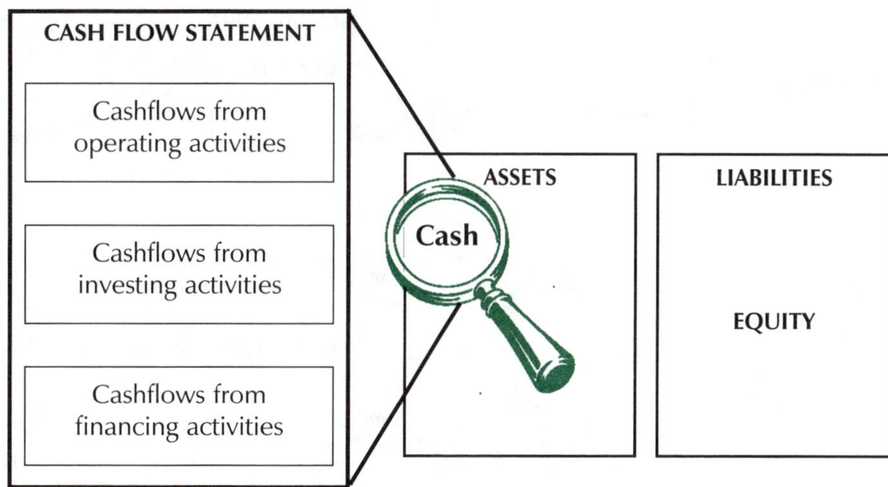

The cash flow statement is a detailed analysis of the cash account

Why financial analysts focus on cash

Cash flow statements are important to financial analysts for two reasons:·

Financial analysis tip

- Companies can manipulate net income by changing their accounting policies (e.g., they can choose FIFO or LIFO), but they can't manipulate cash flows to the same extent.
- Financial analysts use cash flows in valuation and to measure cash generation when assessing a company's credit risk.

Start with the cash account

To understand the cash flow statement, start with the cash account on the balance sheet. Almost every account on the balance sheet is linked to cash. Remember sources and uses of funds?

Example

Sources of cash	**Uses of cash**
Increases in liabilities & equity	Increases in assets
Decreases in assets	Decreases in liabilities & equity

Sources of cash		
Debt increases	You take out a loan.	*Cash goes up.*
Accounts receivable fall	Customers pay their bills.	*Cash goes up.*
Uses of cash		
Inventory rises.	You pay for raw materials.	*Cash goes down.*
Retained earnings falls	You pay dividends.	*Cash goes down.*

The cash flow statement is a summary

Income statement:	Summary
Balance sheet:	Snapshot
Cash flow statement:	Summary

The cash flow statement summarizes the effect on cash due to changes in the balance sheet from the beginning of the period to the end.

Example

B/S Year 1	
Cash	70
Prepaid expenses	10
Mktable securities	30
Total assets	**110**
Paid-in capital	110
Total assets	**110**

Snapshot

B/S Year 2	
Cash	85
Prepaid expenses	20
Mktable securities	25
Total assets	**130**
Paid-in capital	130
Total assets	**130**

Snapshot

Cash flow statement	
Change in Ppd. exp.	(10)
Change in Mkt. sec.	5
Change in PIC.	20
Change in cash	**15**

Summary of changes

Insights from the example

- Cash flows are either positive or negative.
  - The change in prepaid expenses increases assets, therefore: It's a ***use of cash*** (negative cash flow).
  - The change in marketable securities decreases assets, therefore: It's a ***source of cash*** (positive cash flow).
  - The change in PIC increases L&E, therefore: It's a ***source of cash*** (positive cash flow).
- The 15 change in cash is positive. Cash rises from 70 to 85.
- You get the same answer two different ways:
  - By analyzing the cash flows from each account on the cash flow statement;
  - By subtracting last year's balance sheet cash from this year's.

  The two answers should always be equal.

EXERCISE 39
First cash flow statement

Your first cash flow statement

Use the following two balance sheets to calculate the cash flow statement.

B/S Year 1	
Cash	90
A/R	30
Inventories	110
Total assets	**230**
Debt	100
Paid-in capital	130
Total L/E	**230**

B/S Year 2	
Cash	20
A/R	50
Inventories	130
Total assets	**200**
Debt	70
Paid-in capital	130
Total L/E	**200**

Cash flow statement	
Change in A/R	
Change in inventories	
Change in debt	
Change in PIC	
Change in cash	

Net or flow?

The example calculated the change between balance sheet accounts from the beginning to the end of a period to find the net effect on cash. Many financial statements will show you the actual cash flows in and out of an account. You can find examples in Coke's financial statements.

Look at Coke's cash flow statement and find the following examples of net changes in cash and cash inflows and outflows.

Net change		Net change in operating assets and liabilities
Cash inflow		Issuance of debt for cash
Cash outflow		Payments of debt

Non-cash accounts

You have just calculated your first cash flow statement. The procedure you used works for most balance sheet accounts. However, some accounts are affected by non-cash entries, so you can't just take the change in the account's balance between the beginning and end of the period:

Retained earnings	Contains non-cash expenses like depreciation, amortization, and loss on sale of assets. Remember that depreciation reduces net income (and therefore retained earnings) but is not a cash cost. The same is true of amortization.
Net PP&E	Accumulated depreciation is a non-cash account. When depreciation lowers the Net PP&E account, the company doesn't actually pay out cash.
Intangibles	Same issue as Net PP&E. Accumulated amortization is a non-cash account.

You'll find more non-cash accounts in your own analyses, but these are the "big three" present in almost every set of financial statements. You will learn to deal with these non-cash accounts as you continue through this section.

Three sections

The cash flow statement has three sections. They organize the cash flows into three parts that give useful information to analysts:

Cash flows from:	
Operating activities	Anything that helps a company carry out its day-to-day activities, such as making sales, purchasing supplies, paying bills to suppliers, and paying salaries.
Investing activities	Anything related to PP&E, investments in stocks and bonds, and other long-term assets.
Financing activities	Anything related to raising money through debt or equity.

CASH FROM OPERATING ACTIVITIES

Cash flow from operating activities shows you how much cash was generated by day-to-day business operations.

Cash flows from operations include:

- Cash received from customers;
- Cash paid out to suppliers, employees, and tax collectors.

Account driver

In a normal profitable company, cash flow from operations should be positive. In some very fast-growing companies it could be negative.

What about net income and retained earnings?

Isn't net income a cash flow into retained earnings? No, because net income includes some non-cash expenses and income, so it's not a true cash figure. You must adjust it to remove any non-cash expenses and income when you calculate cash flow from operations.

How to calculate cash flow from operations

Step 1: Convert net income to cash income

Cashflow from operations starts with net income. Your first step is to "clean" the non-cash items from net income to get **cash income**.

To get cash income, you must add back non-cash expenses and take away non-cash income.

Examples of non-cash items include:

- Depreciation, impairment and amortization
- Losses/gains on sales of assets
- Equity income from accounting for investments using the equity method

Convert net income to cash income

	Net income	Start with net income.
+	**Non-cash expenses**	Add non-cash expenses like depreciation, impairment and amortization. (These items appear on the income statement but don't affect cash.)
–	**Non-cash income**	Subtract non-cash income.

EXERCISE 40
Joe's London bike shop

Calculating cash income

Joe recently purchased a bicycle shop in London. Calculate the shop's cash income from the following information:

- In 2005 the shop made $100,000 in net income.
- Depreciation for the year was $30,000.
- Amortization amounted to $10,000.
- During the year the shop sold its van for $1,000. The van originally cost $6,000 but had $4,000 of accumulated depreciation allocated to it. In the shop's income statement you see a $1,000 loss on sale of van.

Cash income for the bicycle shop

Net income	
Non-cash adjustments	
Cash income	

Step 2: Find changes in B/S accounts driven by operating activities
Operations-driven accounts usually include:

All assets and liabilities driven by the company's operating activities:

- Accounts receivable
- Inventories
- Prepaid expenses
- Other current assets
- Accounts payable
- Accrued expenses
- Other current liabilities
- Deferred tax liabilities
- Other long-term liabilities

Subtract last year's account balance from this year's to find the change (the use or source of cash).

Example

	Last year	This year	Change	Effect on cash
Inventory	5500	6200	700	-700
Deferred tax liability	500	570	70	+70

EXERCISE 41
Operating accounts and cashflows

Operating accounts and cash flows

Use the following balance sheet to calculate the cashflow from assets and liabilities driven by a company's operating activities.

Hint: Careful! Not all the accounts are included in the calculation!

Cash	100	58	
Inventories	203	251	
Receivables	301	340	
Prepaid expenses	28	32	
Net PP&E	489	480	
Long-term investments	323	321	
Total assets	1,444	1,482	
Accounts payable	289	319	
Short-term debt	120	150	
Deferred taxes	54	50	
Long-term debt	500	500	
Other liabilities	83	91	
Equity	398	372	
Total liabilities & equity	1,444	1,482	
Total change in cash from operating assets and liabilities			

Step 3. Account for any non-operating cash flows in cash income
Steps 1 and 2 are the important steps. You must add Step 3 only if the company has non-operating cash flows in its cash income.

Example

Assets are sold for a profit *(amount higher than their book value)*

Suppose you own a car that cost $5,000. You have allocated $4,000 of accumulated depreciation to it and you sell it for $2,000 .

Accounting value	$1,000	Original price – accumulated depreciation
Sale price	$2,000	Cash received
Gain on sale	$1,000	Added to net income.

Important! The $1,000 gain is part of a cash flow, but it's not a cash flow from operating activities. It's a cash flow from an investing activity, so you take it away from cash flow from operating activities.

CASH FROM INVESTING ACTIVITIES

Part of the cash flow statement records the sources and uses of cash from a company's investing activities. Cashflows from investing activities include:

Cash inflows	Cash outflows
Sales of PP&E	Capital expenditure (CAPEX)
Sales of investments	Purchase of investments

You face two problems in finding intangible asset and PP&E cashflows.

- The cash received from the sale of a fixed asset does not necessarily equal its original purchase price minus its accumulated depreciation. Remember that fixed assets are recorded at their original cost, and that you can have a gain or a loss on their sale.
- They are affected by non-cash accounts (accumulated depreciation and amortization).

Example

Caroline owns a chain of copy shops. She has decided to sell one of her photocopiers, which she purchased for $30,000. So far, it has accumulated depreciation of $25,000, giving a book value of $5,000. When she sells it, her net Net PP&E will fall by $5,000 (the book value) no matter what the selling price is.

- If she sells it **below book value** (at a loss of $2,000):
  Cash flow = book value minus loss on sale.
  Cash flow = $3,000 ($5,000 – $2,000)
- If she sells it **above book value** (at a gain of $3,000):
  Cash flow = book value plus gain on sale.
  Cash flow = $8,000 ($5,000 + $3,000)

Use BASE analysis to help find the true cashflows for intangible assets and PP&E.

Example

Jeffrey Hair Products Inc. had the following fixed asset accounts:

All figures in 000's	**2005**	**2006**
Gross PP&E	150	180
Accumulated Depr.	50	65
Net PP&E	100	115
Depreciation expense		35

During the year, Jeffrey sold a bottling machine that originally cost $50,000. No gain or loss was made on the sale.

Use BASE analysis to work out two numbers:

1. Capital expenditure

	Gross PP&E	
B	150	Beginning balance from 2005 balance sheet
A	**80**	**Capital expenditure during the year**
S	50	Original cost of assets sold during the year
E	180	Ending balance from 2006 balance sheet

The B A S E analysis works out the cash spent on fixed assets during the year. Notice that you can use B A S E analysis to solve for any part of the B A S E equation.

2. Cash flows from fixed asset sales

	Accum. depreciation	
B	50	Beginning balance from 2005 balance sheet
A	35	Depreciation expense during the year
S	**20**	**Accum. depn. of bottling machine (sold)**
E	65	Ending balance from 2006 balance sheet

The B A S E analysis works out the accumulated depreciation of the asset Jeffrey sold (the bottling machine).

You need this number to work out the Net PP&E value of the sold asset and the cashflow from fixed asset sales.

Net PP&E of sold asset	**– loss / + gain on sale**	**=**	**Cashflow**
50 – 20 = 30	No loss/gain = 0		30

Reminder

- Increases in fixed assets or investments are a use of cash.
- Decreases (sales) of fixed assets and investments are a source of cash.

EXERCISE 42
Leslie's restaurant

This is easier than it looks!

Cashflow from investing activities

You invest in Leslie's new restaurant. At the end of the year, you inspect the income statement and balance sheet. Using the information below, calculate the cashflow from investing activities. Use the B A S E templates.

I/S			B/S, beg. of year	B/S, end of year
Depn	30	Gross PP&E	900	1,020
		Acc. depn.	100	100
		Net PP&E	800	920

Assume:

Purchase of new chairs	200
Loss on sale of used kitchen equipment	20

	Gross PP&E	Accum. depn.	Sold asset	
Beg	900	100	Gross PP&E	
Add			Acc Depn.	
Sub			Book value	
End	1,020	100	Loss on sale	
			Cashflow	

Now work out the cashflows:

Capital expenditure	
Fixed asset sales	

Investing activities cashflow: positive or negative?

Companies with ***negative*** cash from investing activities include:

- Manufacturing companies with lots of plant and equipment
- Rapidly growing companies

Companies with ***positive*** or ***neutral*** cash from investing activities include:

- Companies that are downsizing and selling off assets
- Service companies with little need for physical plant

Financial analysis tip

CASH FROM FINANCING ACTIVITIES

You must also include *financing* cash flows in your cash flow statement. Financing cash flows include:

Cash inflows	**Cash outflows**
Issuance of new debt	Repayment of existing debt
Issuance of new stock	Purchase of treasury stock
	Payment of dividends

EXERCISE 43
Bedford Biscuits

Calculate financing cashflows

The Bedford Biscuit Company made the following financing decisions during the year.

- They sold 50,000 new shares for $7.10 each.
- The company took out a new loan of $200,000.
- The company reduced its short-term debt by $10,000.
- During the year, Bedford Biscuits spent $500,000 on a new biscuit cutter.
- Retained earnings at beginning of year: $123,000
- Net income during the year: $50,000
- Retained earnings at end of year: $150,000

Calculate the company's cash flow from **financing** activities.

Issuance of new debt	
Repayment of existing debt	
Issuance of new stock	
Purchase of treasury stock	
Payment of dividends	
Cash flow from financing activities	

Warning

Annual reports are ***summaries*** of many different accounts. If you try to reconcile a historical cash flow statement with changes in historical balance sheet accounts, it usually won't work!

Why? Companies don't show you everything in the annual report. Many flows in and out of accounts remain hidden. If you had the full picture then you could reconcile the balance sheet and cash flow statement.

EXERCISE 44
Irreconcilable differences

Financial analysis tip

Irreconcilable differences

1. Use **B A S E** to analyze Coca-Cola's capital surplus and common stock accounts. What is the amount of your irreconcilable difference?

B		Capital surplus and common stock, end of 2003. *Hint: look on the balance sheet*
A		Issuance of stock. *See the financing section of the Cash Flow Statement*
A		Irreconcilable difference.
E		Ending Capital surplus and common stock, 2004. *From the balance sheet*

When you forecast

When you forecast a company's balance sheet and income statement you can calculate a reconcilable cash flow statement because **you** are making the assumptions of the increases or decreases of cash flows.

Your own cash flow template

All cash flow statements are different. You'll get into trouble when you try to reproduce an odd or unique cash flow statement. This book offers you a set of standard templates that will work with almost every set of financial statements.

Use them in the following exercises and in your own analysis. They work!

The templates show you which accounts are normally negative (use of funds). The parentheses in the labels will help you understand if the item is a cash inflow or outflow.

The next 3 exercises use the 1-year projection on the next page to take you through the calculation of a cash flow statement for Coca-Cola. The financial statements of 2004 were forecast by a financial analyst before the actual year-end numbers were published.

Projected 2004 income statement and balance sheet

(Not based on actual Coca-Cola performance)

INCOME STATEMENT	2004 PROJECTED
Sales	22,698
COGS	(7,704)
Gross profit	14,994
SG&A	(8,000)
Operating profit	6,994
Interest income	280
Interest expense	(300)
Other income	500
Income before tax	7,474
Taxes	(1,480)
Net income	5,994

BALANCE SHEET	2004	2003
Cash and cash equivalents	6,407	3,362
Marketable securities	61	120
Trade accounts receivable	2,171	2,091
Inventories	1,420	1,252
Prepaid expenses and other assets	1,735	1,571
Total current assets	11,794	8,396
Equity investments	5,897	5,224
Cost investments & other assets	3,409	3,636
Gross PP&E	10,149	9,622
Accumulated Depreciation	3,758	3,525
Net PP&E	6,391	6,097
Goodwill and other intangibles	3,836	3,989
Total assets	**31,327**	**27,342**
Accounts payable & accrued expenses	4,283	4,058
Loans and notes payable	4,531	2,583
Current maturities of long-term debt	1,490	323
Accrued income taxes	667	922
Total current liabilities	10,971	7,886
Long-term debt	1,157	2,517
Other long term liabilities	2,814	2,512
Deferred income taxes	450	337
Total liabilities	15,392	13,252
Common stock	875	874
Capital surplus	4,928	4,395
Reinvested earnings	29,105	26,687
Less treasury stock and OCI	(18,973)	(17,866)
Total equity	15,935	14,090
Total liabilities and equity	**31,327**	**27,342**

EXERCISE 45
Coke's cash from ops

Calculate Coca-Cola's 2004 cash flow from operations

Calculate Coca-Cola's cash flow from operations in 2004 using the template below, the income statement and balance sheet on the previous page and the following additional information:

Additional information

- Assume Coca-Cola's depreciation in 2004 was $456
- Assume Coca-Cola's amortization in 2004 was $308
- Assume no sales of intangibles
- Assume there were no other non-cash items on Coca-Cola's income statement in 2004.

Operating current assets and liabilities template

To make your cash flow statement shorter, add the cashflows from changes in from operating assets and liabilities.

	(Increase)/Decrease
Trade receivables	
Inventories	
Prepaid expenses	
Total (increase)/decrease in op. assets	
	Increase/(Decrease)
Accounts payable	
Accrued taxes	
Deferred taxes	
Other long-term liabilities	
Total increase/(decrease) in op. liabilities	

Simplified operating cash flow template

Net income *(From I/S)*	
+ Depreciation of PPE *(From assumptions)*	
+ Amortization of intangibles *(From assumptions)*	
+ Other non-cash adjustments *(From assumptions)*	
(Increase) or decrease in operating assets**	
Increase or (decrease) in operating liabilities**	
Cash flow from operations	

***Use the answer from the template above*

EXERCISE 46
Coke's cash flow from investments

Calculate Coke's 2004 cash flow from investments

Calculate Coca-Cola's cash flow from investing activities in 2004 using the projected income statement and balance sheet, the assumptions and B A S E analysis templates below (to derive CAPEX, accumulated depreciation, and intangibles).

Assumptions

- Coca-Cola sold fixed assets which originally cost $350m for cash of $127m. They did not make a gain or loss on the sale.

Simplified investing cash flow template

Capital expenditures	
Fixed asset sales	
Sales (purchases) of intangible assets	
(Increase) or decrease in all investments (Hint: include marketable securities)	
Cash flow from investing activities	

B A S E analysis Intangibles		
B		2003 balance
A		cash flow
S		amortization
E		2004 balance

B A S E analysis Gross PP&E		
B		2003 balance
A		cap. expenditure
S		see assumptions
E		2004 balance

EXERCISE 47
Coke's cash flow from financing

Calculate Coca-Cola's 2004 cash flow from financing

Calculate Coca-Cola's cash flow from financing activities in 2004 using the projected income statement and balance sheet and the B A S E analysis templates in the margin.

Do not include interest payments in your cash flow from financing activities. Interest payments already appeared in net income.

Net increase or (decrease) of short-term debt	
Increase (decrease) in long-term debt	
(Repurchase of shares *(treasury stock)*)	
Equity Issuance	
(Dividends)	
Cash flows from financing activities	

B A S E analysis Retained earnings	
B	
A	
S	
E	

Putting the cash flow statement together

You have calculated the cash flows from:

- Operational activities
- Investment activities
- Financing activities

Now you can put the whole cash flow statement together. When you add up the above three cash flows you get the net cash flow for the year.

How do you know it's right? Check your results against the balance sheet.

Check your results against the balance sheet

How to check your net cash flow results

1. Calculate net change in cash from the balance sheet

	Ending cash	*This year's ending cash balance*
–	Beginning cash	*Last year's ending cash balance*
	Net change in cash	

2. Check net change in cash from the balance sheet against net change in cash from the cash flow statement

Balance sheet		***Cash flow statement***
Net change in cash	***must equal***	Net change in cash

If these two numbers aren't equal, you have made a mistake in your cash flow statement!

EXERCISE 48
Coke's projected cash flow

The cash flow statement: summary

1. Calculate the new cash balance for 2004 using your answers from the previous exercise.

Beginning cash balance *From Coke's 2003 balance sheet*	
Cash flow from operations	
Cash flow from investing activities	
Cash flow from financing activities	
Ending cash balance	

2. Compare your ending cash balance with the cash balance on the 2004 balance sheet. Are they the same? ❑ Yes ❑ No

...because it can't be manipulated

Recap: Why is cash flow so important?

Why do so many managers and experienced financial analysts frequently say that cash is king? Mainly because no one can manipulate cash flows. *(Companies can manipulate their net income figures because GAAP gives them choices about how they can account for transactions. For example, a company can choose between LIFO, FIFO, and the average cost methods when accounting for inventory.)*

Companies who are in financial difficulty pay particular attention to cash flows. If you can't pay your bills on time you risk going into default and out of business even though you might be profitable. Small businesses who have little cash reserves must constantly consider their cash flows.

Lenders are also interested in cash flow because it reflects the ability of a company to repay its debt. In a difficult situation cash flow, not profitability, reflects whether lenders will be repaid or not.

EXERCISE 49
Go for the gold

Cash flow mastery

Use the following balance sheets, income statement and additional information to create a cash flow statement.

Include every balance sheet account except cash! *The check boxes will help you track the accounts you have included on the cash flow statement.*

BALANCE SHEET	2005	2006
Cash and cash equivalents	35,406	39,985
❑ Accounts receivable	12,514	15,450
❑ Inventories	12,616	15,065
❑ Other current assets	7,527	8,000
Total current assets	68,063	78,500
❑ Gross PP&E	100,000	115,000
❑ Accumulated Depreciation	40,400	45,000
Net PP&E	59,600	70,000
❑ Investments	1,000	900
❑ Other non-current assets	2,411	3,000
Total assets	**131,074**	**152,400**
❑ Accounts payable	16,592	18,000
❑ Current portion of long-term debt	448	800
Total current liabilities	17,040	18,800
❑ Long-term debt	31,977	35,000
❑ Other long-term liabilities	3,526	4,500
Total liabilities	52,543	58,300
❑ Common stock	1,000	1,100
❑ APIC	47,761	58,000
❑ Retained earnings	29,770	35,000
Total equity	78,531	94,100
Total liabilities and equity	**131,074**	**152,400**

INCOME STATEMENT	2006
Sales	221,074
COGS excluding depreciation	(178,000)
Depreciation	(5,000)
Gross profit	38,074
SG&A	(23,087)
Operating profit	14,987
Interest expense	(2,679)
Profit before tax	12,308
Taxes	(4,308)
Net income	8,000

continued on next page

Cash flow mastery, *continued*

Assumptions

- No amortization expense
- Other long-term liabilities are related to operating activities.
- The company sold equipment for $200 cash without a gain or loss.
  Hint: Reduction in Gross PP&E = $200 + reduction in Acc. Depn.

CASH FLOW STATEMENT	2006
Net income	
Depreciation	
(Increase) / decrease in operating assets	
Increase / (decrease) in operating liabilities	
Cash from operations	
Capital expenditures	
Fixed asset sales	
(Incr.) / dec. in total investments and other	
Cash from investments	
Increase / (decrease) in long-term debt, including current portion	
Issuance of common stock / APIC	
(Dividends)	
Cash from financing	
Net change in cash	

Check against B/S	
B/S beginning cash *(from previous year)*	
B/S ending cash *(from current year)*	
B/S change in cash	

Does net change in cash = B/S change in cash? ❑ Yes ❑ No

B A S E analysis Accumulated depreciation	
Beg	
Add	
Sub	
End	

B A S E analysis Gross PP&E	
Beg	
Add	
Sub	
End	

B A S E analysis Retained earnings	
Beg	
Add	
Sub	
End	

Deal #9

SCORE PAD

1. ____
2. ____
3. ____
4. ____
5. ____
6. ____
7. ____
8. ____
9. ____
10. ____

Total

Close the deal #9

On to your ninth tombstone! You must make $100,000 to earn this one. If you make less than $100,000, review the material before you go on.

1. Why is the cash flow statement important to financial analysts?

2. What are the three sections of a cash flow statement and what do each of them tell you?

3. Name 3 adjustments you must make to get from net income to cash income.

4. Name three typical investment and three typical financing cash flows:

Investment cash flows	**Financing cash flows**

5. Assume you sold a building for $10m cash. The building originally cost $8m and you had allocated $5m of depreciation to it. Write out the journal entries you would make to record the sale.

Close the deal #9, *continued*

6. If a company's accounts receivable go up, what will happen to cash flow from operations?
   ❑ Go up ❑ Go down ❑ Unaffected

7. At the beginning of the year a company had a negative operating working capital of ($4m). During the year operating working capital changed to ($2.5m). Was this change a source or use of cash?
   ❑ Source of cash ❑ Use of cash

8. A company had other liabilities related to its employee pension plan. Where would changes to this account appear on your cash flow statement?

9. Why are you unlikely to make a published annual report's cash flow statement reconcile to the balance sheet?

10. If a company sells an asset for a loss, is the loss a cash loss or not?
    ❑ Cash loss ❑ Non-cash loss

CHECKOUT TEST FOR PART 2

Section 1 *Understanding the balance sheet and its links with the income statement*

1. If Coca-Cola decided to double its inventories, how would the company's balance sheet and cashflow statement be affected? Give your answer in $000s and assume that Coke uses short-term debt to meet any funding needs.

Balance sheet *Cash flow statement*

2. Assuming all Coca-Cola's sales are made on credit and its sales figure does not change, what average accounts receivable balance would the company have had if its receivable days were 35 in 2004?

3. Assume Coca-Cola adds $400m of patents onto its balance sheet and uses a 40-year period of amortization. What would its amortization expense be each year?

4. What are the benefits and drawbacks of having a large inventory balance? Which is usually preferable, a large or small inventory balance?

Benefits of a large inventory balance

Drawbacks of a large inventory balance

A ❑ large ❑ small inventory balance is usually preferable.

5. a. Which accounts are driven by a company's operations?
   - ❑ A deferred tax asset relating to a recent debt issue
   - ❑ Accounts receivable net of a bad debt allowance
   - ❑ Short-term debt
   - ❑ Prepaid expenses
   - ❑ Accrued expenses
   - ❑ Accounts payable

   b. If the company increased its balance of accrued expenses, what would be the effect on cashflow from operating activities?

   ❑ Go up ❑ Go down

Score template

Section 1
Each correct question is worth $20,000. All parts of the question must be correct.

Your score:

Section 2
Each correct question is worth $25,000. All parts of the question must be correct.

Your score:

Section 3
Questions 1 - 3: $50,000. All parts of the question must be correct.

Question 4: $450,000

Your score:

TOTAL SCORE

6. If Coca-Cola's competitors had lower receivable days, what would this tell you about Coca-Cola?

7. Name the main link between the income statement and these accounts:

Income statement	Account
Cost of goods sold *Example*	Inventories
	Prepaid insurance on the CEO's car
	Accrued rent on the factory
	Accrued rent on the head office
	Wages payable for the sales force
	Accounts receivable
	Deferred taxes
	Cash
	Debt

8. Which are easier to manipulate, accounts driven by...?
   ❑ Operations ❑ Financing activities

9. Suppose Coke decides to increase its long-term debt by an additional $500m borrowed at an interest rate of 7.8%. Which accounts on the balance sheet and income statement would be affected, and by how much?

Balance sheet	**Income statement**

10. a. Assume Coca-Cola built an additional bottling plant in Atlanta for $300m. They decided to depreciate the plant over 15 years using their normal method of depreciation *(see the notes)*. How will this affect the company's PP&E accounts *(show only the extra amounts)* and income statement in over the next three years? Assume the plant will have no salvage value. *(Show answer on next page)*

b. Assume that Coca-Cola decided to sell the bottling plant after one year. The finance department negotiated a sales price of $290m. Write the journal entries for this sale.
(Hint: remember depreciation).

c. If in 2005 Coca-Cola spent $1,000m on capital expenditure, sold no PP&E and expensed $450m worth of depreciation, what would be its ending 2005 net PP&E?

Section 2 *Equity accounts, the income statement and taxes*

1. Assume Coca-Cola issued an additional $100m of equity on January 1 2005. It sold each share for $65. Each share had a par value of $0.25. Show the journal entries.

2. If in 2005 Coca-Cola generated $3,200m net income and paid $1,500 of dividends, what would be its 2005 ending reinvested earnings balance?

3. a. Suppose Coca-Cola purchased $500m of its own shares on January 1 2005. Show the the journal entries for the transaction.

b. When Coca-Cola purchases treasury stock what happens to the number of its outstanding and issued shares?

Issued shares	❑ Increase	❑ Decrease	❑ Remain the same
Outstanding shares	❑ Increase	❑ Decrease	❑ Remain the same

4. a. Where do you think Coca-Cola adds most of its depreciation to its income statement? ❑ COGS ❑ SG&A

b. Where would it expense amortization?
❑ COGS ❑ SG&A

5. a. What type of costs are cost of goods sold?

b. Suppose Coca-Cola found a new way to make Coke which dramatically reduced its production costs. What impact would you expect the new process to have on its income statement?

6. a. Calculate Coca-Cola's average interest expense for 2004. Use the average outstanding debt between 2003 and 2004.

b. A retailing company has a 15% average cost of debt (calculated using the method in 6a. when current interest rates are around 5%). How could you explain this?

7. a. What are the two tests for extraordinary items?

b. Where are extraordinary items normally shown on the income statement?

8. If your tax expense for the year was $100m and you paid the IRS $70m in cash, how would you show the journal entries?

Section 3 *The cash flow statement*

1. If a company has accounts payable of $120m one year and $90m the next year, how much cash was generated or used up during the year?

   ☐ was ❑ generated ❑ used up

2. If a company's capital expenditure is equal to its depreciation charge what does this tell you about its fixed asset investment policy?

3. How would your company's cash flow change if:
   a. You increase your receivables from $40m to $80m. ❑ Up ❑ Down ❑ No change
   b. You embark on a major investment program increasing capital expenditure from $50m to $150m. ❑ Up ❑ Down ❑ No change
   c. Your cost of goods sold as a percentage of sales increases while total sales are static. ❑ Up ❑ Down ❑ No change
   d. You decide to start a share buyback program (treasury stock) amounting to $10m a year. ❑ Up ❑ Down ❑ No change

4. Use the following information to calculate a cashflow statement:

Income statement for the year to December 31 2005

All figures in millions	**12/31/05**
Sales	$1,556
Cost of goods sold	(989)
Depreciation	(100)
Gross profit	467
SG&A	(78)
Amortization	(12)
Operating profit	377
Interest expense	(11)
Interest income	5
Profit before tax	371
Taxation	(130)
Net income	241

Balance sheet

	12/31/04	**12/31/05**
Assets		
Cash	50	208
Accounts receivable	180	210
Inventory	120	150
Total current assets	350	568
Gross PP&E	500	610
Depreciation	(350)	(400)
Net PP&E	150	210
Intangibles	245	233
Total assets	**745**	**1,011**
Liabilities		
Accounts payable	100	114
Accrued expenses	45	54
Deferred tax liability	10	12
Current portion of LTD	100	100
Total current liabilities	255	280
Long term debt	300	340
Other liabilities	20	24
Total liabilities	575	644
Common stock	10	12
APIC	20	24
Treasury stock	(5)	(5)
Retained earnings	145	336
Total equity	170	367
Total liabilities & equity	**745**	**1,011**

Additional information

a. Capex was $180m in 2005.
b. You sold equipment for $20m cash (its book value) in 2005.
c. Your deferred tax liability was created by an operating activity.

Cash flow template

Net income	
+ Depreciation of PPE	
+ Amortization	
+/-Other non-cash adjustments	
(Incr.) / decr. in operating assets	
Incr. / (decr.) in operating liabilities	
Cash from operations	
Capital expenditures	
Fixed asset sales	
(Incr.) / decr. in other non-operating assets	
Cash from investments	
Incr. / (decr.) in long-term debt including current portion	
Incr. / (decr.) in common stock / APIC	
Incr. / (decr.) in other equity accounts	
(Dividends)	
Cash from financing	
Net change in cash	

Check against B/S

B/S beginning cash *(from previous year)*	
B/S ending cash *(from current year)*	
B/S change in cash	

Does net change in cash = B/S change in cash? ❑ Yes ❑ No

RATIO ANALYSIS

1. INTRODUCTION TO RATIOS

As a financial analyst, you'll spend a great deal of your time comparing companies and analyzing their performance.

Financial statements are useful raw materials for analysis and comparison. However, comparing different companies' numbers directly is misleading, so you will use ***ratios.*** Ratios help you compare different companies' relative performance even if the companies are very different in size.

The three areas of performance that interest analysts are:

- Profitability
- Capital efficiency
- Financial management

About ratios

Remember that income statements show a summary of an entire time period, while balance sheets are a snapshot of conditions at one moment in time. When you use ratios to determine profitability, follow this general rule:

Financial analysis tip

General ratio rule

When you compare an **income statement** number with a **balance sheet** number, average the balance sheets' current and previous years' figures.

2. PROFITABILITY

Profitability is the core of a company's success. A key measure of profitability is the company's ***return on equity*** (ROE). Return on equity is the percentage of net income divided by average shareholders' equity *(net worth)*:

$$\text{ROE} = \frac{\text{Net income}}{(\text{this year's net worth} + \text{last year's net worth}) \times \frac{1}{2}}$$

Note: Net worth = total shareholders' equity

Ratio driver

If net income **rises** and net worth **remains the same**:	ROE rises
If net income **stays the same** and net worth **falls**:	ROE rises
If net income **falls** and net worth **remains the same**:	ROE falls
If net income **stays the same** and net worth **rises**:	ROE falls

EXERCISE 1
Coke's ROE

Return on equity

1. Calculate Coca-Cola's ROE for the last three years.

2002	2003	2004

2. What drives the ROE number

[ ] *...on the income statement?*

[ ] *...on the balance sheet?*

3. Compare Coca-Cola's ROE for 2004 *(Question 1)* with its major competitor PepsiCo Inc.'s ROE over the last three years:

	2002	2003	2004
Pepsi	30%	31%	31%

Which company is more profitable? ❑ Coca-Cola ❑ PepsiCo

4. Do the same analysis with gross margin for Coca-Cola over the last three years and compare it with PepsiCo Inc:

	2002	2003	2004
Coke			
Pepsi	58.3%	59.7%	61.1%

Which company has a higher gross margin?
❑ Coca-Cola ❑ PepsiCo

5. How could Coca-Cola increase its ROE?
❑ By increasing dividends ❑ By reducing dividends

Return on equity

Companies can increase profitability (ROE) three ways:

- ☑ Generate a higher proportion of net income for each $1 of sales
- ☑ Reduce the amount of assets needed to support a given amount of sales
- ☑ Reduce the proportion of assets funded by equity

Ratio driver

$$ROE = \frac{\text{Net income}}{\text{Sales}} \times \frac{\text{Sales}}{\text{Average assets}} \times \frac{\text{Average assets}}{\text{Average equity}}$$

Companies can have too few assets. If a company has too few assets per $1 of sales it might have trouble responding quickly to customers' needs.

Example If inventory is too low, sudden demand could clean out the company's shelves, leaving customers frustrated.

EXERCISE 2
Coke's vs. Pepsi's ROE

Comparing two companies' ROE's

1. Calculate the components of Coca-Cola's return on equity in 2004:

Net income / Sales	*Sales / Avg. assets*	*Avg. assets / Avg. total equity*

2. Compare them to PepsiCo Inc's numbers:

PepsiCo ROE (2004) = 31% = 10.7% **x** 1.139 **x** 2.540

What drives the difference between Coke's and Pepsi's ROE?

3. If you were the CEO of PepsiCo, what would you do?

3. CAPITAL EFFICIENCY

It's easy to assume that the more assets a company has the better. However, as a financial analyst you are only interested in the asset value of the business ***if you are going to break it up and sell it***. Otherwise you are more interested in the cash and ultimately the dividends the company can generate over time for its stockholders.

Funding costs money

Financial analysis tip

Assets need to be funded and funding with debt and equity costs money.

- If your company takes out a loan, it must pay interest. If it doesn't, the bank can sue.
- If you raise money from investors in the form of equity, they expect you to pay them dividends, although they can't force you to do so. If you want to raise equity in the future and increase the price of your equity in the market, you will make sure your returns to your investors are as high as possible.

More assets require more funding, which means...

More **debt**, which means...

Higher interest expense, which means...

Lower net income, which means...

Lower ROE

OR

More funding means...

More **equity**, which means...

Lower ROE.

You'll hear this a lot on the Street

Shareholder value

Wall Street measures shareholder value through the stock market and a company's share price. You'll hear financial analysts talk about maximizing shareholder value. A company increases shareholder value by increasing returns to its shareholders.

EXERCISE 3
Coke's shareholder value

Shareholder value

1. [ ] How much money did Coca-Cola pay to its debt holders in 2004?
2. [ ] What dividends did Coca-Cola pay to its equity holders in 2004?
3. If you increase shareholder value, will your stock price
   ❑ Fall ❑ Rise ❑ Remain unchanged

Current assets and shareholder value

You've already seen how reducing assets can increase a company's profitability. A critical day-to-day responsibility of management is keeping current assets as low as possible without affecting customer service.

Low assets per $ of sales means...

Higher profitability, which means...

Higher share price, which means...

Greater shareholder value.

EXERCISE 4
CA levels and profitability

Current asset levels

1. Calculate Coca-Cola's inventory days and receivable days for 2004. Use the average balance of inventories and receivables.

   [ ] Inventory days   [ ] Receivable days

2. a. [ ] If Coca-Cola averaged receivables days of 42, *(if management chased people who owed them money more slowly)*, what would their new average receivables be in 2004?

   b. [ ] How much more funding would Coca-Cola need? *(use average numbers)*

   c. [ ] If Coca-Cola financed the funding with debt costing 4% per year, how much more interest would they have to pay?

   d. Would shareholders benefit from this move? ❑ Yes ❑ No

3. [ ] Using the same assumptions as in Question 2, find the extra cost to Coca-Cola if its inventories spent on average ten days longer in the warehouse.

4. Using the following information calculate PepsiCo's inventory and receivable days:

	2004	**2003**
Inventories	1,541	1,412
Receivables	2,999	2,830
COGS	13,406	
Sales	29,261	

   [ ] Inventory days   [ ] Receivable days

Long-term assets

The company uses long-term assets to help manufacture its products and house its head office and sales staff. To stay competitive you must continually invest in fixed assets. If you don't, you may find yourself left behind by other companies in the same sector.

Financial analysis tip

If a company's depreciation charge is higher than its capital expenditure, you know the company is using up its fixed assets faster than it is replacing them. In the short term a company can probably get away with this practice. In the long term its competitive position will be eroded.

EXERCISE 5
Teasing information out of CAPEX

Hidden meanings in capital expenditure

1. Compare Coca-Cola's depreciation charge to its capital expenditure over the last three years. Is Coca-Cola increasing its fixed assets? *Hint: Find depreciation and CAPEX in Selected Financial Data.*

   ❑ Yes ❑ No

2. [ ] How much net fixed assets did Coca-Cola have in 2004 to support each $1 of sales? *Divide 2004 Net PP&E by 2004 sales.*

3. [ ] Use the numbers below to calculate how much net fixed assets PepsiCo needs to support $1 of sales.

PepsiCo	**2004**
Sales	29,261
Net PP&E	8,149

Current liabilities and shareholder value

Beware of *too much* free funding

Now jump across to the liability side of the balance sheet. Accounts payable is a big number for Coca-Cola. Normally companies will try to increase their payables number as this is "free funding." However, you must be careful not to annoy your suppliers by paying them too late or they might decide not deal with you.

More payables means ...

More free funding, which means...

Greater returns to shareholders, which means...

Higher shareholder value

EXERCISE 6
The payoff in days payable

Days payable and shareholder value

$$\text{Days payable} = \frac{\text{Avg. accounts payable}}{\text{COGS}} \times 365$$

1. [ ] What was Coca-Cola's days payable in 2004? *(Use the accounts payable and accrued expenses figure in Note 5.)*

2. Does Coca-Cola have to pay interest on its accounts payable?
   ❑ Yes ❑ No

3. Use your answer to Question 1 and the information below to compare Coca-Cola's and PepsiCo's average days payable to sales.

PepsiCo	**2004**	**2003**
Accs. payable & accruals	5,599	5,213
COGS	13,406	

Which company has a higher days payable?
❑ Coca-Cola ❑ PepsiCo

4. FINANCIAL MANAGEMENT

Debt and shareholder value

The owners of debt have first claim on the assets of a company. They can also demand the interest payments due to them. In return for these benefits, they accept a lower return on their investment than owners of equity. The benefit for the company is that debt is cheaper funding than equity.

Capital structure

Companies can increase their profitability by adjusting their ***capital structure*** *(proportion of debt to equity on the balance sheet)* to provide a higher proportion of debt funding.

Terms you should know

Net debt	=	Total debt – cash
Total capital	=	Net debt + equity

EXERCISE 7
What does cost of debt do to ROE?

Cost of debt and ROE

1. [ ] Calculate Coca-Cola's average cost of debt for 2004. Include all debt and use the average balance between 2003 and 2004.

2. [ ] What was its return on equity in 2004?

3. [ ] What was the total capital (total net debt plus total shareholders' equity) that Coca-Cola "employed" (this is the financial term) in 2004?

4. Calculate Coca-Cola's net income in 2004 if the company had replaced $2bn of its equity with debt. Use your average cost of debt for Coca-Cola in 2004 *(from Question 1)* and assume a tax rate of 22%.

   [ ] Step 1. Find the increase in interest expense.

   [ ] Step 2. What was Coca-Cola's original income before tax in 2004?

   [ ] Step 3. Subtract the increase in interest expense from income before tax.

   [ ] Step 4. Calculate net income using a 22% tax rate.

   [ ] Step 5. Recalculate Coca-Cola's ROE using your new net income and total stockholders' equity figures. *(Assume retained earnings does not change.)*

5. You have swapped equity for debt. What happened to Coke's ROE?
   ❑ Went up ❑ Went down

Debt's cheap but risky *(to the company)*

Consequences of debt funding

Why don't companies raise funds just from debt? Because a higher level of debt has consequences:

Consequence 1: The company's interest cost (as a % of debt raised) rises *(**leverage** costs).*

Consequence 2: The company is more vulnerable in downturns *(measured by interest **coverage**).*

Leverage

A high proportion of debt scares a company's debt holders. They are concerned that if the company ceases to trade, they may not get all their money back.

When a company fails, the assets are sold for cash. The cash is then returned, first to the debt holders, then to the equity holders. But sometimes the cash received from the assets is not enough to pay everyone back. The larger the debt, the more likely that the debt holders could be in the group that loses out and doesn't get paid back.

Financial analysis tip

Analysts use leverage to measure this risk. The proportion of debt to equity capital is called a company's ***leverage ratio***. The higher a company's leverage, the higher a company's cost of debt, as the debt holders' risk increases.

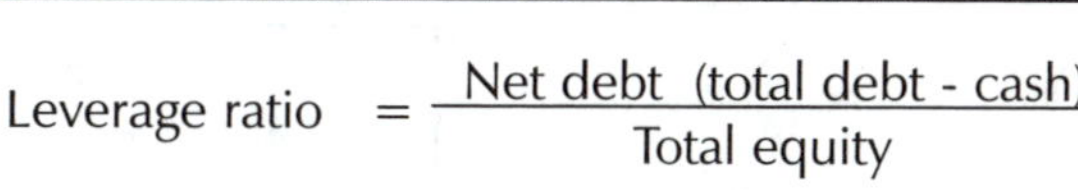

$$\text{Leverage ratio} = \frac{\text{Net debt (total debt - cash)}}{\text{Total equity}}$$

EXERCISE 8
Bankruptcy risk

Leverage ratio

1. Calculate Coca-Cola's leverage ratio for the last two years.

	2004	2003
Coke's leverage ratio		

2. Compare your answer to question 1 with PepsiCo's leverage ratio for the last two years:

	2004	2003
Net debt / total equity	16%	12%

Which company has a riskier debt-to-equity ratio?

❑ Coke ❑ PepsiCo

GULP! I *have* to pay that interest...

Interest and risk assessment

Another aspect of risk that concerns debt holders is a company's ability to pay interest. The greater proportion of debt a company has, the more pretax income it will have to use to pay interest to its debt holders.

Interest payments are compulsory. A company can't "choose" to pay them like dividend payments. Therefore if a company's earnings take a downturn, its interest payments may eat up all the company's net income, and then some.

One way to measure a company's ability to meet its interest payments and still make a profit is to calculate ***interest coverage*** *(how many times its interest payment is "covered" by earnings available to pay interest).*

One ratio you can use to calculate coverage is ***times interest earned***.

$$\text{Times interest earned} = \frac{\text{Earnings before int. exp and tax (EBIT)**}}{\text{Interest expense}}$$

***Note: Includes interest income*

Ratio driver

Companies with stable earnings, like utility companies, can support a low ***times interest earned*** ratio. They can be relatively certain that their earnings won't fluctuate and they can manage to pay interest without losses in nearly all years. Companies with unstable earnings such as airlines can't profitably carry such high levels of debt.

EXERCISE 9
Times interest earned

Times interest earned

1. Calculate Coca-Cola's times interest earned for the last three years.

	2004	2003	2002
Times interest earned			

2. Compare the answer to Question 1 with Pepsi's times interest earned:

	2004	2003	2002
Times interest earned	34.2x	31.7x	25.9x

Which company's debt holders face more risk in 2004?

❑ Coca-Cola ❑ PepsiCo

Deal #10

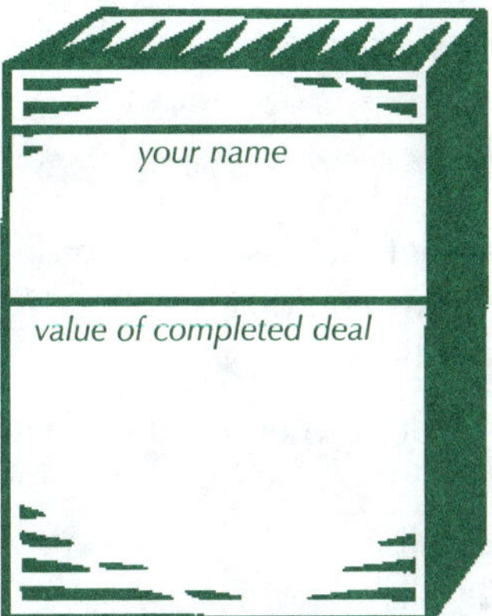

SCORE PAD

1. ____________
2. ____________
3. ____________
4. ____________
5. ____________
6. ____________
7. ____________
8. ____________
9. ____________
10. ____________

Total

Close the deal #10

It's time for you to earn your last tombstone! You must make $100,000 to earn this tombstone. If you make less than $100,000, review the material before you go on.

1. Name three ways a company can increase its profitability:
   Hint: Think about the components of ROE

2. Examine the following companies. Which one has the highest ROE?

	Net income / Sales	Sales / Average assets	Average assets / Average total equity
❑ A.	25.0%	0.20	2.00
❑ B.	10.0%	1.54	3.25
❑ C.	5.0%	2.00	3.25

3. At the beginning of the year a company's average days payable is 60 days. During the year its average days payable falls to 40 days. How does this change affect the company's financing needs and income statement? Assume any new funding it requires will be met by additional debt.

Debt funding	❑ rises	❑ falls
Net income	❑ rises	❑ falls

4. Companies can increase their profitability if they increase their leverage. Then why don't all companies fund themselves with 100% debt?

5. What are the positive and negative impacts of having high levels of current assets?

Positive

Negative

6. Consider the following capital expenditure and depreciation schedule for a large manufacturing company:

	2001	2002	2003	2004	2005
Capex	100	120	150	130	145
Depn.	150	140	120	120	125

[ ] What is the net increase / (decrease) in net PP&E between 2001 and 2005? Assume there are no sales and retirements.

7. If a company increases its proportion of debt to equity, how will this decision affect the following?

ROE	❑ rises	❑ falls
Net income	❑ rises	❑ falls

8. [ ] A company's net earnings before interest expense and tax are $2,000. Its interest expense is $500. What is its times interest earned?

9. Two firms have the following leverage ratios. Which is riskier to debt holders?

Leverage	**2004**	**2005**
❑ Company A	150%	140%
❑ Company B	20%	40%

10. Two firms have the following times interest earned ratios. Which is riskier to debt holders?

Times interest earned	**2004**	**2005**
❑ Company A	4.5	5.0
❑ Company B	0.9	1.0

The end – almost

That's it! You have covered the essential aspects of accounting that you need to know for financial analysis. The last task you have to do is complete your last deal – it's for a billion dollars – and check your score.

YOUR BILLION DOLLAR DEAL

Your last deal is the big one: it's worth $1,000,000,000.

If you are not clear about any of the subjects you've covered, review them now.

Good luck!

Instructions

You will need:

- ❑ Pen or pencil
- ❑ Paper
- ❑ Calculator
- ❑ Your copy of Coca-Cola's 2004 annual report

The final bonus exam is split into two parts:

- ❑ Basic accounting
- ❑ Understanding the financial statements

Answers are in the answer booklet.

Turn the page to begin

SCORE PAD

Give yourself $100,000,000 for each completely correct answer.

1. ____________
2. ____________
3. ____________
4. ____________
5. ____________
6. ____________
7. ____________
8. ____________
9. ____________
10. ____________

Total

1. BASIC ACCOUNTING

1. Look at Coca-Cola's equity accounts for 2004. Use the assumptions below to forecast the company's equity accounts for 2005. Then calculate the return on equity for 2005.
   - $200m of new equity was issued for $58 per share with a par value of $0.25.
   - Accumulated comprehensive income stayed constant throughout the year.
   - Assume Coca-Cola generated $5,300m of net income in 2005.
   - Assume that Coca-Cola purchased 9,500,000 of its own shares at $59 each during the year.
   - Assume that Coca-Cola declared and paid dividends amounting to $2,600m during 2005.

Account	**Amount**
Common stock	
Capital surplus	
Reinvested earnings	
Other comprehensive income	
Treasury stock	
Total equity	

Equity accounts, 2005

Return on equity, 2005

2. a. [ ] Using the following assumptions for Coca-Cola's current asset and liability accounts in 2005, calculate Coke's new working capital balance.
   - In 2005 Coca-Cola's inventory, trade receivables and accounts payable remain the same percent of sales as in 2004.
   - In 2005 Coca-Cola increases its sales by $3,545m.
   - Cash and marketable securities remain the same percent of sales as in 2004.
   - Accrued taxes are 7.55% of sales.
   - Prepaid expenses and other assets increase by $537m in 2005.
   - Coke increases its short-term debt financing by $139m in 2005.
   - Find current maturities of long-term debt in the notes.

   b. If a company has a higher receivables-to-sales ratio than its main competitors, what does this suggest?

3. Assume that Coca-Cola began a major capital expenditure program in 2005, outlined below. Assume all new assets are depreciated over four years and have a salvage value of 15% of their original cost. Determine the additions to Coca-Cola's PP&E accounts.

$ millions	**2005**	**2006**	**2007**
New CAPEX at beg. of year	950	1,000	1,050

Additions to Gross PP&E:

Additions to Accum. Depn

4. a. Assume Coca-Cola improved its gross margin by 1.5% in 2005. Name two possible reasons for the improvement.

   b. If Coca-Cola's depreciation expense was $498m instead of $715m in 2004, how would the following numbers change, if at all?

I/S		Operating income *(op. profit)*
B/S		Net PP&E
CFS		Net cash flow (assume no tax effect)

4. c. Suppose Coca-Cola decided to use its $6,707m of cash and cash equivalents and its $61m worth of current marketable securities to pay off first its short-term debt and then its long-term debt balances. What would happen to:

Total assets?	❑ Rise	❑ Fall	❑ Remain the same
Interest income?	❑ Rise	❑ Fall	❑ Remain the same
Interest expense?	❑ Rise	❑ Fall	❑ Remain the same
Leverage ratio?	❑ Rise	❑ Fall	❑ Remain the same

d. Assume Coca-Cola uses straight-line depreciation for its GAAP financial statements that it shows to its shareholders and accelerated depreciation for calculating taxes due to the government. If Coca-Cola undertook a large CAPEX program, would its net income be higher under its GAAP financial statements or its tax accounts next year?

❑ GAAP ❑ Tax

5. Using some of the information below, calculate SoupCo's cash provided by operating activities in 2005:

- SoupCo reduced its account receivable balance by $33m in 2005.
- Amortization was $29m in 2005.
- Long-term deferred income taxes (liability) increased by $59m in 2005.
- Capital expenditure was $441m in 2005.
- During the year SoupCo repaid $41m of long-term borrowings.
- Depreciation expense was $332m in 2005.
- Inventories increased by $45m in 2005.
- During the year SoupCo repurchased $19m of treasury stock.
- In 2005 SoupCo's other current assets increased by $41m. Its other current liabilities fell by $14m. Both accounts were driven by operating decisions.
- Other long-term liabilities related to employee pension obligations increased by $15m during the same year.
- Net income was $632m in 2005.

[ ] Cash provided by operations

2. FINANCIAL STATEMENTS

1. Use the following information to project Coca-Cola's income statement and balance sheet through 2005.

Show your answers in millions.

Income statement assumptions for 2005

- During the year Coca-Cola generated $25,000m of sales.
- Coca-Cola's SG&A expense was $9,452m *(includes amortization)*.
- There was no other income, equity income or gain on issuance of stock.
- Coca-Cola's COGS was $10,807m *(includes depreciation)*.
- Assume interest income was $150m and interest expense was $180m.
- Coca-Cola's effective tax rate was 22% in 2005.
- Other operating charges remained the same.
- Ignore other forms of income and expenditure such as equity income

Balance sheet assumptions for 2005

- Coca-Cola paid $2,500m of dividends.
- On December 31 2005 Coca-Cola had increased its inventory balance by $381m and its trade accounts receivable by $405m.
- Coca-Cola's current marketable securities increased by $22m during the year and its long-term marketable securities and other assets increased by $19m.
- Coca-Cola's accounts payable and accrued expenses increased by $1,606m in 2005.
- Coca-Cola spent $1,200m on capital expenditure during 2005 and its depreciation expense was $597m. Coca-Cola sold PP&E for $140m cash. It originally cost $540m and had $400m of accumulated depreciation allocated to it.
- During the year assume Coca-Cola purchased no other companies or patents and its amortization expense was $50m.
- Coca-Cola issued an additional $400m of long-term debt. *Remember you can find the repayment schedule of Coca-Cola's existing long-term debt in the notes.*
- Coca-Cola bought $897m of its own stock during the year.
- Accrued taxes increased by $73m and deferred taxes increased by $11m.
- Coca-Cola issued no new shares during the year.
- Other liabilities related to employee pensions fell by $(124)m.
- There was no change to unearned compensation related to outstanding restricted stock.
- Prepaid expenses and other assets increased by $89m in 2005.
- There was no change to equity method or cost method investments.
- Cash and equivalents grew to $7,660m.
- Assume Coca-Cola issued notes payable to make up any funding shortfall.

Coca-Cola
Projected income statement, 2005

Coca-Cola Projected balance sheet	2004	2005 (Proj.)
	Assets	

Coca-Cola Projected balance sheet	2004	2005 (Proj.)
	Liabilities & Equity	

2. Calculate a cashflow statement for 2005 using the format you learned in Part 2. Check your answer against the change in cash from your balance sheet. Check off each balance sheet account to make sure you have included them all.

Coca-Cola **Cash flow statement, 2005**

3. a. Calculate the constituents of ROE for Coca-Cola in 2005. How has it changed from 2004? Explain why the numbers have changed.

2004 ROE

$$\frac{\text{Net income}}{\text{Sales}} \times \frac{\text{Sales}}{\text{Average assets}} \times \frac{\text{Average asset}}{\text{Average equity}} = 32.3\%$$

22.1%		***0.749***		***1.954***	

2005 ROE

Why ROE changed

b. Calculate Coca-Cola's gross and operating margins in 2005.

Gross margin	*Operating margin*

c. Calculate Coca-Cola's working capital in 2004 and 2005.

Working capital, 2004	*Working capital, 2005*

4. Calculate the following ratios for Coca-Cola in 2005:

Depreciation / capital expenditure	
Accum depn / Gross PP&E	

5. a. Calculate Coca-Cola's leverage ratio in 2004 and 2005. Why has it changed?

Leverage ratio, 2004	*Leverage ratio, 2005*

Why the numbers changed

b. Calculate Coca-Cola's times interest earned in 2004 and 2005. Why has it changed?

Times interest earned, 2004	*Times interest earned, 2005*

Why the ratio changed

END OF BILLION DOLLAR DEAL

DEBITS AND CREDITS

Try these drills if you are having trouble with debits and credits. The best way to grasp debits and credits is through practice. The concept isn't hard; it just doesn't make sense at first.

Just keep doing the exercises and the concept will sink in.

DRILL 1
Debits and credits

Debits and credits

Below is a list of increases and decreases in balance sheet accounts. Would the entry be a debit or credit?

1. You increase your cash balance by $10,000.
   ❑ Debit ❑ Credit
2. You reduce your long term debt by $30,000.
   ❑ Debit ❑ Credit
3. You increase your paid-in-capital by $5,000.
   ❑ Debit ❑ Credit
4. You pay dividends of $1,000.
   ❑ Debit ❑ Credit
5. You increase inventories by $500.
   ❑ Debit ❑ Credit
6. You decrease inventories by $2,000.
   ❑ Debit ❑ Credit
7. You increase accounts receivable by $8,000.
   ❑ Debit ❑ Credit
8. You decrease cash by $300.
   ❑ Debit ❑ Credit
9. You pay back $2,000 of short term debt.
   ❑ Debit ❑ Credit
10. You purchase a car for $10,000.
    ❑ Debit ❑ Credit

DRILL 2
Low-cost housing

Low-cost housing in New York

Assume you invest in a new building company providing low-cost housing in New York City. You volunteered to help with the bookkeeping for the company.

Part 1

Complete the journal entries. You'll use them to build your balance sheet.

1. You and four friends each invest $200,000 in the new company in return for shares.

2. A plot of development land comes up for sale. The company purchases it using $100,000 of cash and a 5-year loan of $300,000.

3. The company purchases a small digging machine for $50,000. The manufacturer gives free credit for 90 days (accounts payable). You expect the machine to last at least 3 years.

4. The company makes the following purchases of building materials (inventory).
   - $40,000 worth of bricks, paying in cash
   - $35,000 worth of cement. The supplier gives 90 days credit.
   - $7,000 worth of glass. You pay in cash.

5. Two more sites come up for sale. One costs $200,000, the other $300,000. The first site is paid for in cash. The second is paid for using $150,000 of cash and a new $150,000 long-term loan.

continued on next page

DRILL 2, *continued*
Low-cost housing

Low-cost housing in New York, *continued*

Part 2

First make sure your debits equal your credits, then use your journal entries to help create a balance sheet for the company after the five transactions shown in part 1.

1. [ ] Total debits = [ ] Total credits

   Correct any problems so that total debits = total credits.

2. Create a balance sheet for the company based on the information in part 1.

Balance sheet

Assets		Liabilities	
Cash	[ ]		[ ]
	[ ]	**Total CL**	[ ]
Total CA	[ ]		
	[ ]		[ ]
Tot. NCA	[ ]	**Tot. Liabs.**	[ ]
			[ ]
		Tot. Eq.	[ ]
Tot. Assets	[ ]	**Tot. L&E**	[ ]

DRILL 3
More debits and credits

Debits and credits and the income statement

Write out the journal entries for each transaction.

1. You purchased a new car for $30,000 paying in cash.

2. You make $100,000 worth of sales, all paid for in cash.

3. The goods you sold cost $80,000 to manufacture.

4. You paid your accountant a $1,000 fee in cash.

5. The bank charged you interest of $1,000. You paid in cash.

6. You purchased inventory worth $5,000. The supplier gave you credit.

7. You take out a long term loan for $50,000. The bank gives you cash.

continued on next page

DRILL 3, ***continued***
More debits and credits

Debits and credits and the income statement, *continued*

8. During the year you pay $8,000 worth of dividends in cash.

9. The Internal Revenue Service charges you $8,500 in tax. You pay them in cash.

10. You make a further $30,000 in sales. This time you give all your customers credit.

Drill 4
Building a balance sheet and income statement using debits and credits

Building a balance sheet and income statement

First write out the journal entries for the transactions below. You'll use them to create a balance sheet and income statement.

1. You invest $1,000,000 of cash to set up your new computer retailing business. You record your investment as paid-in capital on the balance sheet.

2. You purchase a warehouse for $500,000, paying cash.

3. You take out a long-term loan from your bank for $2,000,000. The bank gives you cash.

4. You purchase $1,750,000 worth of inventory (computers) during the year. You are given credit for $500,000 of the purchase. You pay the remainder in cash.

5. During the year you make $2,500,000 worth of sales. Half of these sales were for cash and half on credit.

6. You employed 2 administrative staff and 2 salespeople. Their salaries totalled $200,000 during the year. Record this as an SG&A expense. You pay all salaries with cash.

continued on next page

Drill 4, *continued*
Building a balance sheet and income statement using debits and credits

Building a balance sheet and income statement, *cont.*

7. The bank charged you $200,000 worth of interest. You paid them in cash.

8. The sales you made during the year cost you $1,500,000 to generate.

9. The government charged you $200,000 in taxes during the year. You paid them in cash.

10. You purchased a car for $30,000 paying in cash.

INCOME STATEMENT
Revenue/sales
Cost of goods sold
Gross profit
SG&A
Operating profit
Interest expense
Profit before tax
Tax
Net income

Drill 4, *continued*
Building a balance sheet and income statement using debits and credits

Building a balance sheet and income statement, *cont.*

BALANCE SHEET

ASSETS	*$000s*	*LIABILITIES*	*$000s*
Total curr. assets		Total curr. liabs	
Total NCA		Total NCL	
		TOT. LIABILITIES	
		TOTAL EQUITY	
TOTAL ASSETS		TOTAL L&E	

DRILL 5
Advanced debits and credits

Using debits and credits to organize your work

Assume you recently purchased a greeting card company called Franky C Cards Inc. First write out the debits and credits on the table provided. Then recalculate the balance sheet and prepare an income statement. Assume all figures are in millions.

Franky C Cards Balance Sheet at purchase

ASSETS	*$000s*	*LIABILITIES*	*$000s*
Cash	100	A/C Payable	670
A/C receivable	700	Accrued exp.	60
Inventories	550	Short-term debt	500
Prepaid expenses	50	**Total current liabs.**	**1,230**
Total current assets	**1,400**		
		Long-term debt	700
Net PP&E	960	Other liabilities	89
Investments	570	**Total liabilities**	**2,019**
		Paid-in capital	480
		Retained earnings	431
		Total equity	**911**
Total assets	**2,930**	**Total liabs. & equity**	**2,930**

1. During the year Franky C Cards generated $1,500 of sales. 30% of these sales were on credit and 70% were for cash.
2. The cards sold cost $700 to manufacture.
3. Franky C Cards added $650 to its inventory. The supplier gave Franky C $325 of credit, the remainder was paid in cash.
4. Investments increased by $100, paid for in cash.
5. Franky C's existing investments generated $57 of interest income, paid in cash.
6. Franky C instructed their advertising agency to start an advertising campaign. So far the agency has spent $70. Franky C has accrued this expense on their balance sheet. (Hint: increase SG&A and accrued expenses).
7. The company raised an additional $500 of long-term debt. It received cash from the bank.
8. Franky C reduced its short-term debt by $100.
9. They company paid $309 in taxes in cash.
10. Other SG&A expenses amounted to $50 paid in cash.
11. Franky C paid interest of $120 in cash to the bank.
12. Assume no dividends were paid and there was no depreciation recorded.
13. Assume all other accounts remained the same.

continued on next page

DRILL 5, *continued*
Advanced debits and credits

Using debits and credits to organize your work, *cont.*

1. Dr ____________________ __________
   Dr ____________________ __________
   Cr ____________________ __________
2. Dr ____________________ __________
   Cr ____________________ __________
3. Dr ____________________ __________
   Cr ____________________ __________
   Cr ____________________ __________
4. Dr ____________________ __________
   Cr ____________________ __________
5. Dr ____________________ __________
   Cr ____________________ __________
6. Dr ____________________ __________
   Cr ____________________ __________
7. Dr ____________________ __________
   Cr ____________________ __________
8. Dr ____________________ __________
   Cr ____________________ __________
9. Dr ____________________ __________
   Cr ____________________ __________
10. Dr ____________________ __________
    Cr ____________________ __________
11. Dr ____________________ __________
    Cr ____________________ __________

continued on next page

DRILL 5, *continued*
Advanced debits and credits

Using debits and credits to organize your work, *cont.*

INCOME STATEMENT

Revenue/sales	
Cost of goods sold	
Gross profit	
S,G&A	
Operating profit	
Interest income	
Interest expense	
Profit before tax	
Tax	
Net income	

BALANCE SHEET

ASSETS	*$000s*	*LIABILITIES*	*$000s*
Cash		A/C Payable	
A/C receivable		Accrued exp.	
Inventories		Short term debt	
Prepaid expenses			
Total current assets		**Total current liabs.**	
Net PP&E		Long term debt	
Investments		Other liabilities	
		Total liabilities	
		Paid in capital	
		Retained earnings	
		Total equity	
Total assets		**Total liabs. & equity**	

THE CASH FLOW STATEMENT

If you need more practice with cash flow statements, try this additional cash flow exercise.

DRILL 1
Colin's diving business

Colin's cash flow statement

Colin recently established a diving business in Key West. Using his balance sheet and income statement below calculate his cash flow statement. Use the BASE tables to help you. Assume the following:

- Colin spent $20 on new equipment.
- There were no sales of fixed assets or intangibles.
- There were no purchases of intangibles.

All figures in thousands.

INCOME STATEMENT

	2005
Sales	110
COGS	(55)
Depreciation	(5)
Gross profit	50
SG&A	(15)
Amortization	(2)
Operating profit	33
Interest income	2
Interest expense	(5)
Profit before tax	30
Tax	(10)
Net income	20
Dividends	5

DRILL 1, *cont.*
Colin's diving business

Colin's cash flow statement, *continued*

Balance sheet	**2004**	**2005**
Assets		
Cash	5	10
Trade accounts receivable	50	55
Inventories	35	40
Prepaid expenses	10	12
Total current assets	100	117
Gross PP&E	100	120
Accumulated Depreciation	(50)	(55)
Net PP&E	50	65
Intangibles	10	8
Total assets	**160**	**190**
Liabilities		
Accounts payable & accrued expenses	35	40
Loans and notes payable	10	15
Total current liabilities	45	55
Long term debt	25	30
Total liabilities	70	85
Equity		
Common stock	5	5
Additional paid-in capital	45	45
Reinvested earnings	40	55
Total equity	90	105
Total liabilities and equity	**160**	**190**

continued on next page

DRILL 1, *cont.*
Colin's diving business

Gross PP&E

Beg

Add

Sub

End

Accumulated depn.

Beg

Add

Sub

End

Net intangibles

Beg

Add

Sub

End

Colin's cash flow statement, *continued*

Now build Colin's cash flow statement, using the available information.

Cash flow statement	**2005**
Net income	
Depreciation	
Amortization	
(Increase) decrease in operating assets	
Increase (decrease) in operating liabilities	
Cash from operating activities	
Capital expenditure	
Sales of fixed assets	
(Purchase) sale of Intangibles	
Cash from investing activities	
Increase (decrease) in debt	
Increase (decrease) in cmn. stock & APIC	
Dividends	
Cash from financing activities	
Net cash flow	
Beginning cash balance from B/S	
Ending cash balance from B/S	
Difference	

Does Net cash flow = Difference? It should.

DRILL 2
Patricia's nail salons

Patricia Reed's cash flow statement

Patricia Reed set up a chain of nail salons. Using her balance sheet and income statement, calculate her cash flow statement for 2005. Assume:

- Patricia has no intangible assets.
- There were no sales of fixed assets during the year.
- Other long-term liabilities were related to the company's operating activities

All figures in thousands

Income statement	**2004**	**2005**
Sales		1,200
COGS		(900)
Depreciation		(45)
Gross profit		255
SG&A		(89)
Operating profit		166
Interest income		10
Interest expense		(25)
Profit before tax		151
Tax		(47)
Net income		104
Dividends		25
Balance sheet		
Assets		
Cash	47	86
Trade accounts receivable	360	400
Inventories	150	152
Prepaid expenses	15	12
Total current assets	572	650
Investments	74	95
Gross PP&E	213	265
Accumulated Depreciation	(123)	(168)
Net PP&E	90	97
Total assets	736	842
Liabilities		
Accounts payable & accrued expenses	210	215
Loans and notes payable	50	56
Total current liabilities	260	271
Long term debt	251	269
Other long-term liabilities	10	8
Total liabilities	521	548
Equity		
Common stock	5	5
Additional paid-in capital	60	60
Reinvested earnings	150	229
Total equity	215	294
Total liabilities and equity	736	842

DRILL 2, *cont.*
Patricia's nail salons

Gross PP&E

Beg

Add

Sub

End

Accumulated depn.

Beg

Add

Sub

End

Cash flow statement	**2005**
Net income	
Depreciation	
(Increase) decrease in operating assets	
Increase (decrease) in operating liabilities	
Cash from operating activities	
Capital expenditure	
Sales of fixed assets	
(Increase) decrease in other assets	
Cash from investing activities	
Increase (decrease) in debt	
Increase (decrease) in cmn. stock & APIC	
Dividends	
Cash from financing activities	
Net cash flow	
Beginning cash balance from B/S	
Ending cash balance from B/S	
Difference	

Does Net cash flow = Difference? It should.

DRILL 3
Julie's boutiques

Julie's boutiques

Julie Curtis established a chain of women's clothing boutiques across New York State. Using her balance sheet and income statement below calculate her cash flow statement. Assume:

- There were no sales of fixed assets during the year.
- Julie has no intangible assets.

All figures in thousands

Income statement	**2004**	**2005**
Sales		12,500
COGS		(9,000)
Depreciation		(300)
Gross profit		3,200
SG&A		(2,000)
Operating profit		1,200
Interest income		10
Interest expense		(350)
Profit before tax		860
Tax		(301)
Net income		559
Dividends		140
Balance sheet		
Assets		
Cash	800	919
Trade accounts receivable	3,750	4,000
Inventories	3,000	3,500
Prepaid expenses	100	150
Total current assets	7,650	8,569
Investments	100	100
Gross PP&E	5,000	5,500
Accumulated Depreciation	(4,000)	(4,300)
Net PP&E	1,000	1,200
Total assets	8,750	9,869
Liabilities		
Accounts payable	700	800
Loans and notes payable	3,000	3,100
Total current liabilities	3,700	3,900
Long-term debt	3,000	3,500
Total liabilities	6,700	7,400
Equity		
Common stock	50	50
Additional paid-in capital	1,000	1,000
Reinvested earnings	1,000	1,419
Total equity	2,050	2,469
Total liabilities and equity	8,750	9,869

DRILL 3, *cont.*
Julie's boutiques

Gross PP&E

Beg

Add

Sub

End

Accumulated depn.

Beg

Add

Sub

End

Cash flow statement	**2005**
Net income	
Depreciation	
(Increase) decrease in operating assets	
Increase (decrease) in operating liabilities	
Cash from operating activities	
Capital expenditure	
Sales of fixed assets	
(Increase) decrease in other assets	
Cash from investing activities	
Increase (decrease) in debt	
Increase (decrease) in cmn. stock & APIC	
Dividends	
Cash from financing activities	
Net cash flow	
Beginning cash balance from B/S	
Ending cash balance from B/S	
Difference	

Does Net cash flow = Difference? It should.

DRILL 4
Bet's Burger Bars

Bet's Burger Bars

Using the balance sheet and income statement for Bet's Burger Bars below calculate her cash flow statement. Use the BASE tables to help you. Assume:

- There were no sales of PP&E during the year.
- There were no purchases of intangibles during the year.

All figures in thousands

Income statement	**2004**	**2005**
Sales		89,000
COGS		(50,000)
Depreciation		(9,000)
Gross profit		30,000
SG&A		(8,900)
Amortization		(1,300)
Operating profit		19,800
Interest income		345
Interest expense		(3,487)
Profit before tax		16,658
Tax		(5,830)
Net income		10,828
Dividends		2,707
Balance sheet		
Assets		
Cash	1,437	5,017
Trade accounts receivable	26,700	35,000
Inventories	25,015	26,987
Prepaid expenses	2,500	2,645
Total current assets	55,652	69,649
Gross PP&E	78,920	79,420
Accumulated Depreciation	(45,652)	(54,652)
Net PP&E	33,268	24,768
Investments	3,697	2,540
Intangibles	8,975	7,675
Total assets	101,592	104,632
Liabilities		
Accounts payable & accrued expenses	21,458	25,897
Loans and notes payable	8,975	5,174
Total current liabilities	30,433	31,071
Long term debt	56,789	49,856
Total liabilities	87,222	80,927
Equity		
Common stock	125	128
Additional paid in capital	5,648	6,859
Reinvested earnings	8,597	16,718
Total equity	14,370	23,705
Total liabilities and equity	101,592	104,632

DRILL 4, *cont.*
Bet's Burger Bars

Cash flow statement	2005
Net income	
Depreciation	
Amortization	
(Increase) decrease in operating assets	
Increase (decrease) in operating liabilities	
Cash from operating activities	
Capital expenditure	
Sales of fixed assets	
(Increase) decrease in other assets	
(Purchases) sales of intangible assets	
Cash from investing activities	
Increase (decrease) in debt	
Increase (decrease) in cmn. stock & APIC	
Dividends	
Cash from financing activities	
Net cash flow	
Beginning cash balance from B/S	
Ending cash balance from B/S	
Difference	

Does Net cash flow = Difference? It should.

Gross PP&E

Beg

Add

Sub

End

Accumulated depn.

Beg

Add

Sub

End

Net intangibles

Beg

Add

Sub

End

DRILL 5
The auction house

The auction house

Julie Ann Ward owns a large auction house in Boston. Using her balance sheet and income statement below calculate her cash flow statement for 2005. Assume the following:

- Her capital expenditure for the year was $12,760.
- She sold some fixed assets for their book value (use the BASE tables to determine how much cash she received).
- She did not sell any intangible assets.

All figures in thousands.

Income statement	**2004**	**2005**
Sales		103,876
COGS		(81,265)
Depreciation		(8,756)
Gross profit		13,855
SG&A		(1,274)
Amortization		(908)
Operating profit		11,673
Interest income		3,456
Interest expense		(8,761)
Profit before tax		6,368
Tax		(2,229)
Net income		4,139
Dividends		1,345
Balance sheet		
Assets		
Cash	64,141	52,321
Marketable securities	1,234	908
Trade accounts receivable	54,098	65,908
Inventories	34,567	32,196
Prepaid expenses	5,671	3,467
Total current assets	159,711	154,800
Gross PP&E	78,920	88,224
Accumulated Depreciation	(45,652)	(52,063)
Net PP&E	33,268	36,161
Investments	12,375	15,832
Intangibles	10,983	22,420
Total assets	216,337	229,213
Liabilities		
Accounts payable & accrued expenses	45,982	49,081
Loans and notes payable	34,093	26,092
Total current liabilities	80,075	75,173
Long term debt	109,234	123,098
Total liabilities	189,309	198,271
Equity		
Common stock	121	134
Additional paid in capital	3,456	4,563
Reinvested earnings	23,451	26,245
Total equity	27,028	30,942
Total liabilities and equity	216,337	229,213

DRILL 5, *cont.*
The auction house

Gross PP&E

Beg

Add

Sub

End

Accumulated depn.

Beg

Add

Sub

End

Net intangibles

Beg

Add

Sub

End

Cash flow statement	**2005**
Net income	
Depreciation	
Amortization	
(Increase) decrease in operating assets	
Increase (decrease) in operating liabilities	
Cash from operating activities	
Capital expenditure	
Sales of fixed assets	
(Increase) decrease in other assets	
(Purchases) sales of intangible assets	
Cash from investing activities	
Increase (decrease) in debt	
Increase (decrease) in cmn. stock & APIC	
Dividends	
Cash from financing activities	
Net cash flow	
Beginning cash balance from B/S	
Ending cash balance from B/S	
Difference	

Does Net cash flow = Difference? It should.

A

B

C

D

E

P

R

S

T

U

V

W

Supplement
for use with

Introduction to Accounting for Finance

Alastair Matchett

Cover design:	Loraine Machlin Marsha Cohen
Illustrations:	Jacque Auger
Proofreaders:	Mary Jane Kaplan Katharine McMaster Truly Donovan
Content review:	Ross Wisdom, CPA
Editor:	Kieran Maguire

Published by Adkins Matchett & Toy LLC

Manufactured in the United States of America

ISBN 1-891112-67-8

Fourth edition, 2007
Originally published in 1997 and revised and republished in 2002 as *Accounting: A Brief Introduction* by South-Western, a division of Thomson Learning, and offered as a college text without answer keys. The fourth edition is not substantially revised from the third edition but like the first and second editions includes answer keys and can be used as a self-study text.

Toll-free order line: **1 888 414 0999**

Visit us at **www.amttraining.com**
www.crunchthenumbers.com

Offices in: London, New York, Mumbai, Italy, Bangkok

Contents

Extracts from the 2004 Coca-Cola Report

ITEM 6. SELECTED FINANCIAL DATA

The Coca-Cola Company and Subsidiaries

(In millions except per share data and growth rates)	Compound Growth Rates 5 Years	Compound Growth Rates 10 Years	Year Ended December 31, 2004[2]	Year Ended December 31, 2003[3]
SUMMARY OF OPERATIONS				
Net operating revenues	5.5 %	4.2%	**$ 21,962**	$ 21,044
Cost of goods sold	4.9 %	2.2%	**7,638**	7,762
Gross profit	5.9 %	5.5%	**14,324**	13,282
Selling, general and administrative expenses	6.4 %	5.5%	**8,146**	7,488
Other operating charges			**480**	573
Operating income	7.4 %	4.6%	**5,698**	5,221
Interest income			**157**	176
Interest expense			**196**	178
Equity income (loss)—net			**621**	406
Other income (loss)—net			**(82)**	(138)
Gains on issuances of stock by equity investees			**24**	8
Income before income taxes and changes in accounting principles	10.3 %	5.3%	**6,222**	5,495
Income taxes	(0.2)%	1.6%	**1,375**	1,148
Net income before changes in accounting principles	14.8 %	6.6%	**$ 4,847**	$ 4,347
Net income	14.8 %	6.6%	**$ 4,847**	$ 4,347
Average shares outstanding			**2,426**	2,459
Average shares outstanding assuming dilution			**2,429**	2,462
PER SHARE DATA				
Net income before changes in accounting principles—basic	15.3 %	7.3%	**$ 2.00**	$ 1.77
Net income before changes in accounting principles—diluted	15.3 %	7.4%	**2.00**	1.77
Basic net income	15.3 %	7.3%	**2.00**	1.77
Diluted net income	15.3 %	7.4%	**2.00**	1.77
Cash dividends	9.3 %	9.9%	**1.00**	0.88
Market price on December 31,	(6.5)%	4.9%	**41.64**	50.75
TOTAL MARKET VALUE OF COMMON STOCK[1]	(7.0)%	4.3%	**$ 100,325**	$ 123,908
BALANCE SHEET DATA				
Cash, cash equivalents and current marketable securities			**$ 6,768**	$ 3,482
Property, plant and equipment—net			**6,091**	6,097
Depreciation			**715**	667
Capital expenditures			**755**	812
Total assets			**31,327**	27,342
Long-term debt			**1,157**	2,517
Shareowners' equity			**15,935**	14,090
NET CASH PROVIDED BY OPERATIONS			**$ 5,968**	$ 5,456

[1] Refer to Glossary on pages 119 and 120.

[2] In 2004, we adopted FSP No. 106-2, "Accounting and Disclosure Requirements Related to Medicare Prescription Drug, Improvement and Modernization Act of 2003."

[3] In 2003, we adopted SFAS No. 146, "Accounting for Costs Associated with Exit or Disposal Activities."

The Coca-Cola Company and Subsidiaries

2002[4,5]	2001[6]	2000	1999	1998[7]	1997[7]	1996[7]	1995[7]	1994[7,8]
$ 19,564	$ 17,545	$ 17,354	$ 16,767	$ 16,301	$ 16,611	$ 16,635	$ 16,283	$ 14,570
7,105	6,044	6,204	6,009	5,562	6,015	6,738	6,940	6,168
12,459	11,501	11,150	10,758	10,739	10,596	9,897	9,343	8,402
7,001	6,149	6,016	5,963	5,699	5,535	5,597	5,231	4,765
—	—	1,443	813	73	60	385	86	—
5,458	5,352	3,691	3,982	4,967	5,001	3,915	4,026	3,637
209	325	345	260	219	211	238	245	181
199	289	447	337	277	258	286	272	199
384	152	(289)	(184)	32	155	211	169	134
(353)	39	99	98	230	583	87	86	(25)
—	91	—	—	27	363	431	74	—
5,499	5,670	3,399	3,819	5,198	6,055	4,596	4,328	3,728
1,523	1,691	1,222	1,388	1,665	1,926	1,104	1,342	1,174
$ 3,976	$ 3,979	$ 2,177	$ 2,431	$ 3,533	$ 4,129	$ 3,492	$ 2,986	$ 2,554
$ 3,050	$ 3,969	$ 2,177	$ 2,431	$ 3,533	$ 4,129	$ 3,492	$ 2,986	$ 2,554
2,478	2,487	2,477	2,469	2,467	2,477	2,494	2,525	2,580
2,483	2,487	2,487	2,487	2,496	2,515	2,523	2,549	2,599
$ 1.60	$ 1.60	$ 0.88	$ 0.98	$ 1.43	$ 1.67	$ 1.40	$ 1.18	$ 0.99
1.60	1.60	0.88	0.98	1.42	1.64	1.38	1.17	0.98
1.23	1.60	0.88	0.98	1.43	1.67	1.40	1.18	0.99
1.23	1.60	0.88	0.98	1.42	1.64	1.38	1.17	0.98
0.80	0.72	0.68	0.64	0.60	0.56	0.50	0.44	0.39
43.84	47.15	60.94	58.25	67.00	66.69	52.63	37.13	25.75
$ 108,328	$ 117,226	$ 151,421	$ 143,969	$ 165,190	$ 164,766	$ 130,575	$ 92,983	$ 65,711
$ 2,345	$ 1,934	$ 1,892	$ 1,812	$ 1,807	$ 1,843	$ 1,658	$ 1,315	$ 1,531
5,911	4,453	4,168	4,267	3,669	3,743	3,550	4,336	4,080
614	502	465	438	381	384	442	421	382
851	769	733	1,069	863	1,093	990	937	878
24,406	22,417	20,834	21,623	19,145	16,881	16,112	15,004	13,863
2,701	1,219	835	854	687	801	1,116	1,141	1,426
11,800	11,366	9,316	9,513	8,403	7,274	6,125	5,369	5,228
$ 4,742	$ 4,110	$ 3,585	$ 3,883	$ 3,433	$ 4,033	$ 3,463	$ 3,328	$ 3,361

[4] In 2002, we adopted SFAS No. 142, "Goodwill and Other Intangible Assets."

[5] In 2002, we adopted the fair value method provisions of SFAS No. 123, "Accounting for Stock-Based Compensation," and we adopted SFAS No. 148, "Accounting for Stock-Based Compensation—Transition and Disclosure."

[6] In 2001, we adopted SFAS No. 133, "Accounting for Derivative Instruments and Hedging Activities."

[7] In 1998, we adopted SFAS No. 132, "Employers' Disclosures about Pensions and Other Postretirement Benefits."

[8] In 1994, we adopted SFAS No. 115, "Accounting for Certain Investments in Debt and Equity Securities."

CONSOLIDATED STATEMENTS OF INCOME

The Coca-Cola Company and Subsidiaries

Year Ended December 31,	2004	2003	2002
(In millions except per share data)			
NET OPERATING REVENUES	**$ 21,962**	$ 21,044	$ 19,564
Cost of goods sold	**7,638**	7,762	7,105
GROSS PROFIT	**14,324**	13,282	12,459
Selling, general and administrative expenses	**8,146**	7,488	7,001
Other operating charges	**480**	573	—
OPERATING INCOME	**5,698**	5,221	5,458
Interest income	**157**	176	209
Interest expense	**196**	178	199
Equity income — net	**621**	406	384
Other income (loss) — net	**(82)**	(138)	(353)
Gains on issuances of stock by equity investees	**24**	8	—
INCOME BEFORE INCOME TAXES AND CUMULATIVE EFFECT OF ACCOUNTING CHANGE	**6,222**	5,495	5,499
Income taxes	**1,375**	1,148	1,523
NET INCOME BEFORE CUMULATIVE EFFECT OF ACCOUNTING CHANGE	**4,847**	4,347	3,976
Cumulative effect of accounting change for SFAS No. 142, net of income taxes:			
Company operations	**—**	—	(367)
Equity investees	**—**	—	(559)
NET INCOME	**$ 4,847**	$ 4,347	$ 3,050
BASIC NET INCOME PER SHARE:			
Before accounting change	**$ 2.00**	$ 1.77	$ 1.60
Cumulative effect of accounting change	**—**	—	(0.37)
	$ 2.00	$ 1.77	$ 1.23
DILUTED NET INCOME PER SHARE:			
Before accounting change	**$ 2.00**	$ 1.77	$ 1.60
Cumulative effect of accounting change	**—**	—	(0.37)
	$ 2.00	$ 1.77	$ 1.23
AVERAGE SHARES OUTSTANDING	**2,426**	2,459	2,478
Effect of dilutive securities	**3**	3	5
AVERAGE SHARES OUTSTANDING ASSUMING DILUTION	**2,429**	2,462	2,483

Refer to Notes to Consolidated Financial Statements.

CONSOLIDATED BALANCE SHEETS

The Coca-Cola Company and Subsidiaries

December 31, (In millions)	2004	2003
ASSETS		
CURRENT		
Cash and cash equivalents	**$ 6,707**	$ 3,362
Marketable securities	**61**	120
	6,768	3,482
Trade accounts receivable, less allowances of $69 in 2004 and $61 in 2003	**2,171**	2,091
Inventories	**1,420**	1,252
Prepaid expenses and other assets	**1,735**	1,571
TOTAL CURRENT ASSETS	**12,094**	8,396
INVESTMENTS AND OTHER ASSETS		
Equity method investments:		
Coca-Cola Enterprises Inc.	**1,569**	1,260
Coca-Cola Hellenic Bottling Company S.A.	**1,067**	941
Coca-Cola FEMSA, S.A. de C.V.	**792**	674
Coca-Cola Amatil Limited	**736**	652
Other, principally bottling companies	**1,733**	1,697
Cost method investments, principally bottling companies	**355**	314
Other assets	**3,054**	3,322
	9,306	8,860
PROPERTY, PLANT AND EQUIPMENT		
Land	**479**	419
Buildings and improvements	**2,853**	2,615
Machinery and equipment	**6,337**	6,159
Containers	**480**	429
	10,149	9,622
Less allowances for depreciation	**4,058**	3,525
	6,091	6,097
TRADEMARKS WITH INDEFINITE LIVES	**2,037**	1,979
GOODWILL	**1,097**	1,029
OTHER INTANGIBLE ASSETS	**702**	981
TOTAL ASSETS	**$ 31,327**	$ 27,342

Refer to Notes to Consolidated Financial Statements.

The Coca-Cola Company and Subsidiaries

December 31, (In millions except share data)	2004	2003
LIABILITIES AND SHAREOWNERS' EQUITY		
CURRENT		
Accounts payable and accrued expenses	**$ 4,283**	$ 4,058
Loans and notes payable	**4,531**	2,583
Current maturities of long-term debt	**1,490**	323
Accrued income taxes	**667**	922
TOTAL CURRENT LIABILITIES	**10,971**	7,886
LONG-TERM DEBT	**1,157**	2,517
OTHER LIABILITIES	**2,814**	2,512
DEFERRED INCOME TAXES	**450**	337
SHAREOWNERS' EQUITY		
Common stock, $0.25 par value		
Authorized: 5,600,000,000 shares;		
issued: 3,500,489,544 shares in 2004 and 3,494,799,258 shares in 2003	**875**	874
Capital surplus	**4,928**	4,395
Reinvested earnings	**29,105**	26,687
Accumulated other comprehensive income (loss)	**(1,348)**	(1,995)
	33,560	29,961
Less treasury stock, at cost (1,091,150,977 shares in 2004; 1,053,267,474 shares in 2003)	**(17,625)**	(15,871)
	15,935	14,090
TOTAL LIABILITIES AND SHAREOWNERS' EQUITY	**$ 31,327**	$ 27,342

Refer to Notes to Consolidated Financial Statements.

CONSOLIDATED STATEMENTS OF CASH FLOWS

The Coca-Cola Company and Subsidiaries

Year Ended December 31,	2004	2003	2002
(In millions)			
OPERATING ACTIVITIES			
Net income	**$ 4,847**	$ 4,347	$ 3,050
Depreciation and amortization	**893**	850	806
Stock-based compensation expense	**345**	422	365
Deferred income taxes	**162**	(188)	40
Equity income (loss), net of dividends	**(476)**	(294)	(256)
Foreign currency adjustments	**(59)**	(79)	(76)
Gains on issuances of stock by equity investees	**(24)**	(8)	—
(Gains) losses on sales of assets, including bottling interests	**(20)**	(5)	3
Cumulative effect of accounting changes	**—**	—	926
Other operating charges	**480**	330	—
Other items	**437**	249	291
Net change in operating assets and liabilities	**(617)**	(168)	(407)
Net cash provided by operating activities	**5,968**	5,456	4,742
INVESTING ACTIVITIES			
Acquisitions and investments, principally trademarks and bottling companies	**(267)**	(359)	(544)
Purchases of investments and other assets	**(46)**	(177)	(141)
Proceeds from disposals of investments and other assets	**161**	147	243
Purchases of property, plant and equipment	**(755)**	(812)	(851)
Proceeds from disposals of property, plant and equipment	**341**	87	69
Other investing activities	**63**	178	159
Net cash used in investing activities	**(503)**	(936)	(1,065)
FINANCING ACTIVITIES			
Issuances of debt	**3,030**	1,026	1,622
Payments of debt	**(1,316)**	(1,119)	(2,378)
Issuances of stock	**193**	98	107
Purchases of stock for treasury	**(1,739)**	(1,440)	(691)
Dividends	**(2,429)**	(2,166)	(1,987)
Net cash used in financing activities	**(2,261)**	(3,601)	(3,327)
EFFECT OF EXCHANGE RATE CHANGES ON CASH AND CASH EQUIVALENTS	**141**	183	44
CASH AND CASH EQUIVALENTS			
Net increase during the year	**3,345**	1,102	394
Balance at beginning of year	**3,362**	2,260	1,866
Balance at end of year	**$ 6,707**	$ 3,362	$ 2,260

Refer to Notes to Consolidated Financial Statements.

CONSOLIDATED STATEMENTS OF SHAREOWNERS' EQUITY

The Coca-Cola Company and Subsidiaries

Year Ended December 31,	2004	2003	2002
(In millions except per share data)			
NUMBER OF COMMON SHARES OUTSTANDING			
Balance at beginning of year	**2,442**	2,471	2,486
Stock issued to employees exercising stock options	**5**	4	3
Purchases of stock for treasury[1]	**(38)**	(33)	(14)
Adoption of SFAS No. 123	**—**	—	(4)
Balance at end of year	**2,409**	2,442	2,471
COMMON STOCK			
Balance at beginning of year	**$ 874**	$ 873	$ 873
Stock issued to employees exercising stock options	**1**	1	1
Adoption of SFAS No. 123	**—**	—	(1)
Balance at end of year	**875**	874	873
CAPITAL SURPLUS			
Balance at beginning of year	**4,395**	3,857	3,520
Stock issued to employees exercising stock options	**175**	105	111
Tax benefit from employees' stock option and restricted stock plans	**13**	11	11
Stock-based compensation	**345**	422	365
Adoption of SFAS No. 123	**—**	—	(150)
Balance at end of year	**4,928**	4,395	3,857
REINVESTED EARNINGS			
Balance at beginning of year	**26,687**	24,506	23,443
Net income	**4,847**	4,347	3,050
Dividends (per share—$1.00, $0.88 and $0.80 in 2004, 2003 and 2002, respectively)	**(2,429)**	(2,166)	(1,987)
Balance at end of year	**29,105**	26,687	24,506
OUTSTANDING RESTRICTED STOCK			
Balance at beginning of year	**—**	—	(150)
Adoption of SFAS No. 123	**—**	—	150
Balance at end of year	**—**	—	—
ACCUMULATED OTHER COMPREHENSIVE INCOME (LOSS)			
Balance at beginning of year	**(1,995)**	(3,047)	(2,638)
Net foreign currency translation adjustment	**665**	921	(95)
Net loss on derivatives	**(3)**	(33)	(186)
Net change in unrealized gain on available-for-sale securities	**39**	40	67
Net change in minimum pension liability	**(54)**	124	(195)
Net other comprehensive income adjustments	**647**	1,052	(409)
Balance at end of year	**(1,348)**	(1,995)	(3,047)
TREASURY STOCK			
Balance at beginning of year	**(15,871)**	(14,389)	(13,682)
Purchases of treasury stock	**(1,754)**	(1,482)	(707)
Balance at end of year	**(17,625)**	(15,871)	(14,389)
TOTAL SHAREOWNERS' EQUITY	**$ 15,935**	$ 14,090	$ 11,800
COMPREHENSIVE INCOME			
Net income	**$ 4,847**	$ 4,347	$ 3,050
Net other comprehensive income adjustments	**647**	1,052	(409)
TOTAL COMPREHENSIVE INCOME	**$ 5,494**	$ 5,399	$ 2,641

[1] Common stock purchased from employees exercising stock options numbered 0.4 million, 0.4 million and 0.2 million shares for the years ended December 31, 2004, 2003 and 2002, respectively.

Refer to Notes to Consolidated Financial Statements.

NOTES TO CONSOLIDATED FINANCIAL STATEMENTS

The Coca-Cola Company and Subsidiaries

NOTE 1: ORGANIZATION AND SUMMARY OF SIGNIFICANT ACCOUNTING POLICIES

Organization

The Coca-Cola Company is predominantly a manufacturer, distributor and marketer of nonalcoholic beverage concentrates and syrups. In these notes, the terms "Company," "we," "us" or "our" mean The Coca-Cola Company and all subsidiaries included in the consolidated financial statements. Operating in more than 200 countries worldwide, we primarily sell our concentrates and syrups, as well as some finished beverages, to bottling and canning operations, distributors, fountain wholesalers and fountain retailers. We also market and distribute juices and juice drinks, sports drinks, water products, teas, coffees and other beverage products. Additionally, we have ownership interests in numerous bottling and canning operations. Significant markets for our products exist in all the world's geographic regions.

Basis of Presentation and Consolidation

Our consolidated financial statements are prepared in accordance with accounting principles generally accepted in the United States. Our Company consolidates all entities that we control by ownership of a majority voting interest as well as variable interest entities for which our Company is the primary beneficiary. Refer to the heading "Variable Interest Entities" for a discussion of variable interest entities.

We use the equity method to account for our investments for which we have the ability to exercise significant influence over operating and financial policies. Consolidated net income includes our Company's share of the net earnings of these companies. The difference between consolidation and the equity method impacts certain financial ratios because of the presentation of the detailed line items reported in the financial statements.

We use the cost method to account for our investments in companies that we do not control and for which we do not have the ability to exercise significant influence over operating and financial policies. In accordance with the cost method, these investments are recorded at cost or fair value, as appropriate.

We eliminate from our financial results all significant intercompany transactions, including the intercompany transactions with variable interest entities and the intercompany portion of transactions with equity method investees.

Certain amounts in the prior years' consolidated financial statements have been reclassified to conform to the current-year presentation.

Variable Interest Entities

In December 2003, the Financial Accounting Standards Board ("FASB") issued FASB Interpretation No. 46 (revised December 2003), "Consolidation of Variable Interest Entities" ("Interpretation 46" or "FIN 46"). Application of this interpretation was required in our consolidated financial statements for the year ended December 31, 2003 for interests in variable interest entities that were considered to be special-purpose entities. Our Company determined that we did not have any arrangements or relationships with special-purpose entities. Application of Interpretation 46 for all other types of variable interest entities was required for our Company effective March 31, 2004.

Interpretation 46 addresses the consolidation of business enterprises to which the usual condition (ownership of a majority voting interest) of consolidation does not apply. This interpretation focuses on controlling financial interests that may be achieved through arrangements that do not involve voting interests. It concludes that in the absence of clear control through voting interests, a company's exposure (variable interest)

NOTES TO CONSOLIDATED FINANCIAL STATEMENTS

The Coca-Cola Company and Subsidiaries

NOTE 1: ORGANIZATION AND SUMMARY OF SIGNIFICANT ACCOUNTING POLICIES (Continued)

Revenue Recognition

Our Company recognizes revenue when title to our products is transferred to our bottling partners or our customers.

Advertising Costs

Our Company expenses production costs of print, radio, television and other advertisements as of the first date the advertisements take place. Advertising costs included in selling, general and administrative expenses were approximately $2.2 billion in 2004, approximately $1.8 billion in 2003 and approximately $1.7 billion in 2002. As of December 31, 2004 and 2003, advertising and production costs of approximately $194 million and $190 million, respectively, were recorded in prepaid expenses and other assets and in noncurrent other assets in our consolidated balance sheets.

Stock-Based Compensation

Our Company currently sponsors stock option plans and restricted stock award plans. Refer to Note 13. Effective January 1, 2002, our Company adopted the preferable fair value recognition provisions of Statement of Financial Accounting Standards ("SFAS") No. 123, "Accounting for Stock-Based Compensation." Our Company selected the modified prospective method of adoption described in SFAS No. 148, "Accounting for Stock-Based Compensation—Transition and Disclosure." The fair values of the stock awards are determined using a single estimated expected life. The compensation expense is recognized on a straight-line basis over the vesting period. The total stock-based compensation expense, net of related tax effects, was $254 million in 2004, $308 million in 2003 and $267 million in 2002. These amounts represent the same as that which would have been recognized had the fair value method of SFAS No. 123 been applied from its original effective date.

Issuances of Stock by Equity Investees

When one of our equity investees issues additional shares to third parties, our percentage ownership interest in the investee decreases. In the event the issuance price per share is more or less than our average carrying amount per share, we recognize a noncash gain or loss on the issuance. This noncash gain or loss, net of any deferred taxes, is generally recognized in our net income in the period the change of ownership interest occurs.

If gains have been previously recognized on issuances of an equity investee's stock and shares of the equity investee are subsequently repurchased by the equity investee, gain recognition does not occur on issuances subsequent to the date of a repurchase until shares have been issued in an amount equivalent to the number of repurchased shares. This type of transaction is reflected as an equity transaction, and the net effect is reflected in our consolidated balance sheets. Refer to Note 3.

Net Income Per Share

We compute basic net income per share by dividing net income by the weighted-average number of shares outstanding. Diluted net income per share includes the dilutive effect of stock-based compensation awards, if any.

Cash Equivalents

We classify marketable securities that are highly liquid and have maturities of three months or less at the date of purchase as cash equivalents.

NOTES TO CONSOLIDATED FINANCIAL STATEMENTS

The Coca-Cola Company and Subsidiaries

NOTE 1: ORGANIZATION AND SUMMARY OF SIGNIFICANT ACCOUNTING POLICIES (Continued)

Trade Accounts Receivable

We record trade accounts receivable at net realizable value. This value includes an appropriate allowance for estimated uncollectible accounts to reflect any loss anticipated on the trade accounts receivable balances and charged to the provision for doubtful accounts. We calculate this allowance based on our history of write-offs, level of past due accounts based on the contractual terms of the receivables and our relationships with and economic status of our bottling partners and customers.

Inventories

Inventories consist primarily of raw materials, supplies, concentrates and syrups and are valued at the lower of cost or market. We determine cost on the basis of average cost or first-in, first-out methods.

Recoverability of Equity Method and Cost Method Investments

Management periodically assesses the recoverability of our Company's equity method and cost method investments. For publicly traded investments, readily available quoted market prices are an indication of the fair value of our Company's investments. For nonpublicly traded investments, if an identified event or change in circumstances requires an impairment evaluation, management assesses fair value based on valuation methodologies as appropriate, including discounted cash flows, estimates of sales proceeds and external appraisals, as appropriate. If an investment is considered to be impaired and the decline in value is other than temporary, we record an appropriate write-down.

Other Assets

Our Company advances payments to certain customers for marketing to fund future activities intended to generate profitable volume, and we expense such payments over the applicable period. Advance payments are also made to certain customers for distribution rights. Additionally, our Company invests in infrastructure programs with our bottlers that are directed at strengthening our bottling system and increasing unit case volume. Management periodically evaluates the recoverability of these assets by preparing estimates of sales volume, the resulting gross profit, cash flows and considering other factors. Costs of these programs are recorded in prepaid expenses and other assets and noncurrent other assets and are subsequently amortized over the periods to be directly benefited. Amortization expense for infrastructure programs was approximately $136 million, $156 million and $176 million, respectively, for the years ended December 31, 2004, 2003 and 2002. Refer to Note 2.

Property, Plant and Equipment

We state property, plant and equipment at cost and depreciate such assets principally by the straight-line method over the estimated useful lives of the assets. Management assesses the recoverability of the carrying amount of property, plant and equipment if certain events or changes occur, such as a significant decrease in market value of the assets or a significant change in the business conditions in a particular market.

Goodwill, Trademarks and Other Intangible Assets

Effective January 1, 2002, our Company adopted SFAS No. 142, "Goodwill and Other Intangible Assets." The adoption of SFAS No. 142 required an initial impairment assessment involving a comparison of the fair value of goodwill, trademarks and other intangible assets to current carrying value. Upon adoption, we recorded

NOTES TO CONSOLIDATED FINANCIAL STATEMENTS

The Coca-Cola Company and Subsidiaries

NOTE 1: ORGANIZATION AND SUMMARY OF SIGNIFICANT ACCOUNTING POLICIES (Continued)

a loss for the cumulative effect of accounting change for SFAS No. 142, net of income taxes, of $367 million for Company operations and $559 million for the Company's proportionate share of impairment losses from its equity method investees. We did not restate prior periods for the adoption of SFAS No. 142.

Trademarks and other intangible assets determined to have indefinite useful lives are not amortized. We test such trademarks and other intangible assets with indefinite useful lives for impairment annually, or more frequently if events or circumstances indicate that an asset might be impaired. Trademarks and other intangible assets determined to have definite lives are amortized over their useful lives. We review such trademarks and other intangible assets with definite lives for impairment to ensure they are appropriately valued if conditions exist that may indicate the carrying value may not be recoverable. Such conditions may include an economic downturn in a geographic market or a change in the assessment of future operations.

All goodwill is assigned to reporting units, which are one level below our operating segments. Goodwill is assigned to the reporting unit that benefits from the synergies arising from each business combination. Goodwill is not amortized. We perform tests for impairment of goodwill annually, or more frequently if events or circumstances indicate it might be impaired. Such tests include comparing the fair value of a reporting unit with its carrying value, including goodwill. Impairment assessments are performed using a variety of methodologies, including cash flow analyses, estimates of sales proceeds and independent appraisals. Where applicable, an appropriate discount rate is used, based on the Company's cost of capital rate or location-specific economic factors. Refer to Note 4.

Derivative Financial Instruments

Our Company accounts for derivative financial instruments in accordance with SFAS No. 133, "Accounting for Derivative Instruments and Hedging Activities," as amended by SFAS No. 137, SFAS No. 138, and SFAS No. 149. Our Company recognizes all derivative instruments as either assets or liabilities at fair value in our consolidated balance sheets. Refer to Note 10.

Retirement Related Benefits

Using appropriate actuarial methods and assumptions, our Company accounts for defined benefit pension plans in accordance with SFAS No. 87, "Employers' Accounting for Pensions." We account for our nonpension postretirement benefits in accordance with SFAS No. 106, "Employers' Accounting for Postretirement Benefits Other Than Pensions." In 2003, we adopted SFAS No. 132 (revised 2003), "Employers' Disclosures about Pensions and Other Postretirement Benefits," ("SFAS 132(R)") for all U.S. plans. As permitted by this standard, in 2004 we adopted the disclosure provisions for all foreign plans for the year ended December 31, 2004. SFAS No. 132(R) requires additional disclosures about the assets, obligations, cash flows and net periodic benefit cost of defined benefit pension plans and other defined benefit postretirement plans. This statement did not change the measurement or recognition of those plans required by SFAS No. 87, SFAS No. 88, "Employers' Accounting for Settlements and Curtailments of Defined Benefit Pension Plans and for Termination Benefits," or SFAS No. 106. Refer to Note 14 for a description of how we determine our principal assumptions for pension and postretirement benefit accounting.

Contingencies

Our Company is involved in various legal proceedings and tax matters. Due to their nature, such legal proceedings and tax matters involve inherent uncertainties including, but not limited to, court rulings,

NOTES TO CONSOLIDATED FINANCIAL STATEMENTS

The Coca-Cola Company and Subsidiaries

NOTE 1: ORGANIZATION AND SUMMARY OF SIGNIFICANT ACCOUNTING POLICIES (Continued)

2005. Our proportionate share of the stock-based compensation expense resulting from the adoption of SFAS No. 123(R) by our equity investees will be recognized as a reduction to equity income.

In December 2004, the FASB issued SFAS No. 153, "Exchanges of Nonmonetary Assets, an amendment of APB Opinion No. 29." SFAS No. 153 is based on the principle that exchanges of nonmonetary assets should be measured based on the fair value of the assets exchanged. APB Opinion No. 29, "Accounting for Nonmonetary Transactions," provided an exception to its basic measurement principle (fair value) for exchanges of similar productive assets. Under APB Opinion No. 29, an exchange of a productive asset for a similar productive asset was based on the recorded amount of the asset relinquished. SFAS No. 153 eliminates this exception and replaces it with an exception of exchanges of nonmonetary assets that do not have commercial substance. SFAS No. 153 is effective for our Company as of July 1, 2005. The Company will apply the requirements of SFAS No. 153 prospectively.

NOTE 2: BOTTLING INVESTMENTS

Coca-Cola Enterprises Inc.

Coca-Cola Enterprises Inc. ("CCE") is a marketer, producer and distributor of bottle and can nonalcoholic beverages, operating in eight countries. On December 31, 2004, our Company owned approximately 36 percent of the outstanding common stock of CCE. We account for our investment by the equity method of accounting and, therefore, our operating results include our proportionate share of income (loss) resulting from our investment in CCE. As of December 31, 2004, our proportionate share of the net assets of CCE exceeded our investment by approximately $366 million. This difference is not amortized.

NOTES TO CONSOLIDATED FINANCIAL STATEMENTS

The Coca-Cola Company and Subsidiaries

NOTE 4: GOODWILL, TRADEMARKS AND OTHER INTANGIBLE ASSETS (Continued)

equity method investees, the cumulative effect of this change in accounting principle in 2002 was an after-tax decrease to net income of $559 million. The deferred income tax benefit related to the cumulative effect of this change for the Company's intangible assets in 2002 was approximately $94 million and for the Company's proportionate share of its equity method investees was approximately $123 million.

The impairment charges resulting in the after-tax decrease to net income for the cumulative effect of this change by applicable operating segment as of January 1, 2002 were as follows (in millions):

The Company:	
Asia	$ 108
Europe, Eurasia and Middle East	33
Latin America	226
	$ 367
The Company's proportionate share of its equity method investees:	
Africa	$ 63
Europe, Eurasia and Middle East	400
Latin America	96
	$ 559

Of the $108 million impairment recorded as of January 1, 2002 for the Company in Asia, $99 million related to bottlers' franchise rights in our consolidated bottlers in our Southeast and West Asia Division. Difficult economic conditions impacted our business in Singapore, Sri Lanka, Nepal and Vietnam. As a result, bottlers in these countries experienced lower than expected volume and operating margins.

Of the Company's $226 million impairment recorded as of January 1, 2002 for Latin America, approximately $113 million related to Company-owned Brazilian bottlers' franchise rights. The Brazilian macroeconomic conditions, the devaluation of the currency and lower pricing impacted the valuation of these bottlers' franchise rights. The remainder of the $226 million primarily related to a $109 million impairment for certain trademarks in Latin America. In early 1999, our Company formed a strategic partnership to market and distribute such trademarked products. The macroeconomic conditions and lower pricing depressed operating margins for these trademarks.

For Europe, Eurasia and Middle East equity method investees, a $400 million impairment was recorded as of January 1, 2002 for the Company's proportionate share related to bottlers' franchise rights. Of this amount, approximately $301 million related to CCEAG. This impairment was due to a prolonged difficult economic environment in Germany, resulting in continuing losses for CCEAG in eastern Germany. At that time, the market for nonalcoholic beverages was undergoing a transformation. A changing competitive landscape, continuing price pressure and growing demand for new products and packaging were elements impacting CCEAG. The $400 million impairment also included a $50 million charge for Middle East bottlers' franchise rights.

In our Africa operating segment, a $63 million charge was recorded for the Company's proportionate share of impairments related to equity method investee bottlers' franchise rights. These Middle East and Africa bottlers had challenges as a result of political instability and the resulting economic instability in their respective regions, which adversely impacted financial performance.

A $96 million impairment was recorded as of January 1, 2002 for the Company's proportionate share related to bottlers' franchise rights of Latin America equity method investees. In southern Latin America, the

NOTES TO CONSOLIDATED FINANCIAL STATEMENTS

The Coca-Cola Company and Subsidiaries

NOTE 4: GOODWILL, TRADEMARKS AND OTHER INTANGIBLE ASSETS (Continued)

macroeconomic conditions and devaluation of the Argentine peso significantly impacted the valuation of bottlers' franchise rights.

The following tables set forth the information for intangible assets subject to amortization and for intangible assets not subject to amortization (in millions):

December 31,	2004	2003
Amortized intangible assets (various, principally trademarks):		
Gross carrying amount	**$ 292**	$ 263
Accumulated amortization	**$ 128**	$ 98
Unamortized intangible assets:		
Trademarks	**$ 2,037**	$ 1,979
Goodwill[1]	**1,097**	1,029
Bottlers' franchise rights[2]	**374**	658
Other	**164**	158
	$ 3,672	$ 3,824

[1] During 2004, the increase in goodwill primarily resulted from translation adjustments.

[2] During 2004, the decrease in franchise rights primarily related to the impairment charge of $354 million related to CCEAG's franchise rights (see discussion below).

Year Ended December 31,	2004	2003
Aggregate amortization expense	**$ 40**	$ 23
Estimated amortization expense:		
For the year ending:		
December 31, 2005	$ 28	
December 31, 2006	$ 16	
December 31, 2007	$ 16	
December 31, 2008	$ 16	
December 31, 2009	$ 15	

The goodwill by applicable operating segment as of December 31, 2004 was as follows (in millions):

December 31,	2004	2003
North America	**$ 140**	$ 142
Asia	**37**	45
Europe, Eurasia and Middle East	**828**	742
Latin America	**92**	100
	$ 1,097	$ 1,029

In 2004, acquisition of intangible assets totaled approximately $89 million. This amount is primarily related to the Company's acquisition of trademarks with indefinite lives in the Latin America operating segment.

In 2004, our Company recorded impairment charges related to intangible assets of approximately $374 million. The decrease in franchise rights in 2004 was primarily due to this impairment charge, offset by an increase due to translation adjustment. These impairment charges primarily were in the Europe, Eurasia and

NOTES TO CONSOLIDATED FINANCIAL STATEMENTS

The Coca-Cola Company and Subsidiaries

NOTE 4: GOODWILL, TRADEMARKS AND OTHER INTANGIBLE ASSETS (Continued)

Middle East operating segment and were included in other operating charges in our consolidated statement of income. The charge was primarily related to franchise rights at CCEAG. The CCEAG impairment was the result of our revised outlook for the German market that has been unfavorably impacted by volume declines resulting from market shifts related to the deposit law on nonreturnable beverage packages and the corresponding lack of availability for our products in the discount retail channel. The deposit laws in Germany have led to discount chains creating proprietary packages that can only be returned to their own stores. These proprietary packages are continuing to gain market share and customer acceptance.

At the end of 2004, the German government passed an amendment to the mandatory deposit legislation that will require retailers, including discount chains, to accept returns of each type of non-refillable beverage containers which they sell, regardless of where the beverage container type was purchased. In addition, the mandatory deposit requirement was expanded to other beverage categories. The amendment allows for a transition period to enable manufacturers and retailers to establish a national take-back system for non-refillable containers. The transition period is expected to last at least until mid-2006.

We determined the amount of the 2004 impairment charges by comparing the fair value of the intangible assets to the current carrying value. Fair values were derived using discounted cash flow analyses with a number of scenarios that were weighted based on the probability of different outcomes. Because the fair value was less than the carrying value of the assets, we recorded an impairment charge to reduce the carrying value of the assets to fair value. These impairment charges were recorded in the line item other operating charges in the consolidated statement of income for 2004.

In 2003, acquisitions of intangible assets totaled approximately $142 million. Of this amount, approximately $88 million related to the Company's acquisition of certain intangible assets with indefinite lives, primarily trademarks and brands in various parts of the world. None of these trademarks and brands was considered individually significant. Additionally, the Company acquired certain brands and related contractual rights from Panamco valued at $54 million in the Latin America operating segment with an estimated useful life of 10 years.

NOTE 5: ACCOUNTS PAYABLE AND ACCRUED EXPENSES

Accounts payable and accrued expenses consist of the following (in millions):

December 31,	**2004**	2003
Trade accounts payable and other accrued expenses	**$ 2,238**	$ 2,014
Accrued marketing	**1,194**	1,046
Accrued compensation	**389**	311
Sales, payroll and other taxes	**222**	225
Container deposits	**199**	256
Accrued streamlining costs (refer to Note 17)	**41**	206
	$ 4,283	$ 4,058

NOTE 6: SHORT-TERM BORROWINGS AND CREDIT ARRANGEMENTS

Loans and notes payable consist primarily of commercial paper issued in the United States. At December 31, 2004 and 2003, we had approximately $4,235 million and $2,234 million, respectively, outstanding in commercial paper borrowings. Our weighted-average interest rates for commercial paper outstanding were approximately 2.2 percent and 1.1 percent per year at December 31, 2004 and 2003, respectively. In addition, we

NOTES TO CONSOLIDATED FINANCIAL STATEMENTS

The Coca-Cola Company and Subsidiaries

NOTE 6: SHORT-TERM BORROWINGS AND CREDIT ARRANGEMENTS (Continued)

had $1,614 million in lines of credit and other short-term credit facilities available as of December 31, 2004, of which approximately $296 million was outstanding. This entire amount related to our international operations. Included in the available credit facilities discussed above, the Company had $1,150 million in lines of credit for general corporate purposes, including commercial paper back-up. There were no borrowings under these lines of credit during 2004.

These credit facilities are subject to normal banking terms and conditions. Some of the financial arrangements require compensating balances, none of which is presently significant to our Company.

NOTE 7: LONG-TERM DEBT

Long-term debt consists of the following (in millions):

December 31,	2004	2003
Variable rate euro notes due 2004[1]	$ —	$ 296
5⅞% euro notes due 2005	**663**	591
4% U.S. dollar notes due 2005	**750**	749
5¾% U.S. dollar notes due 2009	**399**	399
5¾% U.S. dollar notes due 2011	**499**	498
7⅜% U.S. dollar notes due 2093	**116**	116
Other, due through 2013[2]	**220**	191
	$ 2,647	$ 2,840
Less current portion	**1,490**	323
	$ 1,157	$ 2,517

[1] 2.4 percent at December 31, 2003.

[2] Includes $5 million and $27 million fair value adjustment related to interest rate swap agreements in 2004 and 2003, respectively. Refer to Note 10.

The above notes include various restrictions, none of which is presently significant to our Company.

After giving effect to interest rate management instruments, the principal amount of our long-term debt that had fixed and variable interest rates, respectively, was $1,895 million and $752 million on December 31, 2004, and $1,742 million and $1,098 million on December 31, 2003. The weighted-average interest rate on our Company's long-term debt was 4.4 percent and 3.9 percent per annum for the years ended December 31, 2004 and 2003, respectively. Total interest paid was approximately $188 million, $180 million and $197 million in 2004, 2003 and 2002, respectively. For a more detailed discussion of interest rate management, refer to Note 10.

Maturities of long-term debt for the five years succeeding December 31, 2004 are as follows (in millions):

2005	2006	2007	2008	2009
$ 1,490	$ 43	$ 21	$ 7	$ 406

NOTES TO CONSOLIDATED FINANCIAL STATEMENTS

The Coca-Cola Company and Subsidiaries

NOTE 8: COMPREHENSIVE INCOME

Accumulated other comprehensive income (loss), including our proportionate share of equity method investees' accumulated other comprehensive income (loss), consists of the following (in millions):

December 31,	**2004**	2003
Foreign currency translation adjustment	**$ (1,191)**	$ (1,856)
Accumulated derivative net losses	**(80)**	(77)
Unrealized gain on available-for-sale securities	**91**	52
Minimum pension liability	**(168)**	(114)
	$ (1,348)	$ (1,995)

A summary of the components of accumulated other comprehensive income (loss), including our proportionate share of equity method investees' other comprehensive income, for the years ended December 31, 2004, 2003 and 2002 is as follows (in millions):

	Before-Tax Amount	Income Tax	After-Tax Amount
2004			
Net foreign currency translation adjustment	**$ 766**	**$ (101)**	**$ 665**
Net loss on derivatives	**(4)**	**1**	**(3)**
Net change in unrealized gain on available-for-sale securities	**48**	**(9)**	**39**
Net change in minimum pension liability	**(81)**	**27**	**(54)**
Other comprehensive income (loss)	**$ 729**	**$ (82)**	**$ 647**

	Before-Tax Amount	Income Tax	After-Tax Amount
2003			
Net foreign currency translation adjustment	$ 913	$ 8	$ 921
Net loss on derivatives	(63)	30	(33)
Net change in unrealized gain on available-for-sale securities	65	(25)	40
Net change in minimum pension liability	181	(57)	124
Other comprehensive income (loss)	$ 1,096	$ (44)	$ 1,052

	Before-Tax Amount	Income Tax	After-Tax Amount
2002			
Net foreign currency translation adjustment	$ (51)	$ (44)	$ (95)
Net loss on derivatives	(284)	98	(186)
Net change in unrealized gain on available-for-sale securities	104	(37)	67
Net change in minimum pension liability	(299)	104	(195)
Other comprehensive income (loss)	$ (530)	$ 121	$ (409)

NOTES TO CONSOLIDATED FINANCIAL STATEMENTS

The Coca-Cola Company and Subsidiaries

NOTE 14: PENSION AND OTHER POSTRETIREMENT BENEFIT PLANS (Continued)

Defined Contribution Plans

Our Company sponsors a qualified defined contribution plan covering substantially all U.S. employees. Under this plan, we match 100 percent of participants' contributions up to a maximum of 3 percent of compensation. Company contributions to the U.S. plan were $18 million, $20 million and $20 million in 2004, 2003 and 2002, respectively. We also sponsor defined contribution plans in certain locations outside the United States. Company contributions to these plans were $8 million, $7 million and $6 million in 2004, 2003 and 2002, respectively.

NOTE 15: INCOME TAXES

Income before income taxes and cumulative effect of accounting change consists of the following (in millions):

Year Ended December 31,	**2004**	2003	2002
United States	**$ 2,535**	$ 2,029	$ 2,062
International	**3,687**	3,466	3,437
	$ 6,222	$ 5,495	$ 5,499

Income tax expense (benefit) consists of the following (in millions):

Year Ended December 31,	United States	State and Local	International	Total
2004				
Current	**$ 350**	**$ 64**	**$ 799**	**$ 1,213**
Deferred	**209**	**29**	**(76)**	**162**
2003				
Current	$ 426	$ 84	$ 826	$ 1,336
Deferred	(145)	(11)	(32)	(188)
2002				
Current	$ 455	$ 55	$ 973	$ 1,483
Deferred	2	23	15	40

We made income tax payments of approximately $1,500 million, $1,325 million and $1,508 million in 2004, 2003 and 2002, respectively.

NOTES TO CONSOLIDATED FINANCIAL STATEMENTS

The Coca-Cola Company and Subsidiaries

NOTE 15: INCOME TAXES (Continued)

A reconciliation of the statutory U.S. federal rate and effective rates is as follows:

Year Ended December 31,	2004	2003	2002
Statutory U.S. federal rate	**35.0 %**	35.0 %	35.0 %
State income taxes—net of federal benefit	**1.0**	0.9	0.9
Earnings in jurisdictions taxed at rates different from the statutory U.S. federal rate	**(9.4)**[1,2]	(10.6)[7]	(6.0)
Equity income or loss	**(3.1)**[3,4]	(2.4)[8]	(2.0)[10]
Other operating charges	**(0.9)**[5]	(1.1)[9]	—
Write-down/sale of certain bottling investments	—	—	0.7[11]
Other—net	**(0.5)**[6]	(0.9)	(0.9)
Effective rates	**22.1 %**	20.9 %	27.7 %

[1] Includes approximately $92 million (or 1.4 percent) tax benefit related to the favorable resolution of various tax issues and settlements.

[2] Includes tax charge of approximately $75 million (or 1.2 percent) related to recording of valuation allowance on various deferred tax assets recorded in Germany.

[3] Includes approximately $50 million (or 0.8 percent) tax benefit related to the realization of certain foreign tax credits per provisions of the Jobs Creation Act.

[4] Includes approximately $13 million (or 0.1 percent) tax charge on our proportionate share of the favorable tax settlement related to Coca-Cola FEMSA.

[5] Primarily related to impairment of franchise rights at CCEAG and certain manufacturing investments. Refer to Note 16.

[6] Includes approximately $36 million (or 0.6 percent) tax benefit related to the favorable resolution of various tax issues and settlements.

[7] Includes approximately $50 million (or 0.8 percent) tax benefit for the release of tax reserves due primarily to the resolution of various tax matters.

[8] Includes the tax effect of the write-down of certain intangible assets held by bottling investments in Latin America. Refer to Note 2.

[9] Includes the tax effect of the charges for streamlining initiatives. Refer to Note 17.

[10] Includes the tax effect of the charges by equity investees in 2002. Refer to Note 16.

[11] Includes gains on the sale of Cervejarias Kaiser Brazil, Ltda and the write-down of certain bottling investments, primarily in Latin America. Refer to Note 16.

Our effective tax rate reflects the tax benefits from having significant operations outside the United States that are taxed at rates lower than the statutory U.S. rate of 35 percent. In 2003, our effective tax rate reflects further benefit from realization of tax benefits on charges related to streamlining initiatives recorded in locations with tax rates higher than our effective tax rate.

In 2003, management concluded that it was more likely than not that tax benefits would not be realized on Coca-Cola FEMSA's write-down of intangible assets in Latin America in connection with its merger with Panamco. Refer to Note 2. In 2002, management concluded that it was more likely than not that tax benefits would not be realized with respect to principally all of the items disclosed in Note 16. Accordingly, valuation

NOTES TO CONSOLIDATED FINANCIAL STATEMENTS

The Coca-Cola Company and Subsidiaries

NOTE 15: INCOME TAXES (Continued)

The tax effects of temporary differences and carryforwards that give rise to deferred tax assets and liabilities consist of the following (in millions):

December 31,	2004	2003
Deferred tax assets:		
Property, plant and equipment	**$ 71**	$ 87
Trademarks and other intangible assets	**65**	68
Equity method investments (including translation adjustment)	**530**	485
Other liabilities	**149**	242
Benefit plans	**594**	669
Net operating/capital loss carryforwards	**856**	711
Other	**257**	195
Gross deferred tax assets	**2,522**	2,457
Valuation allowance	**(854)**	(630)
Total deferred tax assets[1]	**$ 1,668**	$ 1,827
Deferred tax liabilities:		
Property, plant and equipment	**$ (684)**	$ (737)
Trademarks and other intangible assets	**(247)**	(247)
Equity method investments (including translation adjustment)	**(612)**	(468)
Other liabilities	**(71)**	(55)
Other	**(180)**	(211)
Total deferred tax liabilities	**$ (1,794)**	$ (1,718)
Net deferred tax assets (liabilities)	**$ (126)**	$ 109

[1] Deferred tax assets of $324 million and $446 million were included in the consolidated balance sheet line item other assets at December 31, 2004 and 2003, respectively.

On December 31, 2004 and 2003, we had approximately $194 million and $160 million, respectively, of net deferred tax assets located in countries outside the United States.

On December 31, 2004, we had $3,258 million of loss carryforwards available to reduce future taxable income. Loss carryforwards of $861 million must be utilized within the next five years; $550 million must be utilized within the next 10 years and the remainder can be utilized over a period greater than 10 years.

NOTE 16: SIGNIFICANT OPERATING AND NONOPERATING ITEMS

Operating income in 2004 reflected the impact of $480 million of expenses primarily related to impairment charges for franchise rights and certain manufacturing investments. These impairment charges were recorded in the consolidated statement of income line item other operating charges.

In the second quarter of 2004, we recorded impairment charges totaling approximately $88 million. These impairments primarily related to the write-downs of certain manufacturing investments and an intangible asset. As a result of operating losses, management prepared analyses of cash flows expected to result from the use of the assets and their eventual disposition. Because the sum of the undiscounted cash flows was less than the carrying value of such assets, we recorded an impairment charge to reduce the carrying value of the assets to fair value.

NOTES TO CONSOLIDATED FINANCIAL STATEMENTS

The Coca-Cola Company and Subsidiaries

NOTE 19: OPERATING SEGMENTS (Continued)

Information about our Company's operations by operating segment is as follows (in millions):

	North America	Africa	Asia	Europe, Eurasia and Middle East	Latin America	Corporate	Consolidated
2004							
Net operating revenues	**$ 6,643**	**$ 1,067**	**$ 4,691**[1]	**$ 7,195**	**$ 2,123**	**$ 243**	**$ 21,962**
Operating income (loss)[2]	**1,606**	**340**	**1,758**	**1,898**	**1,069**	**(973)**[3]	**5,698**
Interest income						**157**	**157**
Interest expense						**196**	**196**
Depreciation and amortization	**345**	**28**	**133**	**245**	**42**	**100**	**893**
Equity income (loss)—net	**11**	**12**	**83**	**85**	**185**[4]	**245**	**621**
Income (loss) before income taxes and cumulative effect of accounting change[2]	**1,629**	**337**	**1,841**	**1,916**	**1,270**[4]	**(771)**[3,5]	**6,222**
Identifiable operating assets	**4,731**	**789**	**1,722**	**5,373**[6]	**1,405**	**11,055**[7]	**25,075**
Investments[8]	**116**	**162**	**1,401**	**1,323**	**1,580**	**1,670**	**6,252**
Capital expenditures	**247**	**28**	**92**	**233**	**38**	**117**	**755**
2003							
Net operating revenues	$ 6,344	$ 827	$ 5,052[1]	$ 6,556	$ 2,042	$ 223	$ 21,044
Operating income (loss)[9]	1,282	249	1,690	1,908	970	(878)[10]	5,221
Interest income						176	176
Interest expense						178	178
Depreciation and amortization	305	27	124	230	52	112	850
Equity income (loss)—net	13	13	65	78	(5)[11]	242	406
Income (loss) before income taxes and cumulative effect of accounting change[9]	1,326	249	1,740	1,921	975[11]	(716)[10]	5,495
Identifiable operating assets	4,953	721	1,923	5,222[6]	1,440	7,545[7]	21,804
Investments[8]	109	156	1,345	1,229	1,348	1,351	5,538
Capital expenditures	309	13	148	198	35	109	812
2002							
Net operating revenues	$ 6,264	$ 684	$ 5,054[1]	$ 5,262	$ 2,089	$ 211	$ 19,564
Operating income (loss)	1,531	224	1,820	1,612	1,033	(762)	5,458
Interest income						209	209
Interest expense						199	199
Depreciation and amortization	266	37	133	193	57	120	806
Equity income (loss)—net	15	(25)	60	(18)	131	221	384
Income (loss) before income taxes and cumulative effect of accounting change	1,552	187	1,848	1,540	1,081	(709)	5,499
Identifiable operating assets	4,999	565	2,370	4,481[6]	1,205	5,795[7]	19,415
Investments[8]	142	115	1,150	1,211	1,352	1,021	4,991
Capital expenditures	334	18	209	162	37	91	851

Intercompany transfers between operating segments are not material.

Certain prior-year amounts have been reclassified to conform to the current-year presentation.

[1] Net operating revenues in Japan represented approximately 61 percent of total Asia operating segment net operating revenues in 2004, 67 percent in 2003 and 69 percent in 2002.

[2] Operating income (loss) and income (loss) before income taxes and cumulative effect of accounting change were reduced by approximately $18 million for North America, $15 million for Asia, $377 million for Europe, Eurasia and Middle East, $6 million for Latin America and $64 million for Corporate as a result of other operating charges recorded for asset impairments. Refer to Note 16.

[3] Operating income (loss) and income (loss) before income taxes and cumulative effect of accounting change for Corporate were impacted as a result of the Company's receipt of a $75 million insurance settlement related to the class-action lawsuit settled in 2000. The Company subsequently donated $75 million to the Coca-Cola Foundation.

[4] Equity income (loss)—net and income (loss) before income taxes and cumulative effect of accounting change for Latin America were increased by approximately $37 million as a result of a favorable tax settlement related to Coca-Cola FEMSA, one of our equity method investees. Refer to Note 2.

[5] Income (loss) before income taxes and cumulative effect of accounting change was increased by approximately $24 million for Corporate due to noncash pre-tax gains that were recognized on the issuances of stock by CCE, one of our equity investees. Refer to Note 3.

[6] Identifiable operating assets in Germany represent approximately 46 percent of total Europe, Eurasia and Middle East identifiable operating assets in 2004 and 50 percent in 2003 and 2002.

[7] Principally cash and cash equivalents, marketable securities, finance subsidiary receivables, goodwill, trademarks and other intangible assets and property, plant and equipment.

[8] Principally equity investments in bottling companies.

[9] Operating income (loss) and income (loss) before income taxes and cumulative effect of accounting change were reduced by approximately $273 million for North America, $12 million for Africa, $18 million for Asia, $183 million for Europe, Eurasia and Middle East, $8 million for Latin America and $67 million for Corporate as a result of streamlining charges. Refer to Note 17.

[10] Operating income (loss) and income (loss) before income taxes and cumulative effect of accounting change were increased by approximately $52 million for Corporate as a result of the Company's receipt of a settlement related to a vitamin antitrust litigation matter. Refer to Note 16.

[11] Equity income (loss)—net and income (loss) before income taxes and cumulative effect of accounting change for Latin America were reduced by $102 million primarily for a charge related to one of our equity method investees. Refer to Note 2.

NOTES TO CONSOLIDATED FINANCIAL STATEMENTS

The Coca-Cola Company and Subsidiaries

NOTE 19: OPERATING SEGMENTS (Continued)

Compound Growth Rate Ended December 31, 2004	North America	Africa	Asia	Europe, Eurasia and Middle East	Latin America	Corporate	Consolidated
Net operating revenues							
5 years	4.2%	9.3%	0.5%	11.8%	3.2%	8.0%	5.5%
10 years	5.0%	6.5%	4.1%	4.1%	1.0%	19.2%	4.2%
Operating income							
5 years	2.1%	9.3%	8.0%	15.9%	5.2%	*	7.4%
10 years	5.7%	5.1%	4.2%	4.3%	3.4%	*	4.6%

* Calculation is not meaningful.

Exercise 1 Accounting entities

2, 4

1. No, relates to the owner not the company.
2. Yes, relates to the activities at Chase.
3. No, relates to the employees not the company.
4. Yes, relates to activities at Chase.

Exercise 2 Find the assets

1, 4, 5, 6

1, 4, 5 and 6 are valuable assets, owned by the firm, acquired at a measurable cost. People and trees near the factory are not owned by the firm and are therefore NOT company assets.

Exercise 3 Find the liabilities

1, 2

Loans and taxes are liabilities, being measurable obligations to other entities. Cash is an asset not a liability. The possibility of an earthquake does not represent a probable, current claim on the firm's assets so it is not a liability.

Exercise 4 CloseShave's equity accounts

1. Paid-in capital since the investor is supplying funds to the business
2. Cash and paid-in capital rise by $200m.
3. Profits retained increase the Retained Earnings account by $900m.

Exercise 5 Equity and risk

1. $5,040m. Liabililty holders can claim the total value they are owed.
2. Liability owners' claims since they precede equity owners' claims.
3. Equity is riskier because the equity owners' claims on assets are ranked after claims by liability holders.

Exercise 6 The clothing company

1. $350m = $10m new loans plus $340m prior funding
2. $350m = $10m in new cash plus $340m in resources.
3. Total resources of $350m = Total funding of $350m
4. $320m = $350m funding less $30m reduction in bank loan
5. $320m = $350m less $30m cash paid to bank
6. Total Resources of $320m = Total Funding of $320m

Exercise 7 Greg's rental agency, part 1

1.

Balance sheet

Assets		Liabilities	
Cash	$1,000		$0
		Equity	
		Paid-in cap.	$1,000
Total assets	**$1,000**	**Total L&E**	**$1,000**

2.

Balance sheet

Assets		Liabilities	
Cash	$2,000	Loan	$1,000
		Equity	
		Paid-in cap.	$1,000
Total assets	**$2,000**	**Total L&E**	**$2,000**

3.

Balance sheet

Assets		Liabilities	
Cash	$1,500	Loan	$1,000
Beach hut	500	**Equity**	
		Paid-in cap.	$1,000
Total assets	**$2,000**	**Total L&E**	**$2,000**

4.

Balance sheet

Assets		Liabilities	
Cash	$1,500	Loan	$1,200
Beach hut	500	**Equity**	
Car	200	Paid-in cap.	$1,000
Total assets	**$2,200**	**Total L&E**	**$2,200**

PART 1

Exercise 7 Greg's rental agency, part 1, *continued*

5.

Balance sheet			
Assets		**Liabilities**	
Cash	$1,400	Loan	$1,200
Beach hut	500	**Equity**	
Car	200	Paid-in cap.	$1,000
Stationery	100		
Total assets	**$2,200**	**Total L&E**	**$2,200**

6.

Balance sheet			
Assets		**Liabilities**	
Cash	$1,350	Loan	$1,000
Beach hut	500	**Equity**	
Bicycle	50	Paid-in cap.	$1,000
Stationery	100		
Total assets	**$2,000**	**Total L&E**	**$2,000**

Exercise 8 Greg's rental agency, part 2

1.

Balance sheet			
Assets		**Liabilities**	
Cash	$1,350	Loans	$51,000
Beach hut	500		
Building	100,000		
Bicycle	50	**Equity**	
Stationery	100	Paid-in cap.	$51,000
Total assets	**$102,000**	**Total L&E**	**$102,000**

2.

Balance sheet			
Assets		**Liabilities**	
Cash	$81,350	Loans	$51,000
Beach hut	500		
Building	100,000		
Bicycle	50		
Furniture	20,000	**Equity**	
Stationery	100	Paid-in cap.	$151,000
Total assets	**$202,000**	**Total L&E**	**$202,000**

Exercise 8 Greg's rental agency, part 2 *continued*

3.

Balance sheet			
Assets		**Liabilities**	
Cash	$91,350	Loans	$11,000
Beach hut	500		
Building	50,000		
Bicycle	50		
Furniture	20,000	**Equity**	
Stationery	100	Paid-in cap.	$151,000
Total assets	**$162,000**	**Total L&E**	**$162,000**

Exercise 9 What can be measured?

1, 3

Financial statements measure only dollar values. Items such as job satisfaction, customer lists, and the number of cars leased do not appear in the financial statements.

Exercise 10 Cleo's relocation service

1.

Balance sheet			
Assets		**Liabilities**	
Cash	$50,000		
		Equity	
		Paid-in cap.	50,000
Total assets	**$50,000**	**Total L&E**	**$50,000**

2.

Balance sheet			
Assets		**Liabilities**	
Cash	$40,000		
Car	10,000		
		Equity	
		Paid-in cap.	50,000
Total assets	**$50,000**	**Total L&E**	**$50,000**

3

Balance sheet			
Assets		**Liabilities**	
Cash	$240,000	Loan	$200,000
Car	10,000		
		Equity	
		Paid-in cap.	50,000
Total assets	**$250,000**	**Total L&E**	**$250,000**

Exercise 10 Cleo's relocation service

4.

Balance sheet			
Assets		**Liabilities**	
Cash	$190,000	Loan	$200,000
Car	10,000		
Building	50,000	**Equity**	
		Paid-in cap.	50,000
Total assets	**$250,000**	**Total L&E**	**$250,000**

5.

Balance sheet			
Assets		**Liabilities**	
Cash	$190,000	Loan	$200,000
Car	10,000		
Building	50,000	**Equity**	
		Paid-in cap.	50,000
Total assets	**$250,000**	**Total L&E**	**$250,000**

Close the deal #1

Give yourself $10,000 for each answer that is completely correct.

1. Items reported on the financial statements must be reliably measured in a monetary form.
2. A liability is a source of funding.
3. Paid-in capital and retained earnings.
4. $155,000
5. No change would appear on its financial statements.
6. Yes, $60,000
7. A balance sheet changes every time you enter a transaction.
8. Liability holders have a prior claim on a company's assets.
9. At least 2
10. a. measurable
    b. valuable to the entity
    c. owned/controlled by the entity

Exercise 11 Long and short-term A & L

1a. CA
b. E
c. CL
d. NCL
e. CA
f. NCA
g. E
h. CL
i. CA
j. CA
k. NCA

2. Assets are resources a company owns, while equity represents the shareholders' investment in a business.
3. Equity is riskier because if the business fails, equity holders are paid after liability holders.

Exercise 12 Sarah's balance sheet

1.

Balance sheet			
Assets		**Liabilities**	
Cash	7,000	Mortgage	110,000
Sketch	10,000		
Apartment	150,000		
Jewels	11,000	Equity	68,000
Total assets	178,000	**Total L&E**	178,000

2. $68,000
3. No
4. Assets are recorded at their original cost, not their market value.

PART 1

Exercise 13 Aunt Kate's balance sheet

Start with the initial cash inflows from Aunt Kate's salary and bonus. Then input all cash flows into the cash balance worksheet and record assets and liabilities on the balance sheet. Any cash inflows increase the cash balance, purchases made with cash reduce the cash balance. Cash and short-term bonds are current assets, all Aunt Kate's other assets are long-term. Current liabilities include household bills and the bank loan due in six months. Aunt Kate's equity is equal to her assets minus her liabilities.

Balance sheet			
Assets		**Liabilities**	
Cash	1,390	Bills	3
Govt. bonds	5	Loans	40
Tot. Curr. A.	**1,395**	**Total Curr. Liab.**	**43**
House	400	Mortgage	400
Apartment	600	Total NCL	400
Drums	10	**Total Liabilities**	**443**
Stocks	50	**Equity**	
Total NCA	**1,060**	Tot. equity	**2,012**
Total assets	**2,455**	**Total L&E**	**2,455**

Close the deal #2

Give yourself $10,000 for each answer that is completely correct.

1. The time they are due. Current liabilities must be paid off within 12 months.
2. Current liability. Bills due within a year or less.
3. Current asset. Goods waiting to be sold.
4. $200,000
5. Assets are recorded at their original cost. Their market value may have changed. Some assets are also not shown on the balance sheet as they have no reliable monetary value.
6. Accounts payable, short-term loan
7. Buildings, equipment, land, furniture, investments
8. The resources the company owns
9. Obligations due to other entities and the funding provided by shareholders. Some assets are also not shown on the balance sheet as they have no reliable monetary value.
10. $13,000

Exercise 14 T&J's balance sheet

Begin with the balance sheet on page 22. For each transaction listed, record the change in accounts, tracking cash changes in the cash balance worksheet. For example, in the first transaction cash increases by $2,000 (record increase in worksheet from $46,591 starting balance to $48,591) and receivables decreases by $2,000 (to $16,833, record on balance sheet). When all entries are recorded, move the cash balance from the worksheet to cash and the final balance sheet is:

T&J's balance sheet			
T&J's balance sheet as of 31 December 2006			
	$000s		***$000s***
Cash & equivs	$43,791		
A/R	16,833		
Inventories	18,937	Accts payable	43,915
Other curr. assets	7,986	Other	5,627
Total curr. assets	**87,547**	**Total curr. liab.**	**49,542**
Ppty. & equip. net	66,557	Long-term debt	11,669
Investments	0	Other L-T liabs	0
Other NCA	6,498	**Total NCL**	**11,669**
Total NCA	**73,055**	**TOT. LIABS**	**61,211**
		Paid-in capital	50,678
		Ret. earnings	48,713
		TOTAL EQUITY	**99,391**
TOTAL ASSETS	**160,602**	**TOTAL L&E**	**160,602**

Exercise 15 Journal entries

1.	Debit	Cash	$1,000	
	Credit	Paid-in capital		$1,000
2.	Debit	Inventory	$4,000	
	Credit	Cash		$4,000
3.	Debit	PP&E	$10,000	
	Credit	Loan		$8,000
	Credit	Cash		$2,000
4.	Debit	PP&E	$5,000	
	Credit	Cash		$3,000
	Credit	Loan		$2,000

Close the deal #3

Record the entry for each transaction in the worksheet, then move the final account balances to the balance sheet. The entries and balance sheet appear below.

Give yourself $10,000 for each answer that is completely correct.

		Debit	Credit
1a.	Dr Cash	80,000	
	Cr Pd-in-Capital		80,000
1b.	Dr Cash	50,000	
	Cr Loan		50,000
1c.	Dr Equipment	20,000	
	Cr Cash	20,000	
1d.	Dr Inventory	4,000	
	Cr Acc. Pay		4,000
1e.	Dr Equipment	2,000	
	Cr Cash		2,000
1f.	Dr Property	10,000	
	Cr Cash		10,000
1g.	No entry		
1h.	Dr Equipment	1,000	
	Cr Cash		1,000
1i.	No entry		
1j.	Dr Loan	20,000	
	Cr Cash		20,000

Close the deal #3
Question 1

Balance sheet
All figures in $s

Assets		**Liabilities**	
Cash	77,000	Acc/Pay	4,000
Inventory	4,000	Loan	30,000
Prop. & Equip.	33,000	**Total Liabilities**	**34,000**
		Equity	80,000
Total Assets	**114,000**	**Total L&E**	**114,000**

2. Credit (Accounts Payable)
   Loans
   Retained earnings
   Paid-in capital

3. Increase its total funding
4. Timing: a current asset is expected to be used up or turned into cash in 12 months. A long-term asset is not.
5. Cash, Inventory, Other, Accounts receivable

Exercise 16 Chugger's

Sales	50,000
Cost of goods sold	(10,000)
Gross profit	40,000
SG&A	(3,000)
Operating profit	37,000
Other income or expense	0
Interest inc. and exp.	(2,000)
Income before tax	35,000
Tax	(4,000)
Net Income	31,000

Exercise 17 New York supermarket

1. No entry. The ice cream wasn't delivered.
2. Sales $3,000
   Cost of sales $2,000
3. No, the ice cream was not delivered.

Exercise 18 Disneyland

Revenues and expenses are recognized when the product is delivered. Cash falls in March when the milk is purchased and rises in August when the firm is paid

1.	Mar	Apr	May	Jun	Jul	Aug
Sales			$100K	$50K	$50K	
Milk expenses			$50K	$25K	$25K	
Change in cash	($100K)					$200K

2.	Mar	Apr	May	Jun	Jul	Aug	Sept
Insurance expense			$120	$120	$120	$120	$120
Change in cash	($600)						

PART 1

Exercise 19 Kalvin Kleen

1. When the socks were delivered
2. The same day
3. June $1,000
   July $1,000
   August $1,000
   September $1,000
   October $1,000
   November $1,000

Exercise 20 The clueless bookkeeper

1. COGS
2. SG&A
3. Neither
4. SG&A
5. Dr Equipment 100,000
   Cr Cash 100,000

Exercise 21 Credits and debits

1. increase / credit
2. decrease / debit
3. decrease / debit
4. increase / credit

Close the deal #4

Give yourself $10,000 for each answer that is completely correct.

1. When the product is delivered or the service is performed
2. Equity
3. Rise
4.

Revenue	5,000
COGS	(1,000)
Gross profit	4,000
SG&A	(3,100)
Operating profit	900
Interest income	500
Earnings before tax	1,400
Tax	(700)
Net income	700

5. Account for revenues when reasonably certain; account for losses when reasonably possible.
6. Cost of Goods Sold
7. Sales, General and Administrative costs
8. Remain unchanged
9. Remain unchanged
10. Inventory and Accounts Payable

Exercise 22 T&J's retained earnings

B $48,713,000
A $10,567,000
S $6,000,500
E $53,279,500

Exercise 23 Ice cream sales

1. Dr A/Rec. $30,000
   Dr Cash $20,000
   Cr Sales $50,000
2. Dr Cash $25,000
   Cr A/Rec. $25,000
3. $5,000
4. Nothing. Equity already went up when the sale was recorded.

Exercise 24 Avocado Explosion

The avocado and milk are inventory ($7,000). Since they are purchased on credit, accounts payable are $7,000. The inventory balance is decreased by $3,000 when delivered to leave an inventory balance of $4,000. Sales are $5,000, $2,500 of this is paid in cash (cash balance) and $2,500 in receivables (AR balance). Finally, since the value of the inventory sold was $3,000 and the sales price was $5,000, net income is $2,000 and retained earnings is $2,000.

1.

Assets	
Cash	2,500
Inv	4,000
Acct Recv	2,500
Total	**9,000**

L & E	
Acct Pay	7,000
Ret earnings	2,000
Total	**7,000**

Inc. statement	
Sales	5,000
COGS	(3,000)
Net income	**2,000**

2. $2,000

Exercise 25 Interest income and expense

1. Interest expense will increase if interest rates stay constant.
2. If interest income rises with stable rates, the amount of interest-bearing assets must have risen.
3. Dr Int. expense $2,800
   Cr Cash $2,800
4. Dr Cash $4,154
   Cr Int. income $4,154

Exercise 26 Links: B A S E analysis

Retained earnings

B	48,713
A	5,149
S	1,000
E	52,862

Inventories

B	13,937
A	150,000
S	130,000
E	33,937

Exercise 26 Links: Cash template

Receipts	Payments
190,890	80,000
	49,000
	2,000
	1,000
	10,890
	3,851
Net change	44,149

Exercise 26 Links: Journal entries

Begin with the journal entry corresponding to each transaction. As you record the transactions, complete the BASE analysis for retained earnings and inventory, and update the cash balance. When the entries are completed, fill in the balance sheet and income statement.

Dr	Inventory	$150,000	
Cr	Accounts payable		$150,000
Dr	PP&E	$80,000	
Cr	Cash		$80,000
Dr	SG&A	$49,000	
Cr	Cash		$49,000
Dr	Interest expense	$2,000	
Cr	Cash		$2,000
Dr	Cash	$190,890	
Dr	Accounts receivable	$10,000	
Cr	Sales		$200,890
Dr	COGS	$130,000	
Cr	Inventory		$130,000
Dr	SG&A	$10,890	
Cr	Cash		$10,890
Dr	Dividends	$1,000	
Cr	Cash		$1,000
Dr	Tax	$3,851	
Cr	Cash		$3,851
Total debits		**$627,631**	
Total credits			**$627,631**

Exercise 26 Links: Income statement

Revenues	200,890
COGS	(130,000)
Gross profit	70,890
SG&A	(59,890)
Operating profit	11,000
Interest expense	(2,000)
Profit before taxes	9,000
Tax	(3,851)
Net income	5,149

Exercise 26 Links: Balance sheet

B&J's balance sheet as of 31 December 2006

ASSETS	*$000s*	*LIABILITIES*	*$000s*
Cash & equivs	90,740	Accts. payable	188,915
Accts. recv.	28,833	Other curr. liabs	5,627
Inventories	33,937	**Total CA**	**194,542**
Other current assets	7,986		
Total current assets	**161,496**	Long term debt	16,669
Ppty & equip. net	136,557	Other L-T liabs	0
Investments	200	**Total NCL**	**16,669**
Other NCA	6,498	**TOTAL LIABS**	**211,211**
Total NCA	**143,255**		
		Paid-in capital	40,678
		Ret. earnings	52,862
		TOTAL EQUITY	**93,540**
TOTAL ASSETS	**304,751**	**TOTAL L&E**	**304,751**

Exercise 26 Links: B/S and I/S

2. a. Retained earnings

Dr Ret. earnings	28,000	
Cr Cash		28,000

b. 3,244,895

3. a. Link: Inventories + COGS

Link: A/C Receivable + Sales

Link: Net income + Retained earnings

b. Accounts receivable is the amount people owe you. Accounts payable is the amount you owe other people.

4. a.

Dr Inventory	100,000	
Cr A/C Pay		100,000

b.

Dr COGS	3,589	
Cr Inventory		3,589

Checkout test, part 1, section 1

The income statement is fairly straightforward.

On the balance sheet, remember to use BASE analysis for retained earnings ($4,878 + $2,049 in net income – $796 in dividends = $6,131). Cash is beginning cash of $2,126 – dividends of $796 = $1,330.

Question 1: Income statement

Sales	20,438
COGS incl. depn	(7,943)
Gross profit	12,495
SG&A	(9,136)
Other op. costs	(138)
Operating profit	3,221
Interest income	76
Interest expense	(221)
Profit before taxes	3,076
Tax	(1,027)
Net income	2,049

Question 1: Balance sheet

Assets		**Liabilities**	
Cash	1,330	Acct. payable	3,815
Acct. receivable	1,764	Other CL	120
Inventory	905	**Total CL**	**3,935**
Other current assets	570	Long-term debt	2,346
Total current assets	**4,569**	Other NCL	4,908
Investments	2,978	**Total liabs.**	**11,189**
Net PPE	5,438	Paid-in capital	984
Other L-T assets	5,319	Ret. earnings	6,131
		Total equity	**7,115**
Total assets	**18,304**	**Total L & E**	**18,304**

Check-out test, part 1, section 2

1. Expenses are recorded at the same time as the revenues they helped to generate.
2. | | | | |
   |---|---|---|---|
   | Dr | Accts receivable | 140,000 | |
   | Dr | Cash | 260,000 | |
   | Cr | Sales | | 400,000 |
3. GAAP Generally Accepted Accounting Principles
4. None
5. Accounting represents information about entities, not about their owners or customers. Entities can be companies, governments, or non-profit organizations.
6. | **Current assets** | **Current liabilities** |
   |---|---|
   | Inventories | Accounts payable |
   | Cash | Short-term debt |
   | Accounts receivable | |
7. Equity represents the owners' investment in the business and the equity holders' claim on the balance sheet assets. It is also the difference between assets and liabilities.
8. a. The customers a company has
   b. A company's reputation
   c. The quality of people a company employs

Checkout test, part 1, section 3

1. COGS shows the cost of manufacturing the good sold.

   SG&A represents costs that are not directly linked to production (overhead, administration, salaries).
2. False. The balance sheet is only a snapshot.
3. Retained earnings
4. Changes in equity
5. When the goods are delivered or the service is performed
6. Non-cash current assets are resources that will be used up or will turn into cash within one year.
7. By COGS
8. Interest income should rise.
   Interest expense will not change.

Exercise 1 Coke's cash

1. $6,707m
2. Large, 30.5%
3. Potentially. PepsiCo have been successful with their acquisitions and Coca Cola have been encouraged by many analysts to follow suit. In December 2005 PepsiCo's market capitalization exceeded that of Coca Cola for the first time in the two companies history.
4. Marketable securities that are highly liquid and have maturities of three months or less at purchase

Take a look Coke's annual report

Trade accounts receivable totaled $2,171m.

Take a look Coca-Cola's accounts receivable

Gross accounts receivable totaled $2,240m. The allowance for bad debt is $69m.

Exercise 2 Bad debts

1. $24,000

Debit	SG&A	$24,000	
Credit	Bad debt allowance		$24,000

2. You had estimated bad debt at 3.1% or $69m (=0.31 **x** $2,240), now the allowance increases by 1.9% or $43m (=0.19 **x** 2,240).

	Existing	+ Add Allowance	= Ending
Gross AR	2,240		2,240
Bad debt allow.	69	43	112
Net AR	2,171	29	2,128

3. Debit Bad debts (SG&A) $2m
   Credit Accounts receivable $2m
4. $2,128m = $2,240 – 112

Exercise 3 Coke's receivable days

1. 35 = ((2,171 + 2,091)/2) / 21,962 **x** 365
2. Coke manages its receivables comparatively well.

Take a look Inventory

Raw materials, supplies, concentrates and syrups

Exercise 4 Inventory detection

1. Inventory was $1,420m.
2. Coke started 2004 with $1,252m in inventory (2003 year-end value).
3. Coke took $7,638m out = COGS.
4. B 1,252
   A 7,806
   S (7,638)
   E 1,420

Exercise 5 Inventory party

This exercise shows the impact of the inventory method on COGS and net income.

1 a. Average cost method: $1,600

Derivation:	$630	
	600	
	1,400	
	410	
	$3,040	Total spent on inventory
	300	
	200	
	350	
	100	
	950	Total gallons

$\frac{\$3040}{950} = \$3.2$

$3.2 **x** 500=$1,600 Cost of goods sold

b. FIFO method: $1,230

$2.1 **x** 300= $630
$3.0 **x** 200= $600
$1,230 Cost of goods sold

c. LIFO method: $1,960

$4.1 **x** 100= $410
$4.0 **x** 350= $1,400
$3.0 **x** 50 = $150
$1,960 Cost of goods sold

2. FIFO
3. FIFO
4. Higher
5. The company that used LIFO calculates its COGS differently and therefore its net income may be understated if prices are rising.
6. Inventory is valued using the average cost or the FIFO method.

Exercise 6 Inventory days

1. 64 = ((1,420 + 1,252)/2)/ 7,638 x 365
2. Coke's warehouse management was not as good as its competitors'.

Fill in the blank Prepaid expenses

The asset side of the balance sheet

Take a look **Prepaid expenses**

$1,735

Exercise 7 **Your new apartment**

1. Dr Prepaid expenses 10,000
   Cr Cash 10,000

   Remains the same, although inventories rise, either cash falls or payables rise.
2. Dr SG&A (rent) 5,000
   Cr Prepaid expenses 5,000
3. a. No
   b. Yes
   c. No
   d. No
   e. Yes
4. $194m

Exercise 8 **Recap**

1. Yes
2. Yes
3. Yes
4. No
5. No

Exercise 9 **Free credit**

1. $4,283m
2. Accrued marketing $1,194m
   Container deposits 199m
   Accr. compensation 389m
   Taxes 222m
   Streamlining 41m
   Accounts payable 2,238m
3. $667m

Exercise 10 **Working capital**

1. ☑ Yes ☐ No Cash
   ☐ Yes ☑ No Buildings, land & equipment
   ☐ Yes ☑ No Long-term debt
2. Cash 53
   Receivables 68
   Inventory 150
   271

   Short-term debt 80
   Accounts payable 54
   Accrued taxes 20
   154

   Working capital = $117
3. Remains the same, inventories rise and either cash decreases or payables increase.

Exercise 10 **Working capital *continued***

4. Remains the same. The loan increases liabilities but the cash from the loan increases assets.
5. Remains the same, cash and liabilities both decrease.

Exercise 11 **Changes in working capital**

1. Remains the same, inventories increase and either cash falls or short term payables both increase.
2. Remains the same, cash and short term payables both increase by the same amount.
3. Increases, cash increases and there is no change in short term payables. Long term payables increase but are not part of working capital.
4. Increases. Cash and equity both increase.
5. Remains the same. Cash initially rises due to the sale of PPE but then decreases as it is used to repay debt.
6. Remains the same. Receivables increase causing cash to fall. Short term payables rise but this is matched by an increase in cash.

Note the impact on working capital of transaction 3 compared to transaction 2. This is an example of how "window dressing" might be used to "improve" the appearance of a firm's financial condition. Borrowing under a short-term credit facility would not increase working capital since both current assets and current liabilities would increase (as in #2) but by borrowing long-term, current assets rise while current liabilities are constant, thus increasing working capital.

Exercise 12 **Coke's operating working capital**

	2004	2003
Sales	$21,962	$21,044
Accounts receivable	2,171	2,091
Inventories	1,420	1,252
Prepaid expenses	1,735	1,571
Accounts payable	4,283	4,058
Accrued taxes	667	922
Op. working capital =		
AR + Inv + prepaid capital =		
AP – Accr taxes	376	(66)
OWC as % of sales	1.71%	(0.31)%

Exercise 13 **One last time**

1. Sales have risen by $918m while the operating working capital has fallen by $442m.
2. Increase from $510m (8,396-7,886) to $1,123m (12,094-10,971)
3. Coca-Cola has a strong negotiating position with its suppliers due to its large size.

PART 2

Close the deal #5

Give yourself $10,000 for each answer that is completely correct.

1. Op. wk. cap.: $2,075.3m Wk. cap.: $1,497.3m (OWC +81.6+1.6-634.7-26.5)
2. Working capital includes all current assets and liabilities. Operating working capital includes only accounts driven by operating activities. Use OWC when you want to measure a company's efficiency and the investment (or funding) that the company makes in (receives from) its operating activities.
3. Higher
4. Dr Prepaid expenses $10m
Cr Cash $10m
5. Accounts payable
6. Accounts receivable
7. FIFO
8. Marketable securities and cash can be driven by non-operating activities.
Other current liabilities related to new debt financing: Debt financing is not an operating activity.
9. Dr Accounts receivable 100,000
Cr Sales 100,000
Dr Sales 5,000
Cr Bad debt allowance 5,000
10. Rise. More competition probably means you need to give better terms to your customers.

Exercise 14 Debt due in 12 months

1. a. Loans and notes payable
b. Current maturities of long-term debt
2. Within 12 months
3. Mainly commercial paper ($4.2b)

Exercise 15 Long-term debt

1. In 2005, the current portion of long-term debt is $43m (see note 7).
2. On the 2005 balance sheet, the long-term debt will be the current long-term debt of $1,157m less the portion that becomes current, $43m, or $1,114m

Exercise 16 Debt close-up

1. $1,490m
2. $663m 5 7/8% euro notes, $750m 4% US dollar notes. This comes to $1,413m. As the total repayable in one year is $1,490, then there must be $77m included in 'other' debt.
3.

	2005	2006	2007	2008	2009
LT Debt	$1,490m	$43m	$21m	$7m	$406m

4. Assets increased by $400m to $31,727
Liabilities increase by $400m to $15,792m
Equity remains $15,935m
5. Assets decreased by $300m to $31,027m
Liabilities decrease by $300m to $15,092m
Equity remains $15,935m

Take a look Tangible assets

1. Land
2. Buildings and improvements
3. Machinery and equipment
4. Containers

Exercise 17 Watch those legal fees

$314,000; include all costs involved in getting assets ready.

Exercise 18 The logging mills

1. Watermill Logging Inc. since its assets have far less accumulated depreciation
2. Coke has relatively newer PP&E. Accumulated depreciation/Gross PP&E is 48.8% for PepsiCo and 40.0% for Coke.

Take a look Coke's depreciation

$715m

$10,149m

$4,058m

$6,091m

Exercise 19 The bottling machine

$60,800

Take a look Coke's depreciation method

Straight line

Exercise 20 Depreciation workout

1.
	50,000	
–	10,000	
	40,000	
÷	5,000	
=	8	years

2. $5,000 SG&A

3.
	500,000	
÷	10	
=	50,000	
	150,000	
÷	50,000	
=	3	years

4. 50,000

5. 55,000

6. No, the balance sheet asset value reflects cost rather than current worth of assets.

Exercise 21 That bottling machine again

1. B/S	Dr	Acc. depreciation	200	
	Dr	Cash	300	
	Cr	PP&E		500
I/S		No entry		
2.	Dr	Cash	550	
	Dr	Accum. depreciation	200	
	Cr	PP&E		500
	Cr	Gain on sale of asset		250
3.	Dr	Cash	200	
	Dr	Accum depreciation	200	
	Dr	Loss on sale of asset	100	
	Cr	PP&E		500

4. Paper loss

5.
	Gross PP&E	Acc Depr	Net PP&E
B	10,149	4,058	6,091
A	1,000	500	
S	(300)	(100)	
E	10,849	4,458	6,391

Exercise 22 Goodwill

1. $250m. Goodwill is equal to the cost of the business less the value of the net assets acquired. Here the net assets are $150m = $500m assets less $350m liabilities. The purchase price of $400 minus the net assets of $150m is equal to goodwill of $250m.
2. Goodwill represents items that help make the company extra profits. These include elements such as market reputation, product knowledge, customer base, employee skills and knowledge etc. not normally recorded on the balance sheet (except when one firm purchases another).

Exercise 23 Goodwill extravaganza

1. $3,836m
2. Impairment

(figures in millions)

3. **End of**	**Year 1**	**Year 2**	**Year 3**	**Year 4**	**Year 5**
Amort. exp. on the I/S	50	50	50	50	50
Accum. amortization	50	100	150	200	250
Balance of intangible	450	400	350	300	250

4. No
5. $715m
6. $893m
7. $178m

Exercise 24 What's In a name?

1. Because Coca-Cola did not buy it from another company and it is very difficult to value such a unique asset unless someone physically pays a price for it.
2. Dr Intangible assets $70b
   Cr Cash $70b

Take a look Coke's consolidation policy

"Our company consolidates all entities that we control by ownership of a majority voting interest as well as variable interest entities for which our company is the primary beneficiary."

Exercise 25 Equity, cost, or other?

1. $355m
2. $9,367m (Remember the short-term amount)

Close the deal #6

Give yourself $10,000 for each answer that is completely correct.

1. You can touch tangible assets. You can't touch or feel intangible assets.
2. Dr Buildings $1,055,000
   Cr Cash $1,055,000

PART 2

Close the deal #6 *continued*

3.

End of	2005	2006	2007	2008	2009
Original cost of building	560,000	560,000	560,000	560,000	560,000
Accumulated depreciation	34,000	68,000	102,000	136,000	170,000
Net PP&E of building	526,000	492,000	458,000	424,000	390,000
Depreciation expense	34,000	34,000	34,000	34,000	34,000

4. COGS

5. 90% of the trucks' original cost was already depreciated, so they are likely to be old and may need replacement.

6. 21 Park Street, Atlanta

Dr	Cash	$600,000	
Dr	Accum. depn.	$1,000,000	
Cr	PP&E		$1,500,000
Cr	Gain on sale		$100,000

Olympic Towers

Dr	Cash	$1,200,000	
Dr	Loss on sale	$800,000	
Dr	Accum depreciation	$10,000,000	
Cr	PP&E		$12,000,000

Take a look Shares info

$0.25

Exercise 26 Coke's shares

1.

Dr	Cash	$6,000	
Cr	Common stock		$25
Cr	APIC		$5,975

2.

	3,500,489,544
–	3,494,799,258
	5,690,286

3. 3,500,489,544

Take a look Treasury stock

1. $17,625m

2.

	3,500,489,544
–	1,091,150,977
	2,409,338,567

Exercise 27 B A S E for dividends

1.

B	$26,687m
A	$4,847m
S	$2,429m
E	$29,105m

2. 50.1%

3.

B	$26,687m
A	$5,000m
S	$2,000m
E	$29,687m

4. Mature
Middle-aged
Fast growing

Take a look Other equity accounts

Loss on derivatives

Gain on available for sale securities

Foreign currency translation

Change in minimum pension liability

Take a look Other Comprehensive Income

$1,348m loss

Close the deal #7

Give yourself $10,000 for each answer that is completely correct.

1. To analyze risk, calculate the total debt/total equity ratio. The higher the ratio is, the greater the level of financial risk.

NY Building Services = $300m/$200m = 1.5
Bishko SunTan Salons = $1,000m/$5,000m = 0.20
Midwest Farming Inc. = $75,000m/$90,000m = 0.83

NY Building Services 1
Midwest Farming Inc. 2
Bishko SunTan Salons 3

2.

Assets	Liabilities	Equity
$32,327m	$16,392m	$15,935m

3. No
No

4.

Dr	Cash	$5,000m	
Cr	Common stock		$25m
Cr	Capital Surplus		$4,975m

5.

Common stock	Capital surplus
$900m	$9,903m

Close the deal #7*continued*

6. $15,935m
   $15,695m
7. $31,105m
8. 43.5%
9. An adjustment to the equity accounts to reflect exchange rate movements when consolidating the assets of overseas subsidiaries.
   Multinational
10. Riskier to own equity

Exercise 28 Coke's revenue by operating segment

	North America	Latin America
Revenues	6,643	2,123
Operating assets	4,731	1,405
Operating income	1,606	1,069
Op inc/revenues	24.2%	50.3%
Op inc/assets	33.9%	76.1%

	Europe	Asia
Revenues	7,195	4,691
Operating assets	5,373	1,722
Operating income	1,898	1,758
Op inc/revenues	26.4%	37.5%
Op inc/assets	35.3%	102.1%

Europe performed best measured by the dollar volume of profits, but Latin America was best in terms of profit margins.

Exercise 29 COGS recap

1. Inventories
2. When it relates to production assets
3. Revenues
4. Costs are matched to the revenues they helped to create.

Exercise 30 SG&A recap

1. Secretarial costs
   Office rent
2. When it is related to non-production assets, such as trucks, computers, furniture etc.
3. COGS. Coca-Cola is a manufacturing company.
4. In SG&A

Exercise 31 Gross margin

1.

1995	57.4%	2000	64.3%
1996	59.5%	2001	65.6%
1997	63.8%	2002	63.7%
1998	65.9%	2003	63.1%
1999	64.2%	2004	65.2%

2. Production efficiency rose until 1997 and then has been relatively static.
3. COGS will rise because the depreciation added to COGS will also rise.

Exercise 32 Operating margin

1.

1995	24.7%	2000	21.3%
1996	23.5%	2001	30.5%
1997	30.1%	2002	27.9%
1998	30.5%	2003	24.8%
1999	23.7%	2004	25.9%

2. Operating performance is little better than it was ten years ago, although the figures have been erratic over that period.
3. CEO's salary
   Depreciation of Coke's headquarters building
4. 2004: $2.2bn 2003: $1.8bn
   Yes, significant expense

Exercise 33 Average cost of debt

1. 3.11%

   2003 debt ***2004 debt***
   $5,423m $7,178m

   2004 interest expense = $196m

   $$\frac{196}{(5,423 + 7,178) \times \frac{1}{2}} = 3.11\%$$

2. Misleading if Coke had strongly seasonal debt requirements.
3. Interest expense will increase.

Take a look Other expenses and income

1. Equity income-net $621m
2. Other income/(loss) ($82m)
3. Gain on issuance of stock $24m

Exercise 34 Extraordinary!

1. Yes
   No
   Yes
   Yes

PART 2

Exercise 35 EBIT workout

	Scenario 1	Scenario 2	Scenario 3
Outstanding debt	900	450	100
EBIT	100	100	100
Interest expense	90	45	10
Profit before tax	10	55	90
Tax	5	28	45
Net income	5	27	45

Exercise 36 Try your hand at taxes

	2001	2002	2003	2004	2005
1. Profit before tax	40,000	40,000	40,000	40,000	40,000
Tax at 50%	20,000	20,000	20,000	20,000	20,000
2. Income before tax	30,000	35,000	40,000	45,000	50,000
Tax at 50%	15,000	17,500	20,000	22,500	25,000
3. Diff. between tax and GAAP amounts	5,000	2,500	0	(2,500)	(5,000)

Exercise 37 Deferred taxes

1. $1,375m
2. $1,213m
3. $162m
4. No. If the deferred tax liability rises then more tax will be physically paid at a later date.
5. Earlier

Exercise 38 The last tax exercise

22.1% (1,375/6,222)

PART 2

Close the deal #8

Give yourself $10,000 for each answer that is completely correct.

1. Depreciation is included in COGS when you depreciate assets related to production activities.
2. More fixed costs
3. Operating margin: 60% Gross margin: 70%
4. 8%
5. No, depreciation is not a cash expense.
6. Extraordinary items:
   Must be infrequent and
   Must be unusual (not related to the company's oper-'ions)

Close the deal #8 *continued*

7. $6m
8. The Government's tax department (IRS in the U.S.)
9. Dr Tax expense $60m
   Cr Cash $40m
   Cr Deferred tax liability $20m
10. Depreciation of fixed assets

Exercise 39 First cash flow statement

Change in A/R	(20)
Change in inventories	(20)
Change in debt	(30)
Change in PIC	0
Change in cash	(70)

Take a look Net changes

Net change in op. assets & liabilities	$(617)m
Issuance of debt	$3,030m
Payments of debt	$(1,316)m

Exercise 40 Joe's London bike shop

Net income	100,000
Non-cash adjustments	41,000
(= 30,000 depr. + 10,000 amort. + 1,000 van sale)	
Cash income	141,000

Exercise 41 Operating accounts and cash flows

Cash	-NA-
Inventories	(48)
Receivables	(39)
Prepaid expenses	(4)
Net PP&E	-NA-
Long-term investments	-NA-

Exercise 41 Operating accounts and cash flows *continued*

Accounts payable	30
Short-term debt	-NA-
Deferred taxes	(4)
Long-term debt	-NA-
Other liabilities	8
Equity	-NA-
Total change in cash from operating assets and liabilities	(57)

Exercise 42 Leslie's restaurant

Begin with the Gross PP&E template and add in the 200 purchase of new chairs. This addition should push gross PP&E up to 1,100 (900 + 200) but the year-end figure is 1,020) so the kitchen equipment sold must have had a gross value of 80 (1,100 – 1,020); record the 80 as gross PP&E of sold asset. Note also that accumulated depreciation remains constant but there was depreciation expense of $30 on the I/S. This means the accumulated depreciation on the sold equipment must have been 30, so plug this in under sold asset. Record the loss on sale. You should get the following:

	Gross PPE	Accum depn.		Sold asset
B	900	100	Gross PP&E	80
A	200	30	Accum. depn.	30
S	80	30	Net PP&E	50
E	1,020	100	Loss on sale	20
			Cashflow	30

Cashflows

Capital expenditure	200
Fixed asset sales	30

Exercise 43 Bedford Biscuits

You will need to set up the BASE analysis on retained earnings to back out the dividend value of 23,000. Note also that the purchase of a biscuit cutter is NOT a financing cash flow.

Issuance of new debt	200,000	
Repayment of existing debt	(10,000)	
Issuance of new stock	355,000	
Purchase of treasury stock	0	
Payment of dividends	(23,000)	(123+50-150)
Cash flow from financing activities	522,000	

Exercise 44 Irreconcilable differences

Remember, the irreconcilable difference is a plug.

1. B Cap. surp. and com. stock end 2003	$5,269m
A Additions	$193m
A Irreconcilable differences	$341m
E Cap. surplus and com. stock end 2004	$5,803m

Exercise 45 Calculate Coke's cash flow From ops

Trade Receivables	(80)
Inventories	(168)
Prepayments	(164)
Op assets movement	(412)
Accounts payable	225
Accrued income tax	(255)
Deferred tax	113
Other LT liabs	302
Op liabs movement	385

Net income	$5,994
+ Depreciation of PPE	456
+ Amortization of intangibles	308
+ Other non-cash adjustments	0
(Increase) or decrease in operating assets	(412)
Increase or (decrease) in operating liabilities	385
Cash flow from operations	6,731

Exercise 46 Coke's cash flow from investments

CAPEX	($877)
Sale of fixed assets	127
Other investing activity assets	
(inc) / dec in investments, equity and marketable securities	(387)
Sales (purchases) of intangibles	(155)
Cash flow from investing activities	**($1,292)**

B A S E analyses

	Intangibles		Gross PP&E
B	3,989	B *(Check the B/S)*	*9,622*
A	155	A *(CAPEX)*	*877*
S	(308)	S *(What did Coke sell?)*	(350)
E	3,836	E *(Check the B/S)*	10,149

Exercise 47 Coke's cash flow from financing

Net inc / (dec) of short-term debt	3,115
Increase/(decrease) of long-term debt	(1,360)
Repurchase of shares (treasury stock)	(1,107)
Issuance of equity	534
Dividends	(3,576)
Cash flows from financing activities	(2,394)

B A S E analyses

Retained earnings

Beg	26,687
Add	5,994
Sub	3,576
End	29,105

PART 2

Exercise 48 Coke's projected cash flow

1. | | |
|---|---|
| Beg cash balance | $3,362m |
| Cash flow from ops | $6,731m |
| Cash flow from inv | ($1,292m) |
| Cash flow from fin | ($2,094m) |
| Ending cash balance | $6,707m |

2. Yes. If they're not the same, you've made a mistake.

Exercise 49 Go For the gold

Net income	8,000
Depreciation	5,000
(Inc) / dec in operating assets	(5,858)
Inc / (dec) in operating liabilities	2,382
Cash from operations	9,524
CAPEX	(15,600)
Fixed asset sales	200
(Inc) / dec in total investments	(489)
Cash from investments	(15,889)
Inc / (dec) in long-term debt (including current portion)	3,375
Inc / (dec) in common stock / APIC	10,339
Dividends	(2,770)
Cash from financing	10,944
Net change in cash	**4,579**

Check against B/S

B/S beginning cash (from previous year)	35,406
B/S ending cash (from current year)	39,985
B/S change in cash	4,579

Yes. They must be equal or you have make a mistake.

P A R T 2

B A S E analyses

Gross PP&E		**Accum. depreciation**	
Beg	100,000	Beg	40,400
Add	15,600	Add	5,000
Sub	(600)	Sub	(400)
End	115,000	End	45,000

Retained earnings

Beg	29,770
Add	8,000
Sub	(2,770)
End	35,000

Close the deal #9

Give yourself $10,000 for each answer that is completely correct.

1. Because companies cannot manipulate cash flows.
2. Operating activities: Cash flows generated by a company's operating activities.
   Investing activities: Cash flows generated by a company's investment decisions.
   Financing activities: Cash flows generated from a company's financing decisions.
3. a) Add back depreciation
   b) Add back amortization
   c) Add back losses on the sale of assets
   d) Subtract non-cash income
4. | Investment | Financing |
   |---|---|
   | CAPEX | Issuance of equity |
   | Sales of fixed assets | Issuance of debt |
   | Increase in investments | Dividends |
5. | | | | |
   |---|---|---|---|
   | Dr | Cash | $10m | |
   | Dr | Acc depn | $5m | |
   | Cr | Gross PP&E | | $8m |
   | Cr | Gain on sale | | $7m |
6. Go down
7. Use of cash
8. Cash from operating activities
9. Some cashflows between the accounts don't appear in the published reports.
10. Non-cash loss

Checkout test for part 2, section 1

1. B/S Dr Inventories $1,420m
   Cr Short-term debt $1,420m
   CFS Cash from operations would fall by $1,420m
   Cash from financing would increase by $1,420m
2. $2,106m ((Average Receivables/21,962)x365=35 so Average receivables= 35/365 x 21,962)
3. $10m
4. Benefits: You can meet customers' needs quickly.
   Drawbacks: You must fund the inventory, which costs money and reduces profitability.
   A small balance is usually preferable.
5. a. Accounts receivable
   Prepaid expenses
   Accrued expenses
   Accounts payable
   b. Go up
6. The competitors are better than Coca-Cola at managing money due from customers.
7.

SG&A	Prepaid insurance on CEO's car
COGS	Accrued rent on factory
SG&A	Accrued rent on head office
SG&A	Wages payable for the sales force
Revenues	Accounts receivable
Tax expense	Deferred taxes
All the accounts	Cash
Interest expense	Debt

8. Accounts driven by financing activities
9.

Balance sheet		**Income statement**	
Cash	+$500m	Int. expense	+$39m
LT debt	+$500m		

10. a.

	Year 1	**Year 2**	**Year 3**
I/S			
Depreciation exp.	20	20	20
B/S			
Gross PP&E	300	300	300
Accum. depn.	20	40	60
Net PP&E	280	260	240

   b. $6,641m

   c.

Dr	Cash	$290m	
Dr	Acc. depn	$20m	
Cr	PP&E		$300m
Cr	Gain on sale		$10m

Checkout test for part 2, section 2

1.

Dr	Cash	$100m	
Cr	Common stock		$0.4m
Cr	APIC		$99.6m

2. $30,805m

B	29,105
A	3,200
S	1,500
E	30,805

3. a. Dr Treasury stock $500m
   Cr Cash $500m
   b. Issued shares remain the same
   Outstanding shares decrease
4. a. COGS
   b. SG&A
5. a. Production costs
   b. Gross margin would increase as COGS would fall as a % of sales. Net margin would increase too.
6. a. 3.1% (196/6,300.5 x 100)
   b. It has a large seasonal debt need that occurs between 2 successive balance sheet dates.
7. a The item must be:
   Infrequent and
   Unusual
   b. After tax expense, before net income
8.

Dr	Tax expense	$100m	
Cr	Cash		$70m
Cr	Deferred tax liability		$30m

Checkout test, section 3

1. $30m of cash was used up.
2. It is at a maintenance level (or just under, if you take inflation into account).
3. a. Down
   b. Down
   c. Down
   d. Down
4.

Net income	241
Depreciation	100
Amortization	12
Other non-cash adjustments	0
(Inc) / dec in operating assets	(60)
Inc / (dec) in operating liabilities	29
Cash from operations	322
CAPEX	(180)
Fixed asset sales	20
(Inc) / dec in other non-op. assets	0
Cash flow from investing activities	(160)
Inc / (dec) in long-term debt including current portion	40
Inc / (dec) in APIC and common stock	6
(Dividends)	(50)
Cash flow from financing activities	(4)
Net change in cash	**158**
B/S beginning cash	50
B/S ending cash	208
B/S change in cash	158

Net change in cash = B/S change in cash

P
A
R
T

Exercise 1 Coke's ROE

1.

	2002	2003	2004
ROE	26.3%	33.6%	32.3%

These figures can be derived from the Selected Financial Data. For example, in 2002 net income is $3,050m, and the average shareholder equity figure is (11,800+ 11,366)/2 = $11,583m to give a figure of 26.3%

2. I/S: Net income
   B/S Shareholders' equity
3. Coke since 2003
4.

	2002	2003	2004
Gross margin Coca-Cola	63.7%	63.1%	65.2%

5. By increasing dividends, which would reduce shareholders' equity and increase ROE

Exercise 2 Coke's vs Pepsi's ROE

1. 22.1% x 0.749 x 1.954 = 32.3%
2. Coke generates more profit on each $ of sales, but Pepsi generates more sales per each $ of assets. Lower sales as a proportion of average assets.
3. Try to reduce costs to boost profitability on each $ of sales.

Exercise 3 Coke's shareholder value

1. $1,512m (Debt payment (from CFS) plus interest (from IS))
2. $4,168m (Dividends plus treasury stock purchases)
3. Rise

Exercise 4 CA levels and profitability

1. Inventory days = 63.8 ((1,420m + 1,252m)/2) /7,638m x 365
   Receivable days = 35.4 ((2,171m + 2,091m)/2) /21,962m x 365
2. Average receivables rises to $2,527m; Now receivables days = 42 = avg rec/21,962m x 365. The increase in average receivables is $2,527m – 2,131m = 396m. This additional amount must be funded. $396m x .04 = $15.8m.
   No, shareholders would not benefit because the extra cost of funding the receivables would reduce the profits available to them. The only possible benefit would arise if Coca-Cola deliberately relaxed its credit terms to generate new customers, and therefore make profits on these incremental sales.
3. Average inventory was $1,336m. If inventory days rise by 10 days to 73.8 then 73.8 = avg inv/7,638 x 365 so the new average inventory is $1,544m, inventory rises by $208m. At a cost of 4% this leads to an extra cost of $8.3m.

Exercise 4 CA levels and profitability *continued*

4. Pepsi's inventory days = 40.2 = ((1,541+1,412)/2) /13,406 x 365.
   Pepsi's receivable days = 36.4 = ((2,999 + 2,830)/2) /29,261 x 365.

Exercise 5 Teasing information out of CAPEX

1. Yes, Coke is increasing its assets.

	2004	2003	2002
CAPEX	755	851	769
Depn	715	614	502

2. $0.28 = 6,091 ÷ 21,962
3. $0.28

Exercise 6 The payoff in days payable

1. Coke: $\frac{(4{,}283 + 4{,}058) \times \frac{1}{2}}{7{,}638} \times 365 = 199$ days
2. No
3. Pepsi: $\frac{(5{,}599 + 5{,}213) \times \frac{1}{2}}{13{,}406} \times 365 = 147$ days
4. Coca-Cola

Exercise 7 What does cost of debt do to ROE?

1. 3.1%; Interest expense is $196m. Average debt is ($7,178m + $5,423m)/2 = $6,300m.
   $196/$6,300 = 3.1%.

	2004	*2003*
Loans and notes	4,531	2,583
Current maturity of LTD	1,490	323
Long Term Debt	1,157	2,517
Total debt	$7,178m	$5,423m

2. ROE = 32.3% = $4,847/(15,935 + 14,090)/2
3.

Total debt	7,178
Cash	– 6,707
Shareholders' equity	15,935
Total capital	16,406

4. Step 1. $62m *2,000 x 3.1%*

   Step 2. $6,222m

   Step 3. $6,160m

   Step 4. $4,805m = *6,160 x (1 - 22%)*

   Step 5 36.9% = $\frac{4{,}805}{((15{,}935 + 14{,}090) \times \frac{1}{2}) - 2000}$

5. ROE rises. This is because the cost of debt is cheaper than the cost of equity.

Exercise 8 Bankruptcy risk

1.

2004	2003
3%	15%

3% = (4,531+1,490+1,157-6,707)/15,935

15% = (2,583+323+2,517-3,362)/14,090

2. Coke has a riskier debt-to-equity ratio in 2003, but Pepsi is higher in 2004.

Exercise 9 Times interest earned

1.

	2004	2003	2002
Net earn. before int exp. and tax	6,418	5,673	5,698
Int. expense	196	178	199
	32.7x	31.9x	28.6x

2. Coca-Cola, although the risk is very slight.

Close the deal #10

Give yourself $10,000 for each answer that is completely correct.

1. Increase its margins.
   Increase its debt to equity ratio.
   Reduce its assets per $ of sales.
2. Company B (ROE = 10% x 1.54 x 3.25 = 50.1%)
3. Net income falls (higher interest expense)
   Debt funding rises
4. High leverage and low times interest earned scare debt holders.
5. Positive: It provides liquidity in a downturn.
   Negative: You have to fund them on the balance sheet, which costs money.
6. ($10m)
7. ROE rises
   Net income falls
8. 4 times
9. Company A
10. Company B

BILLION DOLLAR DEAL

Use the scoring template at left to track your score. You should achieve an overall score of $900,000,000 to demonstrate your mastery of the material.

Part 1. Basic accounting

1. | | |
|---|---|
| Common stock | 876 |
| Capital surplus | 5,127 |
| Reinvested earnings | 31,805 |
| Unearned compensation | (1,348) |
| Treasury stock | (18,186) |
| Total equity | 18,274 |

Return on equity: 31.0% (5,300/(15,935+18,274)/2)

2. a.

Cash	7,790	A/P	4,974
Mkt. sec.	71	Loans/notes	4,670
Trade A/R	2,521	Curr. mat.	43
Inventories	1,649	Accrued taxes	1,926
Prepaid exp.	2,272	Total CL	11,613
Total CA	14,303		

Working capital $2,690m

b. They are not demanding payment fast enough.

3.

	2005	2006	2007
Additions to PP&E	950	1,950	3,000
Additions to Accum. depn.	202	414	638

4. a. COGS fell due to improved productivity
Coca-Cola increased its prices

b. Op. income increases by $217m
Net PP&E increases by $217m
Net cash flow would be unaffected.

c. Fall
Fall
Fall
Fall

d. GAAP

5. Cash provided by operations: 1,000

Net Income	632
Accounts receivable	33
Amortization	29
Deferred Tax	59
Depreciation	332
Inventories	(45)
Other CA	(41)
Other CL	(14)
Other LTL	15
Total	1,000

BILLION DOLLAR DEAL *continued*

Part 2. Financial statements and ratios

1. Coca-Cola's income statement and balance sheet

Projected income statement	**2005**
Sales	25,000
COGS	(10,807)
SG&A	(9,452)
Other Op. charges	(480)
Operating profit	4,261
Interest income	150
Interest expense	(180)
Income before taxes	4,231
Tax	(931)
Net income	3,300

Projected balance sheet	**2005**
Assets	
Cash	7,660
Marketable securities	83
Trade accounts receivable	2,576
Inventories	1,801
Prepaid and other assets	1,824
Total current assets	13,944
Equity method investments	5,897
Cost method investments	355
Marketable securities and other assets	3,073
Gross PP&E	10,809
Accum. depreciation	4,255
Net PP&E	6,554
Goodwill and other intangibles	3,786
Total assets	33,609

Projected balance sheet	**2005**
Liabilities	
Accounts payable	5,889
Loans and notes	6,391
Current maturities of long-term debt	43
Accrued taxes	740
Total current liabilities	13,063
Long-term debt	1,557
Other liabilities	2,690
Deferred income taxes	461
Total liabilities	17,771
Equity	
Common stock	875
Capital surplus	4,928
Reinvested earnings	29,905
Unearned compensation	(1,348)
Treasury stock	(18,522)
Total equity	15,838
Total liabilities and equity	33,609

2. Coca-Cola's cash flow statement

Coca-Cola **Cash flow statement**	**2005**
Net income	3,300
+ Depreciation	597
+ Amortization	50
Δ in operating assets	(875)
Δ in operating liabilities	1,566
Operating cash flows	4,638
CAPEX	(1,200)
Fixed asset sales	140
(Increase) / decrease in investments	(41)
Sales / (purchases) of intangibles	0
Cash flow from investing activities	(1,101)
Issue of notes	1,860
Issue of Long-term debt	400
Repayment of long-term debt	(1,447)
Issuance of stock	0
Repurchase of equity	(897)
Dividends	(2,500)
Cash from financing activities	(2,584)
Net cash flow	953
Opening cash	6,707
Closing cash	7,660

3. a. 2005 ROE:
20.8% = 13.2% x 0.77 x 2.04

Despite the profit margin falling, Coke has reduced the amount of assets required to support a given amount of sales.

b.

Gross margin	56.8%	
Operating margin	17.0%	

c.

	2004	2005
Working capital	1,123	881

4.

Depn / CAPEX	50.0%
Accum depn / PP&E	39.3%

5. a.

	2004	2005
Leverage ratio	3.0%	2.1%

Leverage has fallen because net debt has decreased as a result of the cash balance increasing.

b.

	2004	2005
Times interest earned	32.7x	24.5x

Interest coverage has fallen because EBIT has decreased by a greater proportion than the interest charge. However, the ratio is still extremely high indicating that the company has no problems meeting its debt commitments.

Appendix A. Debits and credits

Drill 1 Debits and credits

	Debit	Credit
1. Cash	$10,000	
2. Long term debt	$30,000	
3. Paid-in capital		$5,000
4. Dividends	$1,000	
5. Inventories	$500	
6. Inventories		$2,000
7. Accounts receivable	$8,000	
8. Cash		$300
9. Short term debt	$2,000	
10. PP&E	$10,000	

Drill 2 Low-cost housing

Part 1

1.	Dr	Cash	$1,000,000	
	Cr	Paid in capital		$1,000,000
2.	Dr	PP&E	$400,000	
	Cr	Cash		$100,000
	Cr	Long term debt		$300,000
3.	Dr	PP&E	$50,000	
	Cr	Accounts payable		$50,000
4.	Dr	Inventory	$82,000	
	Cr	Cash		$47,000
	Cr	Accounts payable		$35,000
5.	Dr	PP&E	$500,000	
	Cr	Cash		$350,000
	Cr	Long term loan		$150,000

Part 2

1.	Dr	$2,032,000	
	Cr		$2,032,000

2.

BALANCE SHEET

ASSETS	*$000s*	*LIABILITIES*	*$000s*
Cash	503,000	A/C Payable	85,000
Inventories	82,000		
Total CA	**585,000**	**Total CL**	**85,000**
Net PP&E	950,000	Long term debt	450,000
		Total liabilities	**535,000**
		Paid in capital	1,000,000
		Total equity	**1,000,000**
Total assets	**1,535,000**	**Total L&E**	**1,535,000**

EXTRA DRILLS

Drill 3 More debits and credits

			Debit	Credit
1.	Dr	PP&E	$30,000	
	Cr	Cash		$30,000
2.	Dr	Cash	$100,000	
	Cr	Sales		$100,000
3.	Dr	COGS	$80,000	
	Cr	Inventory		$80,000
4.	Dr	SG&A	$1,000	
	Cr	Cash		$1,000
5.	Dr	Interest expense	$1,000	
	Cr	Cash		$1,000
6.	Dr	Inventory	$5,000	
	Cr	Accounts payable		$5,000
7.	Dr	Cash	$50,000	
	Cr	Long term debt		$50,000
8.	Dr	Dividends (RE)	$8,000	
	Cr	Cash		$8,000
9.	Dr	Tax expense	$8,500	
	Cr	Cash		$8,500
10.	Dr	Accounts receivable	$30,000	
	Cr	Sales		$30,000

Drill 4 Building a balance sheet and income statement

			Debit	Credit
1.	Dr	Cash	$1,000,000	
	Cr	Paid in capital		$1,000,000
2.	Dr	PP&E	$500,000	
	Cr	Cash		$500,000
3.	Dr	Cash	$2,000,000	
	Cr	Long term debt		$2,000,000
4.	Dr	Inventory	$1,750,000	
	Cr	Accounts payable		$500,000
	Cr	Cash		$1,250,000
5.	Dr	Cash	$1,250,000	
	Dr	Accounts rec.	$1,250,000	
	Cr	Sales		$2,500,000
6.	Dr	SG&A	$200,000	
	Cr	Cash		$200,000
7.	Dr	Interest expense	$200,000	
	Cr	Cash		$200,000
8.	Dr	COGS	$1,500,000	
	Cr	Inventory		$1,500,000
9.	Dr	Tax expense	$200,000	
	Cr	Cash		$200,000
		PP&E	$30,000	
		Cash		$30,000

INCOME STATEMENT

Revenue/sales	$2,500,000
Cost of goods sold	$(1,500,000)
Gross profit	**$1,000,000**
S,G&A	$(200,000)
Operating profit	**$800,000**
Interest expense	$(200,000)
Profit before tax	**$600,000**
Tax	$(200,000)
Net income	**$400,000**

BALANCE SHEET

ASSETS	*$s*	*LIABILITIES*	*$s*
Cash	1,870,000	A/C Payable	500,000
A/C receivable	1,250,000		
Inventories	250,000		
Total CA	**3,370,000**	**Total CL**	**500,000**
Net PP&E	530,000	Long-term debt	2,000,000
		Total liabilities	**2,500,000**
		Paid-in capital	1,000,000
		Retained earnings	400,000
		Total equity	**1,400,000**
Total assets 3,900,000		**3,900,000**	**Total L&E**

Drill 5 Advanced debits and credits

All figures in thousands

			Debits	Credits
1.	Dr	Cash	$1,050	
	Dr	Accounts receivable	$450	
	Cr	Sales		$1,500
2.	Dr	COGS	$700	
	Cr	Inventory		$700
3.	Dr	Inventory	$650	
	Cr	Accounts payable		$325
	Cr	Cash		$325
4.	Dr	Long term investments	$100	
	Cr	Cash		$100
5.	Dr	Cash	$57	
	Cr	Interest income		$57
6.	Dr	SG&A	$70	
	Cr	Accrued expenses		$70
7.	Dr	Cash	$500	
	Cr	Long term debt		$500
8.	Dr	Short term debt	$100	
	Cr	Cash		$100
9.	Dr	Tax expense	$309	
	Cr	Cash		$309

10. Dr	SG&A	$50	
Cr	Cash		$50
11. Dr	Interest expense	$120	
Cr	Cash		$120

INCOME STATEMENT

Revenue/sales	$1,500
Cost of goods sold	$(700)
Gross profit	**$800**
S,G&A	$(120)
Operating profit	**$680**
Interest income	$57
Interest expense	$(120)
Profit before tax	**$617**
Tax	$309
Net income	**$308**

BALANCE SHEET

ASSETS	*$000s*	*LIABILITIES*	*$000s*
Cash	703	A/C Payable	995
A/C receivable	1,150	Accrued exp.	130
Inventories	500	Short term debt	400
Prepaid expenses	50		
Total current assets	**2,403**	**Total curr. liabs.**	**1,525**
Net PP&E	960	Long term debt	1,200
Investments	670	Other liabilities	89
		Total liabilities	**2,814**
		Paid in capital	480
		Ret. earnings	739
		Total equity	**1,219**
Total assets	**4,033**	**Total L & E**	**4,033**

Appendix B. Cash flow statements

Drill 1. Colin's diving business

Working capital

Trade accounts receivable	50	55
Inventories	35	40
Prepaid expenses	10	12
Total operating assets	95	107
Accts. payable & accrued expenses	35	40
Total operating liabilities	35	40

BASE analyses

	Gross PP&E	**Accum Depr**	**Net Intangibles**
Beg	100	(50)	10
Add	20	(5)	0
Sub	0	0	(2)
End	120	(55)	8

Cash flow statement

Net income	20
Depreciation	5
Amortization	2
(Increase) decrease in operating assets	(12)
Increase (decrease) in operating liabilities	5
Cash from operating activities	20
Capital expenditure	(20)
Sales of fixed assets	0
(Purchase) sale of Intangibles	0
Cash from investing activities	(20)
Increase (decrease) in debt	10
Increase (decrease) in cmn. stock & APIC	0
Dividends	(5)
Cash from financing activities	5
Net cash flow	5
Beginning cash balance	5
Ending cash balance	10
Difference	5

Drill 2. Patricia's nail salons

Working capital

Trade accounts receivable	360	400
Inventories	150	152
Prepaid expenses	15	12
Total operating assets	525	564
Accts. payable & accrued expenses	210	215
Other long-term liabilities	10	8
Total operating liabilities	220	223

BASE analyses

	Gross PP&E	Accum Depr
Beg	213	(123)
Add	52	(45)
Sub	0	0
End	265	(168)

Cash flow statement

Net income	104
Depreciation	45
(Increase) decrease in operating assets	(39)
Increase (decrease) in operating liabilities	3
Cash from operating activities	113
Capital expenditure	(52)
Sales and retirements	0
(Increase) decrease in other assets	(21)
Cash from investing activities	(73)
Increase (decrease) in debt	24
Increase (decrease) in cmn. Stock & APIC	0
Dividends	(25)
Cash from financing activities	(1)
Net cash flow	39
Balance sheet change in cash	39

Drill 3. Julie's boutiques

Working capital

Trade accounts receivable	3,750	4,000
Inventories	3,000	3,500
Prepaid expenses	100	150
Total operating assets	6,850	7,650
Accts. payable & accrued expenses	700	800
Total operating liabilities	700	800

BASE analyses

	Gross PP&E	Accum Depr
Beg	5,000	(4,000)
Add	500	(300)
Sub	0	0
End	5,500	(4,300)

Cash flow statement

Net income	559
Depreciation	300
(Increase) decrease in operating assets	(800)
Increase (decrease) in operating liabilities	100
Cash from operating activities	159
Capital expenditure	(500)
Sales and retirements	0
(Increase) decrease in other assets	0
Cash from investing activities	(500)
Increase (decrease) in debt	600
Increase (decrease) in cmn. stock & APIC	0
Dividends	(140)
Cash from financing activities	460
Net cash flow	119
Beginning cash balance	800
Ending cash balance	919
Difference	119

Drill 4. Bet's Burger Bars

Working capital

Trade accounts receivable	26,700	35,000
Inventories	25,015	26,987
Prepaid expenses	2,500	2,645
Total operating assets	54,215	64,632
Accts. payable & acc. expenses	21,458	25,897
Total operating liabilities	21,458	25,897

BASE analyses

	Gross PP&E	Accum Depr	Net Intangibles
Beg	78,920	(45,652)	8,975
Add	500	(9,000)	0
Sub	0	0	(1,300)
End	79,420	(54,652)	7,675

Cash flow statement

Net income	10,828
Depreciation	9,000
Amortization	1,300
(Increase) decrease in operating assets	(10,417)
Increase (decrease) in operating liabilities	4,439
Cash from operations	15,150
Capital expenditure	(500)
Sales and retirements	0
(Increase) decrease in other assets	1,157
(Purchases) sales of intangible assets	0
Cash from investing activities	657
Increase (decrease) in Debt	(10,734)
Increase (decrease) in cmn. stock & APIC	1,214
Dividends	(2,707)
Cash from financing activities	(12,227)
Net cash flow	3,580
Beginning cash balance	1,437
Ending cash balance	5,017
Difference	3,580

Drill 5. The auction house

Working capital

Trade accounts receivable	54,098	65,908
Inventories	34,567	32,196
Prepaid expenses	5,671	3,467
Total operating assets	94,336	101,571
Accounts payable & accrued exp.	45,982	49,081
Total operating liabilities	45,982	49,081

BASE analyses

	Gross PP&E	Accum Depr	Net Intangibles
Beg	78,920	(45,652)	10,983
Add	12,760	(8,756)	12,345
Sub	(3,456)	2,345	(908)
End	88,224	(52,063)	22,420

Cash flow statement

Net income	4,139
Depreciation	8,756
Amortization	908
(Increase) decrease in operating assets	(7,235)
Increase (decrease) in operating liabilities	3,099
Cash from operations	9,667
Capital expenditure	(12,760)
Sales and retirements	1,111
(Increase) decrease in other assets	(3,131)
(Purchase) sale of intangible assets	(12,345)
Cash from investing activities	(27,125)
Increase (decrease) in debt	5,863
Increase (decrease) in Cmn. Stock & APIC	1,120
Dividends	(1,345)
Cash from financing activities	5,638
Net cash flow	(11,820)
Beginning cash balance	64,141
Ending cash balance	52,321
Difference	(11,820)